Dreaming
Down
Heaven

First published by O-Books, 2010
O Books is an imprint of John Hunt Publishing Ltd., The Bothy, Deershot Lodge, Park Lane, Ropley,
Hants, SO24 0BE, UK
office1@o-books.net
www.o-books.com

For distributor details and how to order please visit the 'Ordering' section on our website.

Text copyright Gini Gentry 2009

ISBN: 978 1 84694 530 8

A CIP catalogue record for this book is available from the British Library.

Design: Stuart Davies

Printed in the UK by CPI Antony Rowe
Printed in the USA by Offset Paperback Mfrs, Inc

We operate a distinctive and ethical publishing philosophy in all
areas of its business, from its global network of authors to
production and worldwide distribution.

Dreaming
Down
Heaven

Gini Gentry

BOOKS

Winchester, UK
Washington, USA

For
Miguel Angel Ruiz
Who shook me from my slumber and inspired me to awaken.

Heartfelt appreciation to HILLARY WELLS the Godmother
of this book.
Lasting gratitude to the folks who offered critical support
during a rather long gestation: Kathryn and Dannion Brinkley;
Devra Jacobs; Andrew Adleman; Mary Margaret Moore;
Ellen Kleiner; Ted and Peggy Raess; Stephanie Bureau;
Heather Ash Amara; Paulette Millichap; Janet Mills; Diva Slone;
Wendy Keown; Katye Landis; Halo; Terri Negron and
Frank Hayhurst.

Foreword

For over a decade, Gini Gentry has traveled the world, generously sharing her deep understanding, open heart, and humor, inspiring people she meets to transform their confusion into clarity and their helplessness into power. Because of her ability to teach in this way, Gini has been designated as the Nagual Woman in the Toltec Eagle Knight lineage and honored with the title La Doña.

In, *Dreaming Down Heaven*, Gini catalyzes these same effects through theatrical allegory. Here Maya, the Mistress of Illusion, holds court in the Magical Theatre of life as we know it. Through joy, rich insights, and pain, Maya guides readers through the transformation of their own magical theatre. She delights us into moving past our pervasive sense of self-doubt into an illuminating discovery of truths most of us have long ago forgotten.

Drawing on her truth-based imagination and vast experience with the life-changing aspects of Toltec training, Gini invites us to wake up to who we really are—and in the process advance not only our personal evolution but also that of humanity itself. Prepare for an unforgettable encounter with your authentic self as you embark on a journey into the heart of these timeless practical teachings.

Don Miguel Ruiz, NY Times best-selling author of *The Four Agreements; The Fifth Agreement*

Author's note

Since childhood, I've had a gnawing sense that life on earth was not intended to be nearly as painful or serious as it seemed. In my dreams, I often saw life as a game devised by some greater force for our souls' enhancement. But in 1988, a fateful meeting in South America led me to an unexpected confirmation of that belief. During a trip to Peru, I met a woman who would later introduce me to an as-yet unknown Toltec teacher: don Miguel Ruiz.

I first went to Miguel for energy work. During the session, the treatment was so intense it felt like he was peeling layers of fear off of me. After he finished, I felt gloriously renewed and open, and when he invited me to a small outbuilding in his backyard, I agreed, although I had no idea what to expect. I was surprised to enter a small, empty room completely lined with mirrors and lit only with candles. Miguel asked me to sit on a platform in the center of the room, where all I could see were reflections of myself, multiplied endlessly in the candlelight.

Miguel led me through a meditation, then, indicating one of my reflections, asked, "Who is she?" "She's the image of myself as a spiritual seeker," I replied, seeing how I perceived myself from the outside. "And who is she?" Miguel asked, pointing to another reflection. "She's the one who thinks she's too much," I answered. Miguel took me through image after image, prodding me to reveal all the different masks that I called "I am," until I caught a momentary glimpse of my true essence. For a tantalizing instant, I saw that I was none of these reflections—I was something far greater than any of them. "I get it," I cried, elated.

As I reveled in the wonder of my discovery, Miguel shared with me the story of Maya, the powerful Hindu goddess of illusion, who had conspired to create a wonderful game of awakening for humans to play on earth. I felt an immediate connection to Maya, whose story corroborated my inner sense that life was essentially an elaborate game. That night, in the Toltec tradition, I gained a teacher and a benefactor.

Miguel became my teacher, the spiritual guide who would help me navigate my path here on earth; and Maya became my benefactor, who would shepherd my exploration of the Great Mystery in the nighttime dream world. Miguel used his own experiences as a template for my expansion, and Maya embodied what I had long believed: that in this enchanted game of life, our purpose is to awaken to our angelic nature. Maya's knowledge, which stemmed from the wisdom at the heart of Creation, was a perfect balance to Miguel's Toltec teachings, which were derived from the most sacred traditions of humankind. It was this dynamic partnership that catapulted me onto a fast track to awakening.

Eventually I became Miguel's teaching partner, or Nagual Woman, as it is known in the Toltec tradition. After many years our destinies took us in different directions, but Maya remained with me, sharing the "silent knowledge," or universal consciousness, that represents our highest possibility. I am deeply honored to pass on to you the essential nature of the Toltec way of life through Maya's heartfelt lessons, and I intend that they bring as much illumination and joy to you as they have to me.

GG xxoo

Prologue

Gigi sighed, pulled off the black suede Marc Jacobs platform boots, and put them back in their box.

'I guess I won't take them,' she said reluctantly to the bored salesgirl, who gave her the inimitable look of scorn that was obviously a job requirement at every Manhattan boutique.

Ignoring her, Gigi stuffed her aching feet back into her last-year's spike heels with a sigh. Something was seriously off. It was unlike her to resist the temptation of a gorgeous pair of boots. The Gigi of a mere few months ago would, at this very moment, be riding a surge of adrenaline as she swept triumphantly toward the cash register, boots in hand – or possibly still on her feet. She would have told herself something bracing like, 'So what if I'm facing the holidays alone? At least I'll be looking fabulous. And I'd rather spend the money on boots than a stupid turkey dinner.'

So what was wrong? It wasn't that she didn't have the money; of course she didn't! But she had a wallet full of credit cards. It was something worse: Shoe shopping was not making her feel better. Retail therapy had failed her!

Gigi heaved herself off the seat and trailed out of the store. She walked listlessly down the crowded West Village sidewalk, head bent against the brisk November wind. Occasionally she glanced up to peek into a shop window, but instead of admiring the sumptuous array of pre-holiday goods, she could see only her own reflection. To say the least, this did nothing to lighten her mood. Her thick brown hair, shaggy and neglected, was whipping around in the wind like a nest of snakes. The bedraggled black scarf wrapped several times around her neck nicely highlighted the dark circles under her eyes and accented her pasty face, delicately sprinkled with zits from a recent chocolate binge. All in all, she resembled nothing so much as a down-and-out Medusa.

It wasn't exactly the look she'd been going for.

Gigi let out a gusty sigh that startled a toy poodle walking past. The dog strained at its leash, yapping wildly as its owner gave Gigi the stink-eye.

'Sorry for being so hideous I scared your dog,' she muttered under her breath, swallowing the tears of self-pity that threatened to rise.

She'd sincerely hoped a little shopping would pull her out of her slump. But clearly it was going to take a lot more than that. After all she'd been through, feeling better was going to involve a major life change. Like moving to a small tropical island, getting a job serving fruity cocktails at a beachside bar, and flirting with aging playboys. She could almost hear Jimmy Buffett playing in the background and smell the ocean breeze. A mysterious man with a Matthew McConaughey body and a Swiss bank account would rescue her from the clutches of a Hugh Hefner lookalike and whisk her away on his yacht...

'Urgh!' She slammed into something and stumbled backward, flailing wildly to retain balance in her unsteady shoes.

She managed to avoid a serious fall by grabbing a nearby parking meter. Heart pounding, she looked around furtively to see if anyone had noticed. Luckily the Manhattan sidewalk swarm had produced only a couple of quick stares. Everyone kept moving steadfastly, heads down against the chill wind.

Gigi took a deep breath to calm herself and peered at the offending object, a sandwich sign that proclaimed:

Eternity
Used and Rare Books
Come in and Browse! Comfortable Chairs. Free Hot Tea!

Sounded nice. Gigi pictured herself in a worn armchair with a cup of Earl Grey and a shabby old tome. It sounded like just the cure for her chilled bones and aching feet. She had no real desire to go home to her empty apartment yet, and besides maybe they carried travel books! Hadn't she just been thinking about traveling? She owed it to herself to go in.

Somewhat heartened, Gigi pushed open the door. A bell tinkled and warm stuffy air washed over her, ripe with the comforting scent of musty books.

'Good afternoon,' said a sixtyish man behind the counter, peering at her over his bifocals. His eyes were a surprising bright blue, and his voice lilted with a crisp British accent. He wore a neat Harris Tweed blazer with elbow patches atop a sweater vest. Past the counter, unruly rows of bookshelves spilled over with thick, ancient-looking volumes and worn paperbacks. Omigod, it was just like the bookshop in that movie with Hugh Grant – what was it called? *Notting Hill*. As if she'd stepped into Merry Olde England for a moment, where every problem could be solved with a chipped mug of steaming tea. It was just what she needed.

'Hi!' Gigi replied gaily. 'Where are your travel books?'

'Just there, past the fantasy section,' said the bookish gentleman, pointing. 'And please help yourself to tea. I just brewed a fresh pot.' He indicated a table in the corner flanked by two comfortable-looking overstuffed armchairs. It was all just as she'd pictured it.

'Thank you,' she said, and headed to the travel section. She'd just browse a little, get some ideas. Maybe this moving to an island notion was actually feasible. After all, what did she have to lose?

Gigi spent an enjoyable half hour collecting a stack of books to browse through. Most of them looked hopelessly outdated, but who cared? She was just getting ideas. She could hop on the Internet later and get current information. She lugged the books to the corner and plunked them down beside an armchair, then made herself a cup of tea with milk and sank into the chair with a contented sigh.

Immersed in imagined adventures in Bali, Thailand and the

Caribbean, Gigi was only vaguely aware of the bell over the door ringing and people coming and going. She sipped her tea as she worked her way through the stack of books, setting a couple of more recent ones aside for possible purchase. Finally she reached the bottom of the pile and looked at the last book, puzzled. She didn't remember selecting it. It had a faded, gold-embossed cover that had once been elegant. The title, in swirling script, read: *Dreaming Down Heaven*.

Odd, Gigi thought. *It sounds like some kind of spiritual book, or maybe it's supposed to be in the fantasy section. I must have grabbed it by mistake.*

She opened the book idly. The inside cover was inscribed with a handwritten note:

To my beloved student, December 10, 1974
May this book help you awaken to your magnificence.
Love, M.

Gigi's heart skipped a beat. December 10, 1974– the day she was born! What a strange coincidence! Despite the familiar sinking in her stomach that accompanied thoughts about her looming thirty-fifth birthday, Gigi felt a stab of interest. What did *Dreaming Down Heaven* mean? And was the fact that it had been inscribed on her birthday some sort of sign?

The man behind the counter cleared his throat. 'Sorry, miss, but I must close now. It's after six.'

'Oh – is it really?' Gigi shot out of the seat. She'd been here for over two hours. It was really high time to go home and… and do what? Shoving the thought away, she grabbed the three travel books she'd selected and went to the counter.

'I'll take these,' she said. 'Thanks for letting me hang out for so long.'

'Absolutely no trouble,' said the man, smiling. 'People do it all the time.'

He pointed to the book under her arm. 'That one, too?'

Gigi realized she was still holding onto *Dreaming Down Heaven*. Suddenly she was unwilling to let it go.

'Yes, this one too,' she replied.

'Excellent choice,' said the man with a wink as he rang her up. But before Gigi could ask him what he meant, he hustled her out the door and locked it behind her.

Gigi wrapped her scarf around her neck and hurried down the street. She couldn't wait to get home, open a bottle of wine, and find out what *Dreaming Down Heaven* was all about. Then she'd start planning her move to the tropics. After ordering in Chinese, of course.

Chapter One

Gigi opened her eyes – a more difficult task than it sounded since they were gritty with sand and each eyelid weighed at least ten pounds – and stared blearily at the bland white ceiling above her.

That's funny, she thought. *I'm sure my bedroom ceiling is blue.*

Groaning, she heaved herself to a sitting position and beheld not her bedroom, but her living room – or what passed for a living room in this tiny Lower East Side walk-up with its slanted, scarred wood floor and windows that had been painted shut ages ago.

I can't believe I fell asleep out here again, she thought, the familiar self-pity bubbling in her chest, threatening to produce leaky tears. Ever since she'd moved out of the spacious condo she and Keith had shared at 84th and Fifth Avenue, complete with a doorman and a view of Central Park, she'd been unable to sleep in her lonely bed. Instead she would lie on the sofa for hours, curled in a fetal position, reliving every moment of her life with Keith.

Especially the moment she swooped into their apartment with a cheerful, 'Sweetie, I got done early, and I brought...' A sentence doomed never to be finished. Arms laden with bouquets of early daffodils and canvas tote bags filled with organic vegetables for ratatouille, Gigi stood rooted to the spot in the living room doorway, staring in disbelief at the scene in front of her.

She'd expected to find her husband lounging on the black leather sofa with his cowboy boots propped on the chrome-and-glass coffee table, strumming his guitar or reading *Rolling Stone* while sipping a beer – his usual position at the end of a long day at the recording studio. Instead, Keith lay on his back on the floor, jeans pulled down to his boots, beneath a naked, gyrating woman with purple-tipped blond hair and a Marilyn Manson tattoo on her ass. Classy. Through the fog that swept through her brain and rendered her speechless, Gigi dimly recognized the woman as the new backup singer in Keith's band Redeye.

Her mind refused to accept the evidence in front of her eyes. Keith may have done a lot of things, especially with his band's increasing success, but one thing he'd always assured her of was his fidelity. Gigi had done everything she could to remain attractive to him. She knew groupies were always throwing themselves at him; she wasn't born yesterday.

That's why she went to the gym, neurotically watched what she ate, had her hair highlighted every six weeks, got regular manicures, and dressed with a classy yet sexy flair that none of those trailer-trashy teen fans could hope to match. Not to mention that she cooked him fabulous gourmet meals, kept the condo sparkling, entertained his friends and associates at the drop of a hat, and treated him like a king. Oh, and she also worked full time (and often overtime) as executive director of TheaterKids, a nonprofit offering theater programs in inner city schools.

She'd perfected the art of being the ideal wife: undemanding, caring, independent yet nurturing. And, apparently, it hadn't been enough. Because here was her husband, moaning with pleasure, still unaware of her presence as his hands cupped the spike-haired slut's ass and he thrust himself into her enthusiastically.

The tote bags fell from Gigi's slack hands, root vegetables thudding to the ground and rolling everywhere. Keith froze, his eyes locking with Gigi's for an instant before he threw the naked tattooed wonder off him and stumbled to his feet, hastily pulling up his pants. He lurched toward her with a dazed look – a familiar gaze Gigi immediately identified as the result of a potent combination of marijuana and tequila. Nausea rose in her throat and she wondered wildly if she were going to throw up all over him.

Now, sitting on her shabby sofa and surveying the remains of last night's Chinese takeout decorating the coffee table, Gigi put her hands to her temples, willing herself to excise the memory of that horrible day. But it was hard to get rid of the stale vision of Keith trying to assume a nonchalant posture as she faced him with folded arms. Spoiled as always, he'd jutted out his square jaw while zipping up his jeans, saying petulantly in his husky voice, 'Why are you home so early?'

At Gigi's look of scorn, he hastily added, 'It's not what it seems.'

Although she felt like bursting into tears, Gigi was damned if she'd let Keith and this bimbo see how much they'd hurt her. Fighting back the urge to puke, she tossed her head with a snort of derision and turned her withering gaze to the singer, who frantically tugged her slinky silver tube dress over her head. With cool fury, Gigi noted the rolled-up dollar bill and razor blade on the coffee table.

'Well, I'm glad it isn't what it seems,' she heard herself say. 'Because it *seems* to be the end of a lousy marriage. What is it, really – a sound check?'

Keith searched for an answer, a belligerent expression taking over his face. Meanwhile, the girl bolted for the door, forgetting her purse – in which Gigi later discovered a large packet of white powder that she dumped in the toilet, and a wad of fifties that she took vicious pleasure in spending on a divorce lawyer.

That's all over now, Gigi thought firmly, pressing her fingers to her throbbing temples. An empty bottle of Liar's Dice Zinfandel on the floor next to a lipstick-stained wineglass explained only too well the pain in her head and the dry, furry taste in her mouth.

'Shit,' Gigi said aloud, getting up too fast, holding onto the arm of the sofa for support. Obviously she'd gotten into the wine cabinet again. One of the pleasures of being married to Keith had been having the money to build a really good wine collection. The collection had been among the few things she'd taken when she left, but instead of saving the coveted bottles as she had for so many years, she'd been treating herself.

She'd started slowly, savoring the wines and only allowing herself a glass every evening after work – her reward for making it through another miserable, Keithless, lonely, heartbroken day. But three weeks ago, she'd been sitting at her desk, staring at the mountain of unanswered correspondence she hadn't had the energy to tackle, when her assistant buzzed through a call from their corporate sponsor. Gigi shoved the phone between her chin and shoulder and took up her silver letter-opener, figuring she might as well multitask since these calls usually went on for a while. But a moment later, the opener fell to the cement floor with a clang as Gigi clutched the desk for support. TheaterKids had lost their funding, and her job had been cut – effective immediately.

Barefoot, Gigi tottered into the galley kitchen and opened the cabinet beneath the sink. She groaned, wincing as the sound vibrated through her pulsing head. Just as she'd suspected, she had drunk the very last bottle. After losing her job, she'd gone from a glass every evening to several, beginning in the late afternoon when she could no longer pretend that it was just a weekend day and Keith was out of town. Aching with loneliness, she would carefully select a bottle and open it with a satisfying pop – the only sound she welcomed all day.

She could have gone out if she wanted; of course she had many casual friends in Manhattan. But she couldn't bear their sympathy, their pitying, curious looks and questions. She knew they were wondering if what they'd read in the tabloids was really what happened (it was) and she knew that some of them were actually excited at the thought that sexy, almost-famous Keith was now single.

Gross, all of it. The only person she really wanted to see was her best friend Stephanie. Stephanie would know how to make her see the comical side of this miserable existence, coax her to go out and meet some new men, and encourage her to apply for jobs.

But several months previously, Stephanie had disappeared from Manhattan into the Wild West, after having the nerve to elope with a man from Colorado she'd met online. She might as well have relocated to the moon. Although they talked on the phone some, Gigi missed Stephanie almost more than she missed Keith. To have lost both the people closest to her within months seemed unfair. Not to mention the job she loved, the only thing that had made her feel she was making a difference in this messed-up world.

Sensing another onslaught of debilitating self-pity, Gigi filled the coffee pot with tap water and rummaged around in the cupboards for her canister of beans to grind. With enough cream and sugar, her truck-driver-strong brew would surely revive her from this wine-induced stupor.

'Noooo!' she cried, her head throbbing. The tin was empty. This was just too much. No more wine, no more coffee, and all she had to look forward to was another day of feeling sorry for herself, trying listlessly to read the classifieds in search of jobs. Not to mention that the holiday season was fast approaching, with Thanksgiving, like doomsday, marching ever closer to mock her in her solitary splendor. Fat lot she had to be thankful for, this year.

She slumped to the floor, leaning against the stove, and cradled her head between her knees. What had become of her? A few months ago she'd thought she had the perfect life. Granted, she was always tired, always pushing herself, always trying to be a better wife, a more dedicated worker, a more charming hostess. But wasn't that just how life was when you lived in the greatest city on earth, working your way into the charmed circles of the rich and famous?

Clutching the counter to pull herself up, she decided to go to the Starbucks on the corner, treat herself to a caramel macchiato, and read the Sunday classifieds. Maybe she would even take a shower, blow-dry her hair, and pretend to be one of the living (instead of one of the living dead). On second thought though, that seemed like way too much effort. She'd just pull on a jacket over her Chinese-food-stained sweats and shove a knit hat on her greasy hair. Who did she have to impress, anyway?

Fifteen minutes later, she had settled into a brown plush chair in Starbucks' window with the thick Sunday paper. Sipping her vente macchiato, red pen in hand, she started plowing through the help wanted ads: Administrative – possibly, though nothing looked terribly interesting... Food Service – definitely not; she'd put in her time waitressing in college and vowed to polish shoes at Grand Central Station rather than ever have her rear pinched by another creepy old man... Hospitality – no...

Trudging through section after section of depressing-sounding jobs, Gigi felt her newfound resolve begin to fade. Why not just let her bank account run out until she was evicted and became one of those mysterious gap-toothed women who pushed a shopping cart and fed crumbs to pigeons? After so many weeks without a visit to the gym or the hair stylist, she was already beginning to look the part. Might as well go all the way.

Suddenly her eyes lit on an ad that bounced out at her as if in 3-D, pulsing strangely. She shook her head to clear it, but the letters still appeared to be swelling and contracting as if jumping out to get her attention. How was that possible? Was it a hologram of some kind, or some sort of subliminal advertising trick?

She readjusted her gaze, caught an unfortunate glimpse of herself in the window, and quickly looked back down. Now, the letters were glowing with what must be a trick of the light.

Wanted: Enthusiastic individual to oversee restoration of historic Magical Theatre in beautiful Blessings, Maine. Possible long-term management position. Experience not necessary; must be willing to relocate.

Phone calls only: 607-323-4545.

Gigi felt a twinge of excitement. The Magical Theatre! She had no idea what it was, but it sounded great. She pictured a mossy stone building with elaborate carvings adorning its façade, gilt paint peeling off columns in a dusty, velvet-seated auditorium. *I don't have experience running a physical theater, but surely having been executive director for TheaterKids would qualify me for the position. And it says experience not required. Hmm. Willing to relocate?*

Gigi's gaze strayed out the window. As she watched, couple after couple wandered past in relaxed Sunday mode, holding hands or with their arms wrapped around each other, laughing, carrying paper bags of groceries or takeout, their steamy breaths mingling in the chilly air.

Everyone has someone except me, she thought pathetically. Even people walking on their own looked like they were hurrying home to bring their lover eggs to make an omelet, or bagels and the newspaper to share in bed. Someone cared that they were gone, was waiting for them, wanted to enjoy a life together.

Quickly looking away, she realized that she had no real reason to stay in Manhattan. The thought of starting over in a new place – Blessings, Maine, wherever that was – far from the city's driving energy, was suddenly quite appealing. Her sense of devastation, that loss of everything familiar that had anchored her to her life, she now realized was also a sort of freedom. She thought of the words from the Janis Joplin song – what was it – 'Me and Bobby McGee'? 'Freedom's just another word for nothin' left to lose.' Well...

'So call, already,' a throaty voice said in Gigi's ear. She jumped and looked around furtively. The only person near her was an anorexic teenager, in pants that barely covered her rear end, wiping the next table. The voice certainly wasn't *hers*. Was Gigi finally living up to her mother's prediction that using aluminum-based deodorant would make her lose her mind?

Nah, it's just my intuition, telling me to do what I already know I should do, she thought with a curious sense of excitement. *I'm going to call right now.*

She scrabbled in her scuffed purse for her cell phone – making a mental note to get a new bag the minute she got a job since this one had definitely seen better days – and, before she could lose her resolve, punched in the number from the ad.

Chapter Two

The countryside sped by as Gigi leaned back in the squeaky train seat. She hadn't seen so many trees since her childhood in Maryland, and it made her realize just how long it had been since she'd ventured out of Manhattan. And now she was on her way to Blessings, Maine, to start a new life! Maya, the single-named (like Cher or Madonna) director of the Magical Theatre, had been unexpectedly warm and welcoming on the phone. Before she knew it, Gigi had found herself pouring out the story of her life.

Maya was a wonderful listener, and seemed to really care – though why she should be concerned with a stranger's problems was a mystery to Gigi. They talked, or rather Gigi talked, for what seemed like hours. Then Maya had offered her the job, just like that, telling her that with just a bit of training she was sure she would be able to revitalize the Magical Theatre. Gigi had hardly been able to believe her good fortune.

They agreed she would start as soon as she could settle her affairs in the city, which Gigi had grimly reflected should not take long, since there was very little to settle. Ten days later here she was, heart pumping in anticipation and nervousness, on her way to see Godfreys, the driver Maya had told her would meet her at the station. Blessings had a population of 2,500 (Gigi had Googled it) and was a major tourist destination in the summer.

'But this time of year, my dear, you will find it very, shall we say, restful,' Maya had said in her rich voice, her unidentifiable accent betraying inner amusement.

'Restful is perfect,' Gigi had replied. Just perfect.

Breathing a deep sigh of relief and settling deeper into her uncomfortable seat, she allowed herself a small smile of contentment and anticipation. Which, unfortunately, the man sitting opposite her interpreted as an invitation to strike up a conversation.

Gigi wanted nothing more than to sit with her own thoughts, but on second glance the man wasn't bad-looking, and she remembered that she was a single woman again. So falling back on old habits, she tossed her freshly cut and tinted hair (with extra highlights to cover the strands of wiry silver that kept rearing their pesky heads) and gave him her signature dazzling smile.

Being a modern woman with plenty of fashion magazines, models and actresses for comparison, Gigi had, of course, never been happy with her looks: her eyelashes were short and stubby, her nose turned up just a little too much to be classic, her breasts were too small to be noteworthy, and her hips just a tad too wide to fit into those tiny hip-hugging jeans she'd love to be able to wear. However, one thing she always liked was her smile. Blessed with naturally perfect teeth and full lips, she knew her smile was a killer. Or at least it used to be. It had been eons since she'd tried out its effect on anyone of the opposite sex.

Apparently, it still worked. The man smiled back and leaned in closer. His blond hair was perfectly tousled, and his tiny, square, pink-tinted glasses gave him a European look, enhanced by his casual-yet-elegant silk T-shirt and sleek gray trousers. Gigi had to admit that she tended to go for more earthy men, a tad rougher around the edges. Keith's studiously overgrown hair, perfectly broken-in designer jeans and Italian boots had sent her over the moon when she'd met him. But this man was quite good-looking, and clearly friendly. Besides, she was just talking to him.

'Forgive me for staring, but your hair is *fabulous*,' the man said. 'Who does it?'

'Bobby D,' Gigi said, suddenly feeling foolish. The pink glasses, asking about her hair... of course, he was gay! Had her gaydar really gotten so rusty? Despite embarrassment at her mistake, she was relieved. She felt far more comfortable talking to someone who didn't want to get in her pants.

'Oh, Bobby D. Of course! I should have spotted it,' the man said. He leaned in closer, placing his hand on her knee in a confidential gesture. 'Honey, I don't want to freak you out, but you have a piece of spinach or something in your teeth.'

'Really?' Gigi responded, instantly humiliated. Here she'd flashed her 100-watt smile only to reveal a mouthful of salad!

'I'd better go to the bathroom and take care of it,' Gigi said, trying to be civil, though she felt like strangling him. 'Would you mind watching my stuff for a minute?'

'Sure, hon,' he said with a conspiratorial wink.

Gigi walked down the aisle, stumbling as the train began to slow. They must be approaching the last stop before Blessings. Her heart pounding, she made her way through the nearly empty train car. Not many people were heading to Maine in early November, apparently, and she couldn't blame them.

Suddenly, she felt doubt wash over her like a chilly shower. What on earth was she doing? Could she really live in a tiny coastal town, so far from civilization? What did she know about the situation she was getting into? Was she destined to mess up her life yet again? Gratefully, she locked herself in the minuscule, reeking bathroom and felt tears threatening to destroy her eye makeup. Where was Steph when she needed her? What would she say now to make Gigi see the funny side of this? Giving up, Gigi gave in to yet another bout of self-pity, swiping at the tears that seeped unbidden from her eyes.

After what could have been five minutes or a half hour, she was thrown against the sink as the train began shuddering to a stop. Jolted back into the present, she heard the conductor's voice crackle over the intercom: 'Bayville, Bayville. Next stop, Blessings.'

Remembering why she was in the bathroom, Gigi grimaced into the mirror but couldn't see any sign of spinach in her teeth. Strange. Oh well. Maybe all the snot from her crying jag had washed it out. She really ought to go back to her seat, but she didn't want to face anyone just yet.

Oh crap, I'll never be able to do this starting over thing, Gigi thought hopelessly. She'd been with Keith for so long, and before that had had a series of disastrous boyfriends whom she could hardly remember, and now she was – oh, horrors – she was turning thirty-five in two and a half weeks!

'I'm getting old,' she muttered to her face dimly visible in the smudged mirror. 'I'm alone, and no one wants me, and I've never lived as an adult on my own before, and I'm trusting in this job that could be a complete hoax. What the hell is the Magical Theatre anyway, and who is this Maya?'

Someone banged on the door. Gigi gulped and said in as normal a voice as she could, 'I'll be right out.' She stared at her reflection in the grainy mirror as the train slid into motion, gathering speed to take her to the mysterious town of Blessings. She would have to get herself together before meeting Maya. Her mascara was smudged and her lipstick all worn off, and she had left her purse at her seat.

An alarm went off in her head. Left her purse! What if that pink-bespectacled guy had taken it? Maybe telling her about the nonexistent spinach in her teeth had been a ploy to get her to leave so he could steal her things. The thought propelled her out into the corridor, muttering an apology to the glaring woman clutching a small child who was jumping up and down with her hand between her legs, and hastened back to her seat.

When she got there, her heart fell.

The shiny new Kate Spade bag she'd bought as a celebration of her new job was gone. Her ID, her credit cards, her makeup, the key to her storage unit – and omigod, her suitcase too – all gone! She looked around wildly, but the few people in the car were sleeping, listening to headphones or reading magazines. No one looked up at her.

Where was Queenie? He must have gotten off at Bayville. She had to find the conductor and tell him what had happened! Just then an elderly woman coming down the aisle tripped and fell into Gigi, practically knocking her over. Gigi clutched at the seat back and tried to right the woman, who although tiny had a very strong grip on her arms.

'You tripped me!' the woman said accusingly, peering at Gigi with startlingly bright violet eyes.

'No I didn't. I'm sorry, I was just standing here...' Gigi said, flustered.

'You young people, you're all the same,' continued the woman in her raspy voice. 'You gave me such a fright! You think it's funny to trip an old lady?'

'B-but I didn't...' Gigi stammered.

'Well, the least you can do is get out my heart pills for me,' said the woman, lowering herself into the seat opposite Gigi's and thrusting an embroidered bag into her hands.

'Um...' Gigi was floored by the woman's presumption. She had to go and find the conductor!

'Well, are you going to get them for me or not?' the woman snapped. 'They're in the side pocket.'

Wordlessly, Gigi unzipped the side pocket and handed the woman a bottle of pills.

'Now I need some water,' said the woman. 'I suppose it would be too much trouble to ask you to get a bottle from the concessions car. Young people today don't go out of their way to help the elderly. Just wait until you get to be my age and see how you like it!'

'Of course I'll go,' Gigi said hurriedly. She didn't want the woman thinking she was an uncaring 'youngster'. Sighing, she made her way down the aisle again, giving in to the knowledge that her bags were long gone. She'd just have to wait until she got to Blessings to file a police report. Luckily she had a couple of dollars in her pocket to buy the water.

Twenty minutes later the train screeched to a halt at Blessings.

'You'll help me off the train, dear, won't you?' asked the old woman, whose tone had grown friendlier after Gigi brought her the bottle of water, along with a packet of chocolate wafers. With a silent groan, Gigi took her bag and guided her out of the train to the platform.

A commotion at the other end of the platform distracted her for a moment, and when she looked back, the woman had disappeared. Strange – where had she gone so suddenly? Perhaps she'd gone back into the train for something. Gigi considered looking for her, then realized Godfreys would be waiting.

She had no time to lose, so she made her way through the dingy station to the front entrance, feeling curiously light without her bags. She had no ID, no credit cards, no money, no photos, makeup, clothing or books – nothing to define who she was. Somehow that thought cheered her, and she realized she really was starting over. She had left her old identity behind – it was probably being sold to an illegal Ukrainian stripper right now – and she could be whoever she wanted to be. Maybe Queenie had actually done her a favor by so unceremoniously freeing her of her personal history.

Suddenly exhilarated, she flung open the fly-specked station doors and waltzed into the foggy, dreary afternoon, deeply inhaling tangy salt air.

'Ms Lenox?' came a crisp, British-accented voice as an older man emerged from a sleek roadster like the ones she'd seen in 1930s gangster movies. The man himself seemed to come from that era, with slicked-back silver hair, neatly trimmed moustache and a yellow ascot tucked into a double-breasted black blazer.

'Yes, I'm Ms Lenox. Please call me Gigi,' she replied, surprised at the formality of the car and driver.

Something about the man's British accent and white hair was familiar, but she couldn't place it.

The driver's expression softened and Gigi thought she saw the beginnings of a twinkle forming in his bright blue eyes. 'I'm pleased to meet you, Gigi. I'm Godfreys. Maya sent me to transport you to the Magical Theatre.' He paused to chuckle, as if he found the concept amusing. 'Please come with me. Shall I fetch your bags?' He peered around her, scanning the misty light blanketing the platform.

'Umm, I don't have any bags,' Gigi said. 'Wait, I mean, I did, but now I don't. That man on the train... but it's okay... I'm starting over.'

'Ah, I see,' said Godfreys, nodding as if what she'd said made sense. 'Very well. In we go, then.' He held open the back door of the roadster for her and she clambered in, still clutching her coat around her. The maroon leather seat was smooth and bouncy.

She sat in a comfortable stupor during the short ride up the coast in the rapidly fading light. Soothed by the car's smooth progress, she idly watched the ocean waves lap against rocky shores that gradually gave way to a main street dotted with massive black maple trees and quaint shops in beautifully preserved Victorian houses.

They turned down a gracious street, lined with large brick and fieldstone buildings – public library, courthouse, the town hall – and the car slid to a stop in front of the grand façade of an old theater decorated with carvings of angels and gargoyles.

It's exactly as I imagined it, Gigi thought. The marquee read:

The Magical Theatre. Closed for renovations. Reopening SOON.

Godfreys came around to hand her out of the car, then crooked his arm. She let him lead her to the gilded art deco-style doors. Something made her hesitate then; she had a sudden urge to run away, back to her safe cocoon in Manhattan, and curl up on her sofa. But it wasn't there anymore. This was her life now, and she must go ahead with it.

Sensing her hesitation, Godfreys looked down at her questioningly. She gave a small nod, and the theater door flew open as if it had been waiting for her. 'Oh!' Gigi exclaimed, startled. She hadn't expected an automatic door in a theater so old. She peered into the murky depths but couldn't see anything.

'After you, my dear,' said Godfreys, disengaging her arm. Gigi felt her breath come quicker as she stepped over the threshold into the dimness. Immediately a soft light filled the room. She blinked and looked around in awe. The light came from hundreds of gold sconces lining the walls, draped in crimson velvet. The deep blue ceiling was decorated with extraordinarily lifelike constellations that shimmered with their own cool light. The floor was an elaborate mosaic depicting fantastic scenes of jungles, mountains, oceans and all manner of animals.

'Please, proceed, Miss Gigi,' Godfreys prodded gently from behind her. Gigi stepped into the room, craning her neck to look around. 'You may have a seat and wait while I fetch Maya,' he instructed.

The only furniture in this strange room was a velvet sofa that matched the crimson drapes, strewn with invitingly puffy cushions. She sank into it gratefully, tucking her feet underneath her. In the cavernous silence, unmarred by outside sounds, she peered around curiously. Where was Maya going to come from? She saw no door leading to another part of the theater. This was the strangest building she'd ever been in. The animals seemed to be staring at her from the mosaic floor, their eyes glimmering in the candlelight.

'Ah, welcome, my beloved,' sang a rich, strangely accented voice, startling her. Where was the voice coming from? It seemed to fill the entire high-ceilinged room and echo through her body.

Gigi caught a swift movement from the corner of her eye and turned to behold a striking woman with warm café-au-lait skin and a mane of intricately beaded braids. The woman advanced majestically toward her, surrounded by fluttering yards of luminescent purple fabric. Gigi couldn't make out her features in the dim light, but backlit from the glow that surrounded her, she seemed almost to have a halo.

She held out her braceleted arms in greeting. Fascinated, Gigi took a deep breath and realized this must be Maya, the director of the Magical Theatre. No wonder she'd appeared so dramatically. She probably had all sorts of magic tricks up her sleeve, and had prepared this show to demonstrate to Gigi what the theater was capable of.

'Gigi, my love, welcome,' said Maya, pulling her up and sweeping her into a rose-scented embrace. Gigi felt herself stiffen. She was not accustomed to hugging strangers – had never been a touchy-feely type. Almost against her will, she relaxed into Maya's voluminous soft caress, and immediately felt a strong sense of well-being sweep through her.

Maya held Gigi at arm's length to study her.

'Mmm, yes,' she murmured. 'Much as I expected... yes... remedial training essential... must begin immediately.'

Gigi shifted uncomfortably under Maya's scrutiny, trying to screw up the courage to ask Maya what she meant by 'remedial training essential'. Of course she needed training – the classified ad had specified that experience was not required, and she'd made it very clear during their phone interview that this was her first theatrical management position. But *remedial*? That would hardly be necessary.

'Well, no time to lose, my dear,' Maya said briskly, releasing Gigi from her grasp before she could defend herself against the 'remedial' comment. 'Follow me,' she added.

Turning around in a swirl of violet light, she made off swiftly across the room.

Gigi hurried behind Maya, but the woman was a whirlwind. Before Gigi could catch up, Maya seemed to disappear into the velvet-draped wall at the opposite end of the room. There must be a door there that she hadn't noticed before, hidden by the thick curtains. But when Gigi arrived, there was no opening to be seen. She snatched at the curtain, scrabbling for a gap, but there was none. Frantic, she kneeled and lifted the curtain from underneath, peering at the wall behind. It was smooth and dark. Where had Maya gone, and how did she expect Gigi to follow?

'Look beyond the obvious, my sweet,' Maya's voice breathed in her ear. 'Things are not always as they seem. Seek what is beyond the familiar.'

Gigi whipped her head around, but Maya was not there. Her disembodied voice echoed endlessly in Gigi's mind. 'Seek the truth... pierce the veil of the illusion...'

Around and around the voice echoed, causing Gigi to grow dizzy, and her sight to blur. Still kneeling, she felt the room spin around her. When she tried to stand, the floor lurched. She staggered to her feet, swaying, trying to focus on the curtain. There must be a way in, there must...

Godfreys appeared at her elbow, steadying her. 'Can be a bit tricky around here until you get your sea legs,' he murmured. Gigi tried to give him a smile but she felt like crying. What was this place, and why was she here? It was almost as though she was dreaming. But if it was a dream, why did it seem so real?

Godfreys' hand on her elbow, the soft velvet of the curtain in her fist... She realized her hand was grasping the velvet as if it were a lifesaver.

Suddenly she saw the image of a lifesaver in front of her. It grew larger and larger, and in the center was an opening that revealed a yawning black sky dotted with stars – a way through the curtain! Without thinking, Gigi dove through the opening and felt herself tumbling, spinning, falling through space, losing all sense of boundaries, time and fixed reality.

Surrendering to her precipitous flight, the world as she knew it streamed from her, leaving a glittering vapor trail as she tumbled and flipped, then spread her arms and soared through endless black night.

Chapter Three

Gigi landed in a once-plush auditorium chair with a bone-jarring jolt, as if she'd been dropped from a great height. She stared around, disoriented, at a small, old-fashioned, dimly lit playhouse that was half-filled with people of all ages, shapes, sizes and colors. To her astonishment, while she watched, more people began filling the seats – not by walking down the threadbare red-carpeted aisle and pushing through rows, as Gigi would expect, but by dropping, as she must have, from above.

Where had she fallen from? She remembered flying through space, cavorting with stars and whirling with planets, dizzy with euphoria. But the memory was fading, even now. What the hell had that been about? Perhaps the Euro-queen on the train had dropped drugs in her water, and it had all been a giant hallucination. Or else it really was a dream.

Obviously, she couldn't have actually flown through space to get here – wherever 'here' was. Flying was not her favorite activity to begin with. But when she looked up at what should have been the ceiling, she saw that the theater was open to the sky – a sky filled with multitudes of stars – more stars than she'd ever seen in her life. Galaxies upon galaxies spun and pulsed, and she could swear she heard them emitting a deep, comforting hum.

While she watched, spellbound, a star shot across the sky, growing brighter as it approached. *Ooh, I love falling stars!* she thought, then quickly noticed another, and another. They were coming very close. In fact, it looked like the stars were falling right into the auditorium! As they approached, however, they gained solidity and decreased speed, taking the form of humans. She realized with a shock that the people appearing in the seats were falling like stars from the endless sky.

Gigi's eyes widened in surprise as a star whizzed directly

toward her. It began morphing into the shape of a person who was headed, apparently, for Gigi's lap.

Instinctively reverting to elementary-school emergency drills, she ducked and covered. A second later she felt a *thunk!* as the flying person landed in the adjoining seat.

Feeling foolish, Gigi righted herself, shook her hair off her face and stared at her neighbor – a slender youngish woman who seemed utterly composed and not at all put out by her journey. With perfect calm, the woman set down the leather briefcase she was clutching and removed a polka-dotted makeup bag. Surveying herself critically in a compact, she whipped out a brush and ran it through her dark chin-length bob, slicked on shell-pink lip gloss and checked her flawless eyeliner. After putting away the makeup bag, she smoothed her black pencil skirt over slim thighs and surveyed her surroundings with a satisfied smirk.

Finally the woman turned to an open-mouthed Gigi and offered her a small nod and a tight-lipped smile. Gigi returned it weakly, too astounded to speak. Why didn't her neighbor seem discomposed by this bizarre situation?

Whatever! Gigi mentally shook herself. It was time to attempt to make sense of what was happening. *I appear to be at some sort of intimate theatrical event,* she thought. *In space.*

Stunning reasoning. Obviously she was not destined to become a detective. She had a sudden urge to laugh. What would Stephanie say about this? She'd nudge Gigi's arm and whisper something about how the trip through space was obviously hard on the hair. Automatically, Gigi's hand went up to smooth her tresses, and she noticed she was clutching a piece of paper. Huh? She brought the paper close to her eyes, to try and make out its small writing in the dim light.

The paper was folded like a program, and on the front in elaborately curlicued writing it said, 'Remedial Angel Training: The Dreamtime Sessions'. What the heck was Remedial Angel

Training? And dreamtime – well, that clarified things a little, even though she couldn't remember falling asleep. If this was all a dream, that would go a long way toward explaining the unexpected turn of events. But it certainly was the most lucid, tangible dream she'd ever had – space travel aside.

Darting a look at the woman next to her, Gigi noticed she had donned stylish rectangular reading glasses and intently perused her own program, nodding in agreement as she scanned it. She seemed to have some idea of what was going on, but much as Gigi longed to ask her for information, she wasn't going to reveal her own ignorance. She opened the program and read the fanciful print on the inside:

Eons ago, angelic beings of light celebrated each moment in a celestial playground of unending perfection.

Oh no, Gigi thought with rising panic. *Is this some New Age convention or something? Or maybe I'm dead? What is this stuff about angels?* Willing herself to remain calm, she resumed reading.

One particularly sunny afternoon, a gathering of angels began discussing the nature of being an angel. Many good observations were made, but after awhile the group became dissatisfied; it seemed as if there was a limit to what they could truly understand. "You know," one very wise angel finally said. "It's almost as if we would have to experience what it means to not be an angel in order to fully grasp what it means to be one." At that very moment, Maya, Mistress of Illusion and Director of Heavenly Special Effects, happened by. The group turned to her expectantly.

'Maya', the wise angel said, 'would you create an illuminating game for us? We would like to expand beyond our knowing and you're just the person to make learning fun.' The rest of the group nodded in eager assent.

Delighted, Maya agreed. She loved a challenge, and she immediately set out to develop an elaborate game of enchantment that would provide a forum for the angels' learning.

She dreamed a fantasy called life on earth and set it center stage in a fabulous playhouse that she named the Magical Theatre. She lost no time decorating the theater with her favorite creations: mangoes, panda bears, red-breasted newts and rainbows.

Gigi wrinkled her brow, confused. The Magical Theatre! What?

From the crest of heaven the angels peeked eagerly down at the Magical Theatre, watching it fill up with oceans, mountains and crimson sunsets. They couldn't wait to get there.

'Is it ready?' they asked Maya when she emerged, radiant.

'It's ready,' Maya said, 'but you're not. One more thing...' and she wove a magic spell around the eager angels with her golden wand. This spell was an integral part of the game, because it caused the angels to forget everything they knew about the perfection of the universe, including the perfection of themselves. Maya used the fiery tip of her wand, to send forth a smokey screen to cloak the spark of each angel's Divine connection.

Laughing merrily she gleefully proclaimed, "Now, let the game begin!"

Maya then lovingly pushed the angels through the layered mists of her splendid creation. As they tumbled head-over-heels through the void, her fading instructions echoed in their ears: "Go now and play the game of enchantment in the Magical Theatre on earth. But know this: To break the spell of forget-fulness and awaken from the enchantment, you must remember your divine perfection. And you must live the truth of your magnificence!"

Gigi felt her lips take on an Elvis-like sneer. What was this, some kind of a joke? Maybe Maya wanted to see if she had a sense of humor.

As time passed, the initial group of angels was joined by a curious multitude eager to participate in Maya's game. All the angels were certain they would awaken from the enchantment and remember their innate perfection as sparks of the Divine Mystery. They were sure they could withstand the pervasive fears of the human belief system. But few were able to break the spell of forgetfulness.

Instead, the game of enchantment entrapped them in the belief of limitation, and one by one, they fell prey to the illusion of their imperfection. Feeling lost and strangely incomplete, they searched in vain for the missing pieces that might make them whole.

It was fascinating to watch, but ultimately it occurred to Maya that perhaps she'd made her game a little too enticing. Even the angels who wanted most to awaken couldn't seem to get through the beautiful veils Maya had created. The angels needed a clue, she realized. A hint, maybe a website that revealed some intricacies of the game? Finally, Maya decided a remedial training course was exactly the ticket to help those angels who had demonstrated their readiness to awaken. Summoning them in their dreams, she began to teach them about the keystones they needed to master to cast off the spell of forgetfulness and reclaim their authentic natures.

You, Gigi, are one of the earthbound angels, and you're fortunate enough to have been offered the opportunity to attend this course and learn the steps necessary to awaken from the enchantment.

Startled to see her name on the program, Gigi crumpled it in her sweaty hand. What a crock! It had to be some sort of practical joke. Maybe she was on a reality show and any moment the cameramen would break into laughter, and the lights would come on. Remedial angel training, indeed!

Gigi looked around hopefully, but there was no camera crew to be seen, and no one jumped out to yell, 'Punk'd!' Instead, all she could see were more and more flying stars turning into falling people.

Okay, let's think about this rationally, Gigi said to herself sternly.

For argument's sake, let's say I really am an angel.

If so, the idea of her needing remedial *anything* was ridiculous. She'd always been a good student and had graduated from an Ivy League college. If she hadn't been so busy with all her extracurricular activities, she was sure she would have been near the top of her class. The word 'remedial' had never been applied to her in any circumstance, and she certainly wasn't going to stand for it now. She was going to have to ask her prissy-looking neighbor how to get out of here.

But maybe the woman wasn't that intelligent, if she was in remedial angel training too. Still, it was worth a try.

'Hi,' Gigi said, clearing her throat. Her neighbor looked up with an annoyed expression. Gigi plowed ahead. 'I was just wondering, um, if you know how we can get out of this? I mean, I'm obviously in the wrong place, and I need to know who to talk to so I can be excused from the course.' Realizing she hadn't introduced herself, Gigi stuck out her hand and said, 'Oh, and I'm Gigi.'

Reluctantly, her neighbor took her hand and gave it a quick shake, saying, 'I'm Susan' before quickly withdrawing her hand and wiping it on her skirt.

This Susan was really starting to get on Gigi's nerves. Unable to stop herself, she said cheerfully, 'It's great to be able to shake hands with people again since my contagious rash is almost gone.'

Susan froze, then dove into her briefcase and pulled out antiseptic gel, briskly rubbing it on her hands. Gigi watched with satisfaction.

'So, Susan, any idea how to ditch this remedial nightmare?' she asked, trying for a light tone.

Susan raised one perfectly waxed eyebrow. 'Clearly you have no idea where you are. You're here because you have been given a once-in-a-lifetime chance to take this course. Maya probably selected you because you had hit bottom, and were in need of serious help.' She added something under her breath that Gigi was pretty sure was, 'And boy, do you need it.'

Losing patience, Gigi snapped, 'Well, since this is remedial angel training, I guess *everyone* in here needs it. And not just in the social graces, either, though I hope she covers basic politeness.'

Susan sniffed, crossed her arms over her expensive-looking raw silk jacket, and turned away, aquiline nose in the air.

'Smarty-pants,' Gigi muttered, wishing there were someone sitting on her other side, but that seat was empty. Perhaps the dreadlocked Rastafarian sitting in front of her would be able to help.

Before Gigi could tap the man on the shoulder, a screechy sound like the movement of rusty cables drew her attention to the stage. The small proscenium was framed by velvet curtains like the ones in the lobby of the Magical Theatre, but these were suspended in space with no visible means of support. Gilded columns rose from stage right and left, up and up until Gigi's eye could no longer follow them.

An elaborate chandelier was being lowered on invisible cables from the nonexistent ceiling, causing the ghastly screeching noise. It finally reached its destination ten or twelve feet above the stage, whereupon the house lights dimmed and the theater was plunged into blackness.

Then, with silent splendor, the chandelier glowed to life, illuminated by thousands of tiny, swarming lights. Gigi squinted. The lights looked like fireflies, darting in and out of each other in a never-ending pattern.

The audience fell silent, except for a general rustling as everyone settled into their seats expectantly. Gigi held her breath, heart pounding. Although she had no idea what might be coming, she discovered that she was sweating in anticipation. The strangeness of her surroundings and her manner of arrival were no longer her primary concern. She was completely focused on the stage, waiting to see what was next.

The silence stretched on, and just when her inner New Yorker was about to give in to the urge to yell 'Let's get the show on the road!' Gigi heard a swooshing noise from above like the flapping of dozens of wings. She gaped, awestruck, as a golden chariot drawn by winged horses swept across the theater and landed on the stage, accompanied by a collective 'Oooohh!' from the audience.

Then with infinite grace, a figure unfolded from her seat in the chariot – a woman with a mass of swirling braids, cinnamon skin and robes that seemed alive, whipping around her as she grew taller, taller, floating out of the chariot and onto the stage. She snapped her fingers and the chariot disappeared in a puff of pink smoke.

'Welcome, my dear students,' said Maya.

So Gigi *had* followed Maya to the Magical Theatre after all! This must be it. But how could the theater in Blessings, Maine, be located in outer space? Remembering that this was apparently some sort of lucid dream, Gigi decided to stop trying to figure out the details. Instead she would simply wait for the moment when she could get Maya's attention and let her know she was in the wrong place. Maya would surely recognize that she was supposed to be training to manage the Magical Theatre, not enrolled in a remedial angel course.

Maya's rich tones carried effortlessly through the small theater, sounding at once grand and intimate.

'You are probably feeling slightly confused, and I cannot blame you,' Maya began. 'I do apologize if your arrival here was a tad abrupt. But we really have no time to lose. You are all in great need of assistance with your awakening – and since there is only this moment, we may as well seize it!'

Gigi was startled to see a shrieking monkey hop across the stage, chasing an alarm clock running as fast as it could on spindly legs. The monkey caught the clock and grasped it in its long fingers, waving it in the air before leaping offstage.

Maya laughed delightedly. 'Yes, seize the moment, my little band of strays! For you have lost touch with who you really are, and I am here to help you discover the truth.'

'Are you gonna tell us who *you* are?' someone yelled from the balcony in a thick Brooklyn accent.

'Oh yes, thank you, Vinny. Timidity is certainly not one of your limitations, is it? Permit me to introduce myself. I am known as Maya, the Great Mistress of Illusion. As you no doubt read in your programs, I am the creator of the Magical Theatre – and I am here to guide you through a program of dreamtime remedial angel training.' She beamed and dipped her head modestly, as if expecting applause.

A stir rippled through the theater. Emboldened by Vinny's question, Gigi seized the moment to raise her hand, certain that once Maya recognized her she'd send her to wherever she was really supposed to be, to train for her new job. But Maya, either not seeing or ignoring her waving arm, continued.

'Yes, I designed the game of daily life you've been playing!' she declared, clapping her hands and causing a cascade of yellow smiley faces to bounce and twirl around her. 'I am so happy to remind you that what you have thought of as reality until now is a world entirely of your own making, a "reality" that you have created within the enchantment of the Magical Theatre.'

She held up her hand, as if to ward off the unspoken questions of the students. 'We'll answer all your queries, never fear. For now, I ask you only to access the farthest recesses of your mind to remember the eons you lived *before* you began your human experience. As angels, you existed without time or care, each love-filled moment flowing unimpeded into the next, across eternity.'

The word 'eternity' reverberated, booming, around and around the theater. Gigi felt as if she'd encountered that word only recently in a very different circumstance, but she couldn't remember where. Before she could place it, however, she was distracted by a brisk click-click-clicking next to her. Susan had taken her laptop out of her briefcase and was studiously typing away, recording Maya's every word with immaculately manicured fingers.

Gigi rolled her eyes. *God, she's too much. What does she think this is – the Harvard Business School?* She quickly sat on her own bitten, ragged nails and wished she'd thought to get a manicure before departing for Blessings, and also to bring at least a pad of paper and a pen. Annoying as Susan was, she found herself wishing she could be more like her. She really seemed to have it all together – one of those women who'd always had the ability to make Gigi feel instantly dowdy, insignificant and stupid, no matter how good she'd been feeling a moment before.

Strangely, however, the seemingly practical Susan looked like she was buying this eternal life stuff. Her expression in the glowing light from the chandelier was eager and serious.

I've really got to get out of Woo-hoo-ville, Gigi decided, suddenly desperate to escape. She tried to stand, but found herself stuck to her seat as if by a magnetic force. Reluctantly, she turned her eyes back to Maya.

'I know this will challenge your human notions of common sense, but you must hear it,' Maya said sternly, beaming her violet eyes straight at Gigi. Gigi suddenly felt that she'd seen those eyes in someone else's face recently – but the moment passed as Maya continued, 'You are each a spark of the Divine Mystery, cloaked in human form. Perfection is your inheritance!'

Perfect? A spark of the Divine Mystery?

'Please, give me a break,' Gigi groaned, earning a glare from Susan. But against her will, a part of her found Maya's words appealing. It would be nice to be perfect. Then she wouldn't have so much to worry about.

'So Vinny's perfect? I guess that's why he's so conceited,' another Brooklynese voice shouted from the rear of the theater, causing a titter to ripple through the listeners.

Maya put her hands on her hips and shook her head at the culprit. 'Yes, Vinny is perfect, and so are you, Tito – and I would think you'd know enough to keep your comments to yourself, seeing as this is your third trip through Remedial Angel Training.'

'Ah, bull's-eye!' Tito said, drawing more laughter. Gigi had to admire his spunk, but Susan sighed and shot a disdainful look in the direction of the balcony.

'Now, let's get on with the program, shall we?' Maya asked, an aura of indefinable power surrounding her. Her voice took on an echoing quality. 'Although you don't remember it, each of you volunteered to undergo a spell of forgetfulness and enter the Magical Theatre in human form. That is how you arrived on earth.' She paused for dramatic effect.

It all sounded improbable to Gigi, especially the part about volunteering. She picked at her ragged nails as Maya continued. 'You courageously chose to participate in the grand experiment of the Magical Theatre. You agreed to play the game of life on earth, knowing that the rules of the game required you to remember your essential perfection – in spite of all the forces on earth that would collaborate to convince you that you're deeply flawed.'

A murmuring swelled from the crowd and Maya held up her finger, shooting them a playfully stern look before continuing. 'The key to breaking this spell is to rediscover and live the truth of your magnificence.'

Gigi reluctantly admitted to herself that it did sound nice to imagine that life on earth was only a game designed for her to discover her magnificence. If only it were true and not a fairy tale.

'Each of you was certain you'd be the one to withstand the enchantment, break the spell of forgetfulness, and star in your own production without a glimmer of stage fright. But your good intentions weren't enough to keep you from giving in to the illusion, and you began to see life on earth as the only reality. You took it very seriously and developed all kinds of physical and emotional ailments in response to the stress it created. Worse, you became convinced that you were fundamentally flawed, and that to achieve happiness and completion you'd have to change. You began concocting a distorted image of perfection.

'Imagine the lunacy of searching for something outside yourselves to complete you,' Maya sighed. 'My sweet souls, how could you believe you had to do that? How could you spend your whole lifetime in the Magical Theatre trying to be something other than what you are, when you already embody absolute perfection?'

Silence reigned in the theater, even Vinny and Tito sobered by Maya's words. Gigi was torn. It was obvious Maya was sincere, but it was really too much – Maya, talking about logic? As if any of this were logical! Her eyes roved the theater to see if anyone else had noticed the absurdity of Maya's reasoning, but everyone seemed riveted. If others were skeptical, they weren't showing it. Oh, well. She, for one, was not about to accept a load of crap about her own perfection. What a laugh! She used to be an angel – sure, and pigs had wings!

Suddenly, the stage was beset by a flurry of sound and motion that kicked up a cloud of dust. When the dust cleared, Gigi's jaw dropped. Maya's robes had been replaced by overalls and a plaid shirt, and she was surrounded by a flying gaggle of fat pink pigs with madly flapping angel wings, dipping and swirling around her. They snorted gently as they played an airborne game of 'Ring Around the Rosy' with Maya in the center. Gigi couldn't believe her eyes and ears. Flying pigs – it was as if Maya had read her mind. *Could* Maya perceive her thoughts? She slumped down guiltily in her seat.

Looking across the rows of students straight into Gigi's eyes, Maya said steadily, 'Be assured that your current nonsensical thinking is merely a result of the spell you're under. It has led you to search in vain for the missing pieces you hope will create a new, flawless version of yourself. Mark this well, my dear students, and remember it: What you long for already exists within you. You won't find it through relationships, success or riches. You were born a perfect expression of divine love. The wellspring of love, acceptance and happiness you've been madly seeking is already inside you. You are its source!'

The word 'source' echoed around and around the theater as the audience sat in rapt silence. With a shimmer of shifting light, Maya's garb changed back to her goddess robes, and she continued. 'Miracles await you, beloveds, when you remember who you truly are.'

Well, how are we supposed to remember? Gigi thought. *If we really are so perfect – which I doubt – how are we supposed to break the spell of forgetfulness? I mean, I must be under a really strong spell, because I feel about as imperfect as you can get.*

Gigi's heart contracted unexpectedly in reaction to her thought, and a sudden sharp pain assailed her. It hurt to think of herself as massively imperfect. Tears sprang to her eyes and ran down her face, and she allowed herself the indulgence of a silent cry. Then, embarrassed, she darted her eyes around to see if Susan had noticed – but she was looking down at her computer screen, seemingly in deep contemplation.

Then, without warning, a parade of negative thoughts began marching through Gigi's mind, chanting words she had used many times to describe herself: *Dumb, wrong, bad, too much, not enough, too silly, too tall, too fat, too loud, unlovable, undeserving.* The words cut into her now, and the pain in her heart increased. She placed her hand on her chest and breathed deeply, trying to soothe herself.

I don't want to hurt myself anymore with this belief in my imperfection, she thought suddenly, surprising herself with her strength of conviction. A moment ago she'd been scoffing at the idea that she was perfect, yet now she wanted more than ever to believe it. But how could she get there?

As if in answer to her question, Maya said, 'Here in the dreamtime, uninfluenced by the lure of the enchantment, I will reveal to you the secrets you once knew and are now buried deep in your soul. All you need to do is open the barriers in your minds and hearts. What have you got to lose?' She flung her arms wide, and Gigi felt a flood of love pouring over her.

Mesmerized, Gigi nodded yes, in sync with the others yearning for a chance to reconnect with their true natures.

'During this dreamtime course, I will share with you twelve keystones – the foundational principles that will release you from your slumber of forgetfulness and allow you to grow into awareness of your magnificence,' Maya continued. 'Tonight we will explore the first keystone, and your homework will be to find a way to implement it. Then you'll be ready for the second one, and so on. After you begin to absorb the first crucial keystones, you'll be well on your way to awakening, and we will no longer need to meet so formally or have assigned homework. Depending on where your dreams take you, I'll begin visiting you in different ways.'

Susan's hand shot into the air.

'Yes, Susan?' Maya asked.

'So this course will take place completely during the dreamtime?'

'Yes. That is the time when I can most easily reach you, since you are out from under the direct influence of the spell of forget-fulness.'

'But how will we be able to remember what we learn when we wake up?'

Gigi had to admit that was a good question.

'Let us say your memory will be nudged,' Maya said. 'You may not remember it all at once, but the way you've looked at the world will no longer make sense, so you will automatically seek the keystones as you need them. Of course, you will have to practice the lessons of the keystones until you master a new way of life. And maybe there will be some additional help you'll find when you wake up,' she added mysteriously.

Although Gigi was still unsure why she was here, her revelation about believing in her own imperfection had given her an inkling. She decided not to take this opportunity to alert Maya of her mistake. Clearly Maya knew Gigi was here, and it did seem she had some interesting points to make. Gigi settled back to enjoy the lecture as invisible lights began to bathe the stage in an ever-changing spectrum of color.

Chapter Four

'Now, my loves,' Maya trilled, suddenly surrounded by a flock of iridescent songbirds, 'let us begin with the first keystone.' A marble podium appeared in front of her and she stepped up to it, peering at a thick pile of pages that were turning themselves over, one by one, for her perusal.

Gigi felt nervous and excited. Maybe these keystones really could change her life. It was about time. After all, she'd tried it her way, and it hadn't exactly been a smashing success.

'Hrrmm.' Maya cleared her throat dramatically and said, 'Before I start, angel dears, I want you to know that you don't need to worry about taking notes. I want your attention completely present.'

Susan's busy fingers stopped abruptly and she looked abashed. Her hand shot into the air again.

'Yes, Susan?' Maya asked, and Gigi thought she could detect a hint of impatience in her tone.

'Can we take notes if we want to?' Susan asked. 'I think I can do a lot better if I have notes.'

'Certainly,' said Maya. 'But be aware that you cannot absorb this information with your intellect alone. Your mind will want to "figure it out", but true understanding will come from surrendering your need to know and sinking into the wisdom that was yours before you fell under the spell of forgetfulness.'

'So we can take notes, though?' Susan asked. God, this woman was persistent. She was probably a Phi Beta Kappa and had some high-powered job in the city. Against her will, Gigi felt envy gnaw at her gut.

'Yes, you can. However!' Maya eyed them piercingly. 'When you are once again caught by the spell's seduction, you will need to find your way back to a place of true awareness. Knowledge hasn't worked for you yet. In fact, what you *think* you know has been a distraction. Now, you need to take action to reconnect to your authentic nature. Don't worry; the right way will come to you if your awareness stays present.'

Oh no, Gigi thought. *This sounds hard. How am I going to know if I'm aware or not? Maybe I'm the only one that doesn't get it.* Suddenly she felt anxious, and her eye started to twitch involuntarily.

Meanwhile, above the stage a neon-yellow banner unfurled to reveal the following words, written in the same fancy, old-fashioned lettering as the program: 'Keystone 1: You are the playwright of your own life.'

Gigi leaned forward, rested her chin on her fist, and listened intently as Maya began:

'The first thing you must discover, dear students, is that you, and you alone, are *the playwright of your own life*. You write your own script. Yes, you were born into a particular situation, and certain things have happened that might have been beyond your physical control. Yet you are responsible for your reactions and responses to these situations and circumstances. At each juncture of your life, *you* have made decisions and taken actions that propelled your production in a certain direction.

'Tonight I invite you to ask yourself two questions: First, what kind of storyline does my script follow? And second, has it brought me happiness and peace?'

'Not exactly,' Gigi muttered aloud.

To her surprise, Susan shot her what looked like a sympathetic glance. 'I know what you mean,' she whispered, then immediately returned her gaze to the stage.

'Without awareness, you have missed the moments where taking a different action would have shifted the course of your drama,' Maya went on. 'Tonight, I invite you to witness the fact that you are now free to recognize these moments. You can now see that the possibility for reworking your script lies in your hands.'

Gigi felt a small bubble of excitement building inside her. The concept of being free to create a different reality for herself was infinitely appealing.

'Next, ask yourself if your current script accurately reflects who you are,' instructed Maya, pausing to let the students ponder her statement.

No way, thought Gigi. *I know I can be way more than the wronged ex-wife who threw herself a two-month pity party and drank all the wine in the cupboard.*

'If the script you are following is not an accurate reflection of the *real* you, you're free to fashion an entirely new production,' said Maya. 'After all, my dear ones, you alone have the power to recreate the themes that form the foundation of your script.

'Now listen carefully, because I am going to give you your first homework assignment. Before we meet again, I ask that you uncover the truth of the life you are living in the Magical Theatre. Describe the mythical script you've been following by recording the story of *you* in your journal.'

As Susan leaned down to pull out a notebook from her briefcase, Gigi felt a jolt of panic. She didn't have a journal! How had Susan Smarty-pants known to bring one? She thought of asking Susan to borrow a notebook and pen, which she surely had in her briefcase, but she didn't want to give her yet another reason to feel superior.

Just then, she looked down to see a beautiful journal miraculously resting in her lap. The cover of the journal seemed to be a rainbow-hued hologram, the colors shifting and melting into one another in a constantly changing watercolor tableau. She watched, thinking that life was like that – one event melting into another without stopping. Maybe this was her chance to stop long enough to change the course of her script.

Maya's voice cut through her reverie. 'Although I understand that you may find it intimidating to write what you perceive as the flawed story of your life, let me reassure you that it's safe to be honest in your revelation, because I love you unconditionally and will not judge you.'

'Even Tito?' Vinny's voice shouted, causing an outbreak of snorting and guffawing in the back rows.

Ignoring Vinny, Maya continued. 'As you describe your life, I want you to ask yourself the following questions.'

A second banner unfurled above her head, emblazoned with questions that illuminated like neon signs as she spoke:

Who are you, really? What do you claim to believe? How do you feel about the character you've become? What image of yourself do you most stubbornly defend?

A gold pen appeared in midair. Gigi snatched it and scribbled the questions in her journal, grateful she wouldn't have to try to remember them later.

'These questions will lead you to discover what forms the basis of your reality,' Maya continued. 'Be completely open and curious and let your thoughts pour onto the page. Allow yourself to be surprised by what comes out. Act as an investigator and discover the uncensored you. Finally, notice that the person you've called *you* is actually a mythical character of your own creation.'

A fantastic-looking creature danced onstage. It was a life-sized rag doll patched together from all manner of fabrics, with a mop for hair and different-colored buttons for eyes. She danced jerkily, her expression blank. She reminded Gigi of the Patchwork Girl from the *Wizard of Oz* series she'd read as a child.

'It is important to realize that who you *think* you are is merely a composite cobbled together from beliefs you've formed and decisions you've made based on your experiences,' Maya explained. 'Like this patchwork girl, you have pieced yourself together from scraps.'

Gigi felt a gnawing sadness at the pit of her stomach. Had she really doomed herself to such an existence, allowing herself to be a patched-together image rather than a whole person?

'As you write the story of your lives, my dear students,

imagine that you could glimpse your tale from the vantage point of the heart of the Great Mystery. Would your story accurately reflect this legacy or would it show the influence of the enchantment of the Magical Theatre? Musing on this question will help you recognize how far you've drifted from the divine inheritance of your perfection.'

Gigi closed her eyes, trying to take in this seemingly implausible information. While she could intellectually understand that she had made unconscious decisions that determined the course of her life, she had trouble believing she had been the one to make things so difficult. If she could really have written her own script, she would have been a philanthropist or a writer or a famous actress; she would have thrown in world peace for good measure – and certainly Keith never would have left her. Or maybe she would have married George Clooney instead.

How could she have been the 'playwright of her own script' when she would have wanted things to be so different – when *she* would have been so different?

As if in answer, Maya continued. 'I beg you to be stout-hearted, my wayward students, because although it may seem difficult, you must acknowledge that you've been your own scriptwriter. Once you assume responsibility for the story of your life, you'll have the power to break free from the restricted role you've been playing. Remember, I am here to help you awaken, and I would not assign you something that did not have a distinct purpose.

'While you write your story, notice how much of it has been formed out of your mind's often skewed interpretation of past events. Allow yourself to notice that you've stuck to a storyline created from reactions to situations and backed up with inaccurate evidence. Aren't you ready to ditch that muddled mass of fears, wounds and relentless self-criticism?'

Maya chuckled, a sound like water bubbling up from a deep spring. 'Can you imagine how much time and energy you've expended on this tired script? Why not use your vast ingenuity to become the true essence of *you* instead of working so hard to keep yourself small, manageable and predictable? My dears, your script may fit you as comfortably as a pair of well-worn jeans, but it's time to let your boundless magnificence shine. Dare to write yourself a fabulous starring role in a groundbreaking new production!'

Gigi's head was spinning. Had she really been the one to write the script that led her to wake up a week and a half ago, lonely, depressed, and all out of wine and coffee? But what about Keith cheating, Stephanie getting married, and TheaterKids losing its funding? She hadn't made those things happen. How could she have created the parts of the script that were beyond her control?

Answering her silent question, Maya said, 'As the playwright of your own script, your choices are infinite. When life events seem out of your control, remember that even if you can't change them, it is always possible to form a new perception of them. That new perception leads to new choices, which then create new experiences. When you begin to shift your perspective in this way, you will understand that you have the power to continually rework the script of your life, opening yourself to amazing outcomes you've yet to imagine.'

Maya surveyed the audience, her eyes seeming to beam into each individual to convey the clarity of her message. 'Are you ready to throw away your stale, yellowing script and create a fresh and lively one? Can you throw open the stage door and admit the endless possibilities available to you in the Magical Theatre?'

A smattering of 'yeses' emitted from the crowd.

Sure, why not? Gigi acquiesced silently. It couldn't be worse than before, after all.

Suddenly, she realized her vision had grown blurry and everything looked slanted and strange. She blinked, confused, and attempted to rub her eyes. But instead of flesh, her hand encountered cool glass.

Maya laughed her deep, rich laugh. 'Today, my dears, dare to remove the bewitched spectacles you've been wearing. These spectacles have kept you from knowing who you really are!'

Bewitched spectacles! Gigi tried to pluck them off but they were fastened to her ears.

'Perhaps the spectacles caused you to miss the fine print on your production's playbill,' Maya continued. 'It reads: "Magical means anything is possible. You are limited only by your choices." It's high time you smash the lenses that have blinded you and stare in wonder at the millions of options right in front of your face.'

Gigi closed her eyes to block out the warped perspective of the bewitched spectacles, her temples beginning to throb gently. She felt a strange sense of mingled exhaustion and exhilaration. Her mind was tired, but Maya's words had given her a sense of hope.

'That's all for now, my dears,' said Maya briskly, pulling a huge gold pocket watch out of her bosom and consulting it. 'I really must run. So many illusions, so little time.' She added to herself, 'Even eternity sometimes doesn't seem like enough...'

The pocket watch turned into a dove, complete with olive branch, and took a turn around the theater, its wings scattering white confetti.

'Peace, my doves. Have fun with your script! And remember, you are magnificent,' Maya added.

Before Gigi could raise her hand and ask what she was supposed to do next, Maya twirled upward, her robes swirling around her as she spiraled up and up into the endless sky. As she ascended, the bewitched spectacles rose as one, off hundreds of noses, and followed her into space.

Relieved to be able to see normally again, Gigi looked at Susan, who was busily packing up her things.

'Hey, do you know where we're supposed to go now?' she

asked, trying to sound casual. Maybe Susan would be a little nicer now that they'd shared a moment of recognition earlier.

Susan stood, grasping her briefcase. Looking at her hopefully, Gigi couldn't help noticing that she was wearing high-heeled leather boots with her skirt and blazer, the perfect mix of sexy and businesslike that Gigi had never felt she'd truly accomplished.

'If you don't know, then I guess it's up to you to figure it out,' Susan said rather nastily. Just then a scooter swept down from the sky and hovered in front of her. She got on primly and revved the engine, scooting up into space as if it were the most normal thing in the world.

Gigi resisted the impulse to hurl her journal at Susan and knock her off her stupid scooter. So much for a shared bond. Oh well, she didn't want Susan's help anyway.

All around Gigi, strange contraptions were arriving to pick up the students. A camel carried off a stout satin-clad opera singer, a donkey picked up a Japanese man in a business suit, and a purring Harley arrived for a tiny Indian woman. Gigi figured something would come for her since this seemed to be the way out. She hoped it would be a Porsche. She settled in to wait, enjoying the parade of outlandish vehicles and trying to guess which person each vehicle would choose.

Before she knew it, the theater had gradually emptied until she was the only one left. She cried out to the last person to leave, a leather-clad muscleman straight out of The Village People riding on a rocking horse, but he didn't appear to hear her. She was alone in the silent theater. Suddenly frightened, she ran up the aisle to check the doors. Maybe she was supposed to just walk out of here. But the doors wouldn't budge. Fighting a rising sense of panic, she tried jumping up to see if she could fly out the way she'd flown in. But that didn't work either.

Gigi finally sank into a front-row seat. She'd just have to wait and see what happened. There was nothing else to do.

Chapter Five

Feeling small and rather creeped out in the empty theater, Gigi huddled in her seat. To distract herself from her jitters, she figured she'd start on her homework. Opening her journal, she reread the homework questions she'd jotted down on the first page:

Who are you, really?

What do you claim to believe?

How do you feel about the character you've become?

What image of yourself do you most stubbornly defend?

Okay, this shouldn't be too hard, Gigi thought, nibbling on the surprisingly tasty tip of the gold pen. She began to write.

I am Gigi Lenox. Theater manager [writing that gave her a small thrill], divorced, almost 35 years old, formerly of New York and now of Blessings, Maine. I am a caring, often selfless, but sometimes flippant person with a deep desire to trust and help people. I am also a bit of a loner sometimes. I have a good sense of humor, unless the joke's on me (vis-à-vis Slutgate). I am fairly attractive (when I have the right products handy), quite intelligent (except when it comes to my taste in men) and ridiculously loyal. I'm a perfectionist with myself but pretty forgiving with others. And I make a mean vegetarian lasagna.

Gigi paused to read over what she'd written. It was strange to try to sum herself up in a few sentences, and her words seemed inadequate. Still, they gave the general gist. Shrugging, she moved on to the next question.

I believe that:

Someday I'll find a soul mate to complete me.

To effect world change, it is necessary to think globally and act locally.

There is no such thing as coincidence.

Women need to take over the world before it combusts.

You can't count on anyone but yourself.

Fashion rules are made to be broken.

Chocolate won't go to your hips if you eat it standing up.

She thought of crossing out the last two, not wanting to appear frivolous, but then she remembered Maya saying she would never judge anyone and thought, *What the hell. I am a little frivolous, after all. And I think Maya can appreciate that, seeing as she's the one who created flying pigs onstage.*

Moving on, Gigi wrote:

I feel okay about who I've become, considering the cards life has handed me, but I know I have a lot of untapped potential. In other words, I have a long way to go.

The last question stumped Gigi a little. What image of herself did she most stubbornly defend? She couldn't think of an answer. Oh well, she'd move on to writing her script and would get back to that pesky question later.

'Maybe together we could find out a bit more about that image of yourself by investigating your story,' called a crisply accented voice, causing Gigi to jump to her feet, with a little scream, and drop her pen. Heart racing, she turned to see Godfreys walking down the theater aisle toward her, looking like a professor in a gray cardigan and impeccably creased gabardine trousers.

'Sorry if I startled you,' Godfreys said, suppressing a smile at her astonishment. 'I'm here to help you with your homework. In case you haven't figured it out yet, I'm the guardian angel assigned to assist you.'

'But... I thought I was supposed to write my life story,' Gigi said lamely, still shaken up by Godfreys' sudden appearance. Also, something about his tweedy, über-British look reminded her of someone she was sure she'd seen recently...

'Actually, the elements of your story are not as important as understanding that it is just a story,' Godfreys corrected her.

'Oh-kaay,' Gigi said distractedly. Who did he resemble?

Someone in Manhattan, she was sure... someone who had helped her, in some way...

Focus, Gigi, this is important, she admonished herself, and, giving herself a little shake, she honed in on Godfreys' words.

'For instance, you answered the profound question "Who are you, really?" by selecting a few specific details from the millions you could have used to describe yourself,' Godfreys explained. 'These details have become your story.'

'Hmm,' Gigi said, pondering this new information. It was an interesting angle. Why *had* she selected some facts and not others?

'To see how that happened, let's take a look at some key moments in the script you've called your life,' he went on. 'Don't worry about writing it down. Your journal will take care of it for you. Just put it on the seat next to you, then get comfortable and enjoy the show!'

Godfreys sat down in the front row next to Gigi and she put her journal and pen on the empty seat beside her.

'Popcorn?' Godfreys asked, and suddenly Gigi realized she was very hungry.

'Sure,' she said, and a bucket of steaming buttered popcorn appeared on her lap. She shoved a handful in her mouth.

'Jolly good, here we go,' said Godfreys cheerfully, pointing a sleek silver remote control at the stage. He pushed a button and a scene appeared, looking as lifelike as could be. Gigi stared, half-eaten popcorn kernels spilling out of her mouth.

She beheld a hospital room with a woman in labor, panting and moaning while a doctor encouraged her. 'That's right, Mary, push! Just a little more now, here it comes.'

Mary! Gigi thought, astonished, looking closer at the woman's red, sweaty face. *That's my mom! Omigod, she's giving birth to me!* How could this be? How could she be witnessing her own birth?

Gigi heard a rustling noise in the next seat. Startled, she turned to see her journal flip open and hover in the air while the pen started to scratch away busily of its own accord. She barely had time to register surprise before Godfreys began to intone a narrative, sounding like one of those voice-overs in a Discovery Channel documentary.

'On December 10, 1973, Angel Gigi took Maya's challenge to engage in the enchantment of the Magical Theatre and entered the game of life on earth, certain she could maintain the knowledge of her own perfection and awaken from the spell of forgetfulness. But the moment she was born, she realized her human form was completely dependent on those around her for survival.'

The birth scene wavered and went dark. Gigi took a deep breath to steady herself and stuffed another handful of popcorn in her mouth as Godfreys continued.

'Soon, rules were introduced to define acceptable human behavior. The first word Angel Gigi came to understand in her new language was "No!" This word pained her, for it implied that she was wrong to want what she wanted, and she could not make sense of this. When she tried to communicate her needs, she found that only certain forms of expression were acceptable.

'Too often, expressing herself authentically resulted in a disappointed, even angry, response. It appeared that being wrong was bad, and thus provoked a withdrawal of love and approval from those she needed the most – reactions that seemed to threaten her safety.

'Angel Gigi's once indomitable sense of confidence melted into an expanding puddle of fear and confusion.'

The stage lit up again and Gigi beheld her four-year-old self in a discount store, clutching a boxed Barbie doll that her mother was trying to take away from her. Stamping her feet and crying, she refused to give it up. Finally, her mother spanked her bottom in frustration and yanked the doll from her, replacing it on the shelf then dragging her, wailing, to the exit.

Godfreys hit a button and the scene froze. 'This is an example of a life-altering decision you made based on your experience,' he said quietly. 'When your mother punished you for not obeying her, you unconsciously interpreted it to mean that you would get in trouble if you asked for what you wanted. From that time on, you would yearn for things in private, but rarely ask for what you desired.

'Over time you decided that such restraint was commendable, selfless behavior – and you gave up the idea that you could ask for what you wanted, or even needed.'

With sudden tears clogging her throat, Gigi nodded. 'You're right,' she said. 'It felt like a bad thing to ask for anything, and somehow I felt like I didn't deserve it.'

'And that has become part of your story, hasn't it?' Godfreys said, not unsympathetically. 'The role you wrote was powerless – someone who could never have what she wanted. That decision then formed part of your identity as an adult, because you didn't use your awareness to question your point of view as you matured. You just said, "This is who I am." Looking back, can you see that as a child you made a decision about not getting what you wanted and then lived it out?'

Gigi nodded ruefully. Even in the divorce settlement she hadn't asked for anything, and Keith had ended up with all their assets and most of the money.

'Excellent,' Godfreys said, pushing another button on the remote. 'Gigi's early childhood flew by quickly as she learned to navigate the rules and conditions of this enchanted life,' he continued, as an ever-changing series of scenes unfolded onstage. 'She interpreted all new information through the filters based on her perception of her human experience.'

'Like the bewitched spectacles?' Gigi interrupted.

'Exactly. And although her decisions were arbitrarily formed by past emotional responses to similar experiences, she assumed they represented the sum total of life's possibility. Occasionally she would rebel, whereupon she would get into trouble with the adults in her life. They told her things like "You mustn't show off like that," "Who do you think you are?" or "What will people think?" Hearing their words through human ears, Gigi felt ashamed and quickly came to view herself as tragically flawed rather than whole and perfect.'

Godfreys paused on a scene of six-year-old Gigi standing in the principal's office at school, hands clasped behind her back and head bowed as the principal reprimanded her sternly from behind a gigantic steel desk. Gigi remembered that scene all too well. After being ruthlessly physically and emotionally tormented by a group of girls on the playground for the entire first semester of the first grade, she'd finally pushed one of them down. When the teacher came to investigate, the girls banded together and blamed it on Gigi, and she had been ignominiously sent home from school to deal with her parents' wrath.

'From this incident you decided that not only could you not trust people, but you needed to be overly vigilant to protect yourself from the standpoint of a victim,' Godfreys explained.

'Ain't that the truth,' sighed Gigi.

Godfreys nodded. 'Yes, and it was about this time – age six – when the angelic essence of *you* succumbed to the "reality" of life on earth and forgot her part in the divine mystery. The enchantment was cast, and the truth of your magnificence was now hidden deep within.'

Godfreys' words tugged at Gigi's heart, and she instantly mourned the divine innocence lost in childhood. She could almost feel a spark of it inside her, even now. How sad that it had been all but quenched.

'This perception of her imperfection was sharpened at the end of Gigi's first grade year, when her father left home for good.'

Gigi leaned forward in her seat. For a moment, the only sound was the ceaseless scratching of the gold pen. Slowly, a scene appeared: the front lawn of the sprawling ranch house where she'd grown up. Six-year-old Gigi was holding onto her father's leg, tears streaming down her freckled face.

'Please don't go, Daddy,' she pleaded, as her father tried to loosen her grip on him.

'I have to, honey,' he said softly. 'Your mom and I just can't work things out. It will be better this way, trust me. You won't have to hear us fighting anymore. But I'll come back for you. I'll take you to Disneyland, okay?'

'Okay,' said Gigi softly. 'Promise?'

'I promise,' said her father, giving her a kiss, then climbing into the car and driving away. Little Gigi walked slowly into the house and went to her bedroom to sit on her bed, clutching her stuffed panda.

Again Godfreys paused the action. The gold pen, which had been furiously recording each scene, paused too, hovering above the open journal in anticipation. Gigi realized she was holding her breath and exhaled with a sigh. That had been the single most painful moment of her life until she found Keith sprawled naked on the floor with Blondzilla.

Her father had never kept his promise, and she had never figured out if he meant to and couldn't, or if he had just been pacifying her so he could make a clean getaway.

'So,' Godfreys said gently, 'this was obviously another critical juncture in the formation of your script.'

'Yeah, it was pretty pivotal,' Gigi said. 'But I don't see how I could have made it different. The fact is, my dad left and there was nothing I could do about it.'

'True,' said Godfreys. 'But again, you made and reinforced a decision about how it affected you. As a child, you decided that your father's leaving was your fault. You thought about all the times you'd been corrected or reprimanded, particularly the scene I just showed you where you got sent home from school, and you decided that your father left because you were a problem.

'So if you could only be good enough, he would come back

and everything would be okay. And that decision influenced your life from then on.'

'Really?' Gigi asked, a tad skeptical. 'Could the choices I made at such a young age really impact the rest of my life so drastically?'

'Yes, when combined with the choices you made to be powerless and a victim of circumstances,' Godfreys said. 'It was a combination of decisions that led you, after your father's departure, to decide that your only hope for not being abandoned again was to be perfect at everything you did, so you tried even harder to be good. These behaviors quickly became ingrained and you forgot where they started, but you determined unwittingly that the more of your life you could control, the safer you would be.'

'In other words, I started trying to change myself,' Gigi muttered, scrabbling absent-mindedly for a last handful of popcorn. She'd always wished she could just not care what people thought, but it seemed like the more she tried not to care, the more she did care.

'Exactly,' said Godfreys. 'The identity you developed as a "good" girl was accompanied by a strong need to please others and keep them happy.'

Gigi sighed. This was painful, but also cathartic. She watched as a dizzying collage of scenes tumbled past in which she exhausted herself by working incredibly hard to be all things to all people – while consistently ignoring her own needs and desires. Witnessing the sheer pace and desperate eagerness of these past efforts made her feel nauseous. Just when she thought she couldn't watch anymore, Godfreys paused the action and said, 'This was the perfectionist Gigi, the one who projected into the world an image of competence, intelligence, goodness and willingness. This Gigi evolved from the child who used her experiences as evidence that she had to be faultless to win love and acceptance. Do you see how her actions are driven by that childhood decision?'

Gigi nodded slowly, feeling a sinking sense of recognition dawn in the pit of her stomach. Suddenly, she could imagine how many other details of her childhood had also exploded into major themes in her adult script.

'Yes,' she agreed resignedly. 'I chose the good girl role. But I see now how I could just as easily have made a decision to rebel. Since it was hard to be right, I could have said, "Screw it, I'm not going to even try."'

'Excellent insight,' said Godfreys. 'So since you chose the good girl role, your need to be flawless was heightened by the fact that your mother was so hurt and embittered by the divorce that she had very little patience with you, and was notably hard to please.'

'Yeah,' Gigi said. 'I just kept trying to please her by getting good grades and doing well at all my activities. After she remarried when I was eleven, I tried really hard to please my stepfather, too. But the good part was that I went that route instead of rebelling. I mean, I made good choices by striving to do well, didn't I?'

'You should do your best regardless of the circumstances,' said Godfreys. 'But your reasons for excelling kept you in a pattern of self-limitation. For instance, you didn't join the school band simply because you were dying to play the flute, did you?'

'No,' Gigi answered slowly. 'I guess I took clarinet because my junior high boyfriend, David, played drums in the band, and I wanted him to think I was cool.'

'And why did you join the track team instead of the drama club, which is what you really wanted to do?'

'Because my stepfather Bob was assistant coach and he encouraged me to do it,' Gigi said. 'I thought it would help win his approval. You're right, Godfreys – I didn't even realize I could have chosen to do what I really wanted instead of what others wanted me to do.'

'Yes, you placed more importance on wanting approval than on your own desires,' Godfreys said. 'And after puberty hit, you let this desire to look good to others influence you badly at times. Just look.'

Godfreys pressed a button and the parade of scenes resumed, showing Gigi's interactions with her peers: sneaking cigarettes during lunch break with a couple of the popular girls, her desire to be part of the in-crowd overriding her disgust at the taste; smiling and talking with her overweight Advanced Placement English teacher, then performing an admirable impression of her behind her back; pretending she liked drinking beer at frat parties; flirting with a seemingly endless procession of high school and college boys (so desperate for male attention that she would even flirt with her friends' boyfriends); and giving herself to boys with abandon, in cars, in hallways, in messy dorm rooms.

Godfreys paused the action and turned to an inwardly cringing Gigi. The popcorn had congealed in her stomach. Wasn't it bad enough to have experienced these humiliating activities once, without having to go through the torture of watching them again – with her frigging guardian angel, for heaven's sake? It was not pleasant to review just how much integrity she had been willing to give up to be accepted, even while she was generally perceived as 'good' due to her high grade point average, success in extracurricular activities, and volunteer efforts. She wished her journal could have omitted the last few scenes, but the pen had faithfully recorded everything.

Godfreys gently removed the empty popcorn bucket from her lap. She felt embarrassed that she'd eaten every kernel, but she really had been hungry.

'Notice that throughout your life, whenever you were trying to please someone, you were engaged in what we call "selective evidence gathering",' Godfreys said softly. 'Meaning that you made sure your experiences matched your expectations.'

'Really?' Gigi asked. 'You mean I somehow torqued my

experiences so they fit in with my conviction that I needed to work really hard to make people love and approve of me?'

'Exactly,' said Godfreys with a smile. 'It's as if you were walking through an abundant orchard, and instead of reaching for the ripened fruit right in front of you, you searched for the most wizened, rotten remnants you could find. Then when you took a bite, its nastiness confirmed your opinion that rotten fruit was the only kind.'

'Wow,' Gigi said slowly. 'That's really sad.'

'Indeed,' Godfreys agreed. 'And you certainly played out selective evidence gathering in your choice of a husband. Remember that really nice, kind, generous man who worked with you at the drama festival where you served as volunteer coordinator after college?'

'Oh yeah, Steven,' Gigi said. 'He was really sweet and had the hugest crush on me.'

'And he would have done anything for you,' Godfreys said. 'But you overlooked him because he didn't fit your criteria for the familiar rotten fruit – you simply did not see him as someone you could be with. Your idea of men was based on your absent father and your disinterested stepfather. A man had to be distant and difficult to reach before you felt comfortable. And the misery that caused you, bore out your belief that a man's love took great effort to attain.'

Godfreys hit the remote button and the stage lit up to reveal a scene of Gigi at an after-hours party at a hip New York club. Keith's band had been the star attraction and she'd zeroed in on him immediately when she saw him mingling afterward.

Gigi groaned inwardly. Did she have to watch this? It was still too painful.

'Keith was both interested and unavailable,' Godfreys explained. 'When he was in town, he showered you with the admiration and attention you'd sought so desperately for so long. When he was away you pined for him, which made you feel comfortable, since longing for an absent man was so familiar to you.

'You knew he drank too much and did drugs, but figured it was a phase. The glamour of dating a popular musician blinded you to some of his less than admirable qualities – but you just knew that if you could be the perfect girlfriend you could win his love forever. You were sure he'd change for you.'

Gigi watched herself dancing backstage while Keith's band performed at a large outdoor amphitheater. Girls screamed and threw their panties onstage while Keith flashed his sexy smile. One fan jumped up onstage and started grinding her hips against Keith before security dragged her off him. Gigi just shook her head tolerantly, but a brief look of pain flashed across her face as she saw his grin of enjoyment.

'When Keith proposed after returning from a European tour, you were ecstatic. You planned a fancy wedding that became the event of the season. Meanwhile, your own career was going well. You landed a job as assistant to the director of TheaterKids and were being groomed to take his position.'

Godfreys paused the action for a moment and looked directly at Gigi as he continued. 'However, no matter how well your life seemed to be going, you constantly encountered a lingering problem. Each time you made progress on your path to unerring perfection, you discovered your "to do" list had expanded again. The goalposts kept moving, so that no matter how much time passed, you remained separated from your false image of perfection by the same incremental distance. Perhaps you can see that even though you occasionally realized the futility and injustice of your quest, you could never quite give up – or live up to – the ever-increasing standard of perfection you contrived for yourself.'

A barrage of scenes showed Gigi frantically chasing the perfect image: working out at the gym, staying late at the office, lavishly entertaining Keith's friends, saying yes to untimely requests, fundraising for work and political candidates, giving up sleep to rub Keith's feet, spending hours perfecting her daily makeup, hair and nails, starving herself, planning perfect vacations, shopping for the right clothes, cooking, cleaning, and on and on in a constant, dizzying whirlwind of activity.

Gigi closed her eyes against the spinning in her brain. No wonder she'd collapsed in exhaustion and holed herself up in her apartment! Had she really been so intent on proving she was acceptable? It all seemed so far away…

'Finally, it took a drastic series of events to slow Gigi down and allow her the time and space to begin the process of change in which she is currently engaged,' Godfreys intoned.

Opening her eyes, Gigi saw that the whirlwind of images had slowed. Oh no, was she going to have to revisit the scene of Keith and the tattooed wonder sprawled on the sheepskin rug?

But, as if in sympathy, the next few images slid by quickly, leaving tracers of light, and did not come to a stop until Gigi was lying on the sofa, hung over and surrounded by the chaotic dimness of her post-Keith apartment.

As Gigi stared at the fading images on the stage, it all began to make sense. The Magical Theatre represented her own life – the stressful, sometimes euphoric, yet always frantic life she'd chosen for herself.

She saw now that she had truly written her own story. Like a bad play filled with melodrama, her life had just unfolded before her eyes, and she could see now how her own decisions and reactions had created its path. She was indeed the playwright of her life! The realization filled her with a whirlpool of emotions: delight, fear, regret, anger, but most of all, hope.

'So now tell me the answer to that pesky question of Maya's: What image of yourself do you most stubbornly defend?' directed Godfreys.

'The good girl,' said Gigi without hesitation. 'The perfect good girl.'

'Can you see now how you could stop defending that image and rewrite your script from a place of wisdom?' Godfreys asked. 'Imagine if that six-year-old who took responsibility for her father's departure could have made a different decision from the standpoint of a wise thirty-five-year-old.'

'Thirty-four, for another couple of weeks,' Gigi corrected him, then immediately felt foolish. What was the difference?

'Ah, yes, thirty-four,' Godfreys said, humoring her. 'So what would you tell that six-year-old from your perspective as an adult to change her decision?'

Gigi said slowly, 'I guess I would tell her that she was not to blame. She was doing just fine, great in fact, navigating her way through the confusing world of adult rules and expectations. I'd tell her that most things that happen have nothing to do with her. People make their own choices for reasons she might never understand. And that she didn't have to *do* anything to try to make it better. That the best thing she could do would be to honor herself by expressing herself truthfully and following her heart.'

'Ah,' Godfreys said. 'And what might have changed if she had taken that advice to heart?'

'She, I mean, *I* would have been a lot more laid-back, and a lot less stressed out,' Gigi said. 'I would have taken more music and drama classes and less math. I would have stood up for people who got picked on instead of joining in the teasing. I would have cared more about enjoying life and less about getting perfect grades, or looking perfect, or finding the perfect guy. I would have thrown caution to the wind more often and thrown myself at men less often. I would have auditioned for parts in plays instead of staying behind the scenes. I would have been fiercer, wilder, freer and more fun.'

Gigi paused for a deep breath, then finished, 'And I definitely would have worn more spandex and less khaki.'

'Interesting,' said Godfreys, adding dryly, 'and since you are not dead yet, I presume you could still do these things.'

'I could, couldn't I?' Gigi said, understanding dawning. 'Because if I wrote the script of my life up until now, that means I can rewrite it and change my future! I could stop basing my happiness on what people think and start living the way *I* want to. I could channel my inner Katharine Hepburn or even Madonna. I could speak my mind and really reach for my desires.'

She was beginning to truly see the extent to which her childhood decisions about how to interact with the world had created her script. Which might mean – wonder of wonders – that she could still change it.

The thought of being able to change her script at will was thrilling. After all, who did she think was going to do it if she didn't? It was abundantly clear that Prince Charming was in a committed relationship with Cinderella, and was therefore not available to *save*, then sweep Gigi off into the sunset. She could take the reins of her future in her own hands!

As if in agreement, her journal snapped shut, the pen coming to rest on top of it.

'Exactly. Excellent work,' Godfreys said, startling her. She'd forgotten for a moment that he was there. 'And now you are ready to absorb the lesson of the second keystone.'

Chapter Six

Gigi had a feeling of déjà vu. Once again she was sitting in the same seat in the small theater watching the arrival of the other students. But this time she was far better informed, and her former uneasiness was replaced by a sense of anticipation.

She couldn't wait to get Maya's attention and tell her what she'd learned about her script. Maybe now Maya would release her from Remedial Angel Training and let her get on with her life.

I'm sure I've worked my way up from remedial already, she thought smugly. *After all, Godfreys said I learned the keystone really well.*

Gigi surveyed the arrival of the students with equanimity. They were arriving from the sky on the same fantastic contraptions on which they'd left, a circumstance that now seemed almost commonplace. A coffee-skinned man in a wetsuit rode in on a hot pink surfboard; a pair of redheaded twins cruised down on a two-seated bicycle; and a Native American man coasted to his seat on a woven Navajo blanket. More alarmingly, Vinny swept in wildly on an orange dragon, holding on for dear life. The dragon dumped him unceremoniously in the balcony before disappearing in flames.

Predictably, Susan buzzed in on her scooter looking as composed as if she had just ridden down a quiet suburban street. Dismounting neatly, she gave Gigi a cool hello before setting down her shiny briefcase then checking her hair and makeup. Of course, she still looked perfect.

Gigi, on the other hand, had never felt more discomposed and untidy. Not only were her fingernails in a sorry state from nervous biting, but her blouse was rumpled and stained with popcorn grease; her hair was surely a mess, having not seen a comb or mirror since the man on the train stole her purse; and her makeup had to have completely worn off by now.

She surreptitiously tried to untangle her hair with one hand while sucking bits of popcorn from between her teeth, furious at herself for caring and for letting Susan intimidate her. That supercilious know-it-all! Gigi wouldn't want to be like her in a million years.

Unexpectedly, Susan leaned over and offered Gigi her compact and a blue wide-toothed comb she'd pulled from her makeup bag. 'Would you like to comb your hair?' she asked. 'I can see you forgot to bring beauty supplies. Never travel without emergency makeup and toiletries, is my motto. Here, I think I have an extra lipstick you can use too.'

Before Gigi could refuse, Susan had shoved the compact and comb into her hands and was rummaging in her makeup case. Gigi was torn: she hated to take Susan's charity, especially when tempered with her annoying advice, but she really ought to do something with her hair, and who knew when she'd be able to buy beauty products herself? The dreamtime didn't seem overly populated with drug stores, and she didn't have her wallet anyway.

Wincing at her reflection in the compact, she gratefully brushed her hair to a semblance of order then applied the coral-colored lipstick Susan had offered.

'You can keep the lipstick,' Susan said.

'Oh, thanks!' Gigi said, touched, in spite of herself, at Susan's generosity.

'Seeing as you're still recovering from that rash,' Susan added, thrashing Gigi's gratitude. 'And might as well keep that comb too, come to think of it. I have another one.'

'Thanks,' Gigi mumbled grudgingly, shoving the comb and lipstick in her pocket.

'So did you do your homework?' Susan asked conversationally, apparently having decided that Gigi was worth talking to now that she'd tidied up a bit.

'Naturally,' Gigi said with what she hoped was a superior

glance. 'It was easy.'

'Really?' Susan asked. 'I don't think the point was for it to be *easy*. If it was too easy, maybe you didn't really grasp the lesson. Because it's not supposed to be easy to have to reassess the whole script of your life. It takes some work to honestly look at it in its totality, but it will make your life easier once you realize you can rewrite the script.'

'Well, maybe it's harder for some people than for others,' Gigi snapped. 'Some of us might not have as much to rewrite as others do.'

Susan was about to retort when, thankfully, the dimming of the theater's invisible lights followed by a sudden hush signified Maya's imminent arrival. Trying to ignore Susan's malignant presence next to her, Gigi placed her journal and pen on the floor in front of her, and whispered, feeling slightly foolish, 'Alright, journal, get ready to start taking notes.'

Immediately the journal rose to hover above the ground and flipped open to a blank page, the pen poised above it. Gigi flushed with pride and peeked at Susan to see if she'd noticed how brilliant she was – only to see Susan gazing in satisfaction at a black leather-bound journal accompanied by a fountain pen that was already scrawling in its voluminous pages. She should have known Susan would be one step ahead.

Gigi craned her neck to see what Susan's journal was recording so assiduously, but the journal closed with a loud slap. Chastised, Gigi sat back hastily and pretended not to notice. She had to stop letting Susan distract her. More to the point, how would Maya arrive this time?

Her question was soon answered when, with a whoosh of warm air, a brightly decorated hot-air balloon appeared in the sky and descended gently, hovering just above the stage. Maya, clad in emerald green and gold robes, leaned out and blew kisses to all sides of the auditorium, causing chocolate candy kisses to rain down on the assembled students. Gigi jumped up to grab for a candy, caught it, and settled back into her seat, popping it into her mouth with a smug sigh of satisfaction. Her enjoyment was momentarily ruined when she caught Susan staring at her in disgust, but she shrugged it off as Maya began speaking.

'My beloved students, congratulations!' she called. 'You have courageously flung away your bewitched spectacles and begun to see that, although totally engrossing, the script of your life isn't the end-all and be-all of reality.'

A titter rippled through the audience as a pair of chocolate kisses in front of Maya turned into candy lips and began smooching in midair. Maya cleared her throat, and they immediately separated and flew to her, one kissing her on each cheek.

Maya swatted them away playfully. 'To be honest, as you are beginning to understand, most of what you perceive as real in the Magical Theatre is only an illusion. The infamous script you've lived by is an illusion as surely as these chocolate kisses or the quite entertaining methods of transportation that brought you here tonight.'

Two things occurred to Gigi simultaneously: first, how had she been able to taste the candy if it really was an illusion; and second, why was she the only one who had not been provided with an entertaining method of transportation? Were those good signs or bad signs? And might now be a good time to try to catch Maya's attention and let her know Gigi was ready to move on to her real job in Blessings? But Maya sailed ahead. Beside Gigi, Susan's fingernails clacked busily on her laptop.

'In fact, every single soul laboring under the enchantment of the Magical Theatre has meticulously constructed so-called "reality" from his or her own point of view,' continued Maya. 'Look at the people all around you. Each person in this theater has a very different idea of what "reality" is. That's because you have each made it up out of your own experience. But there are millions of options that exist *outside* of your experience. That is why "reality" is not a fixed concept.'

Across the front of the hot-air balloon appeared the words: 'Keystone 2: Your perceptions create your reality.'

'My dear students, allow your minds to open and realize this essential truth: you form, limit and describe reality solely through your perceptions,' Maya declared.

Gigi could feel her mind doing the exact opposite, retracting on itself as it resisted Maya's words. Weren't some things just the way they were, no matter how you looked at them? Yet her recent experiences belied this point of view. After all, she was taking angel lessons in the dreamtime in a theater located in space! How did this fit into her established view of reality? She struggled to clear her mind of skeptical thoughts and allow herself to simply listen as Maya continued.

'Like everyone in the Magical Theatre, you interpret both your physical world and your life experiences through a strong filter created by your thoughts and emotions. This filter easily lets in information that aligns with your past experiences and future expectations based on those same experiences. On the other hand, new or conflicting information often encounters resistance.

'As you might imagine, this greatly limits your possibilities. However, you stubbornly cling to the belief that your interpretation is complete and correct – to the point where you think others' interpretations are wrong and actually work very hard to change them.

'Am I right?' she asked rhetorically, scanning the silent auditorium with piercing eyes.

Gigi fidgeted uncomfortably, thinking of her conversation with Susan. Their interpretations of the remedial training were different, and Gigi was sure hers was the right one. That had to be an example of what Maya was talking about. Then, out of nowhere, a memory from her waking life assailed her: looking at travel brochures with Keith, arguing stridently over a trip to Bangkok he'd proposed. He thought Bangkok would be an exciting adventure, and a place to get exotic drugs. Gigi was sure they would be ripped off, get sick from the food, and possibly get arrested for drug smuggling when Keith forgot he'd stashed cocaine in their bags.

Neither of them changed the other's mind, since their thoughts were a result of their perception.

'Exactly my point,' said Maya, looking directly into Gigi's eyes as if she'd read her thoughts again. 'What you have determined to be real and permanent is only an impression you create by combining your limited perception with your own personal experience. Basically, reality in the Magical Theatre isn't set in stone; it's flexible.'

Suddenly a tuxedo-clad orchestra appeared onstage and the strains of a symphony infused the auditorium with sound. Gigi felt herself swept on a tide of joy as the violins swelled and the haunting melody filled her heart until she thought it would burst. Without thinking, she rose from her seat and began moving ecstatically with the rhythm. As she closed her eyes in ecstasy and twirled, the music lifted her until she felt like she was flying. In fact she *was* flying, spiraling above her seat in wild abandon.

She thought everyone must feel the joy of this music and was surprised to look down and see some people crying, some sitting blankly, and a few visibly nodding off to sleep. Susan was sitting primly with her hands folded in her lap, looking patient, as if the music hadn't touched her at all.

The music stopped suddenly, causing Gigi to thump rather ungracefully back down into her seat. Susan shot her another disapproving look, which Gigi returned with an exaggerated grin as she took out the comb and pointedly dragged it through her disheveled hair.

Maya's voice reverberated around the theater. 'You, my magical beings, have a sense of hearing that can identify a wide variety of sounds. Yet although you each heard the same piece played by the magnificent Magical Theatre Symphony, how you experienced it varied considerably.

'Your interpretation is unique, because you automatically merge your thoughts and feelings to form your perception. And this might be the total opposite of how the person next to you thinks or feels about the same piece of music. This is true for all of the ways you form your entire subjective point of view.'

Ain't that the truth, Gigi thought dryly. *To me the music represented the joy of life, and to Susan it didn't seem to mean anything at all.*

Predictably, Susan's hand had once again shot into the air.

'Yes, Susan?' Maya asked.

'Music is one thing that is certainly open to interpretation,' Susan said. 'But what about other things we experience? What about *objects*, for example? If I look at a table, it looks like a table, and if Gigi or Vinny looks at it I assume it also looks like a table. How can a table be subjective?'

'Excellent question,' said Maya. 'As usual, Susan, you're a step ahead of me. Bear with me and I'll catch up!' And she favored Susan with a brilliant smile.

Gigi burned with unwelcome jealousy. *She* was supposed to be Maya's favorite, not Susan Smarty-pants! Wasn't she the one Maya had hired to manage the theater?

'However, let's not overly intellectualize this,' Maya went on, and Gigi felt a smidgen better. 'Remember, you can't *think* your way through all these points – you have to let your intuition go to work as you absorb them. I know it is not easy to do, but you must trust that what I am telling you is correct.'

Susan nodded thoughtfully. Against her will, Gigi admired the way she seemed to truly absorb Maya's words without feeling either triumphant or downcast. Gigi had always wished she had that kind of objective focus, but she seemed to take everything personally. Still, maybe Susan was just acting calm, and inside was as much of a seething mass of thoughts and emotions as Gigi herself.

As if in answer, Maya continued firmly, 'It is time, my darlings, to release the point of view that your thoughts and emotions form the foundation of an absolute reality that can stand the test of time. Please follow me closely. Everything in the Magical Theatre is composed of particles of light. In contrast to the physical essence you perceive through your five rudimentary senses, your body is comprised of subatomic particles, which you can imagine as very tiny bits of light or pure energy. Your lights take on a different form from, say, a cactus or a cobra. But you are made up of the same substance – energy expressed as light. The spark that gives you life is the same spark that animates all living things. If this seems implausible, it's only because your mind has been conditioned to perceive a different point of view. I encourage you to go beyond these old limits, because only by doing so will you have a chance to break the enchantment.

'Now let's take this a step further. Everyone, soften your eyes to blur your gaze, and imagine moving beyond the reality of your five senses. As you allow your consciousness to expand beyond the physical, I'd like you to consider the seat you are sitting on from the point of view of pure energy. Notice that the cushion and arms of your seat are composed of microscopic twinkling lights.'

What? Gigi narrowed her eyes obediently, but she was certain that, this time, Maya had gone too far. A seat cushion was just a seat cushion, even in the dreamtime. But in an instant, her mind reeled as she looked down and saw the arm of her chair glimmering with infinite bits of light. Was everything really made of light? She certainly must have been experiencing a very limited point of view about reality.

Maya's voice seemed to come from a great distance as she continued.

'Next gaze down at your legs, noting that despite your opinions about how your legs look, there's a more expansive way to see them. Imagine the interaction between empty space and light that creates your physical form. Let your mind quiet. Release the notions you hold about your legs and allow them to become one with the lights that make up the seat. Let the boundary between yourself and your surroundings disappear.'

Looking down at her body, Gigi saw that it, too, was composed of the same vibrating motes of light.

From behind half-closed eyelids, Gigi gazed out and saw that the people, the floor, the seats and the stage all appeared as a single spectacle filled with infinitesimal stars. Maya let out a soft chuckle that seemed to tickle Gigi all over. The particles of light that were her body jiggled and danced in response.

Wow, this is a trip, Gigi thought, seeing her legs shimmer and dissolve into the seat. *I flow into the seat, and the seat is connected to me, and everything is a part of the energy in the universe!*

'Exactly, my dear,' Maya said, as if addressing her alone. Gigi looked up and saw Maya as a brightly pulsating mass of light particles. 'So since you and everything else surrounding you is made up of light, the boundaries you perceive between yourself and other expressions of physical reality are arbitrary.'

Gigi allowed herself to release into the wonder of being part of this endless array of twinkling lights. She felt herself grow lighter as she melded into the larger mass of energy, and she was infused with a flush of delicious joy.

'Reality will not shift so you can witness the vastness of your being,' Maya continued. 'But like the expanded perception of the physical world you have just experienced, your emotional perception can be shifted at any time.'

Suddenly the auditorium lights came up and Gigi blinked. Her legs now looked like her accustomed legs, spread out on the worn seat and clad in faded, skintight jeans. The auditorium was once again filled with people of all shapes, sizes, colors and attitudes, and Maya was still hovering above the stage in the hot-air balloon.

'So, my studious angels – homework!' Maya trilled, twirling in the balloon so her robes billowed out around her and her braids flew in all directions. 'Your assignment is to take a look behind the scenes at your perceptions, so you can get beyond them and create a new reality.

'Have fun, and I'll see you in a twinkling, for our next lesson!' And with that, the hot-air balloon began to rise from the stage, leaving Maya's signature rainbow in its wake.

Gigi looked around her, confused by Maya's sudden departure. The homework assignment seemed a little vague, and she wasn't sure what to do next. She had an uncomfortable sense that once again everyone else knew what to do and she didn't. The others were all busily getting out of their seats, tucking journals under their arms and looking like they were ready to go somewhere. Was she the only one without a clue? She wanted to ask Susan what to do but was stopped by the memory of her brusque rebuff the last time.

In the midst of the hustle and bustle, Gigi became aware of a thin gray mist creeping through the room. Its cold fingers reached out to her and she shivered involuntarily. Abruptly she stood, longing to leave. But she couldn't make her feet move, as if the mist held her rooted to the spot. Meanwhile the gray cloud grew thicker, obscuring the other people and muffling all sounds. She was completely surrounded by thick, silent blankness. She couldn't even see Susan next to her. Panic rose in her throat and she tried to scream to alert others to her predicament, but the sound was quickly deadened by the dense fog.

She clutched her journal to her chest – the only solid object she could still see or feel – and, fighting the fear that threatened to overtake her, took a tentative step forward. Her foot encountered nothing but a vague spongy surface. Looking down, she could see only fog below her. She took another tiny step, then another, expecting to encounter the hard surface of the auditorium chair in front of her, but there was only the insidious fog.

Giving in to panic, Gigi began to run, stumbling over her own feet. She flailed her arms and dropped her journal, not caring, only wanting desperately to find her way out of this chilly, frightening purgatory.

The only sound was the ragged gasping of her breath. She no longer knew up from down or left from right. Was she in hell? Was this some sort of test? She ran for what seemed like ages, until her breath gave out and she had no choice but to let herself sink limply into the fog, down and down, drifting through layers of white and gray...

Suddenly her feet hit solid ground and she flailed for balance then fell on her bottom with a thump. As she gasped for breath, the fog cleared to reveal the grassy backyard of a farmhouse. Heart pounding, Gigi scrambled backward to lean against the sturdy trunk of a nearby oak tree. Once the black spots cleared from her vision, she could see that the yard was swarming with guests being seated in white-cloth-covered chairs. Set in neat rows, the chairs faced a honeysuckle-covered gazebo decked with white and yellow ribbons. A string quartet played softly in the background and a tinkle of glassware could be heard coming from the kitchen window.

In a rush of recognition, Gigi's heart leapt to her throat. This was the day of her wedding to Keith! How could she be sitting under a tree looking at her own wedding eight years before? What was going on? Panicked, she struggled to stand. She had to get inside! What would happen if she wasn't there to marry Keith? But wait – what if she *was* there? What if she came face to face with an earlier version of herself? It was like a bad dream.

Then she remembered this actually *was* all a dream, and she relaxed a little. But knowing she was in the dreamtime didn't make the situation any less strange. It seemed so real, and it was weird to be an outsider at her own wedding. On the actual day, she'd stayed inside getting ready and had missed the guests' arrival. Everything looked different from this new perspective.

'Yes, that's what this lesson is all about – perspective,' a British voice said in her ear, and she jumped, nearly falling down again. Grabbing the tree trunk for support, she turned to behold Godfreys, resplendent in a gray cutaway coat and ascot, with a gold-tipped walking stick.

'God, can't you give a girl a little warning?' Gigi blurted, heart still racing.

'Generally I don't go by my nickname,' Godfreys replied serenely, the ghost of a smile playing around his lips. 'And yes, I suppose I could send a team of angels ahead to warn you of my imminent arrival if you would prefer. But they're all a bit busy just at present.'

'Whatever,' Gigi muttered, slightly put out by Godfreys' attitude. 'Nice outfit, by the way. All you're missing is a top hat.'

'Ah, excellent idea,' said Godfreys, as a sleek gray top hat appeared on his head. 'Now I think we'd better get you dressed for the occasion.' He swept his hands in front of her from head to toe, and everything turned to sparkling light for a moment. Just as suddenly, the lights were gone and Gigi looked down to see that she was dressed in a tea-length dress of pale pink gauzy chiffon. Her perfectly manicured hands clutched a hot-pink purse that matched her four-inch strappy heels.

'Pink, Godfreys?' Gigi moaned, mortified to her Manhattan-chic core. 'Couldn't you at least have put me in black?'

'For a summer afternoon wedding? Absolutely not – Mitchell would kill me!' Godfreys said. 'Now come along, we've a wedding to attend.'

'Wait a minute,' Gigi said. 'We're not going to watch from here? And who's Mitchell?'

'No, of course we're not watching from under a tree, for goodness' sake. And you'll meet Mitchell soon enough. Now please come along.'

'But won't the guests notice? What if I see myself? I'll have a coronary!'

'No one will notice,' Godfreys said calmly. 'They can't see us.'

'Are you kidding? You dressed me in head-to-toe bargain-basement pink for nothing?' Gigi was outraged. He could at least have put her in Prada! But Godfreys ignored her outburst, taking her arm firmly and steering her toward the last row of chairs.

'What exactly are we supposed to be doing here?' Gigi hissed.

'You are here to see how perception – yours and others' – molds what you think of as "reality",' Godfreys said. 'Now do be quiet, my dear girl, and listen carefully.'

'Listen to what? The music?' Gigi asked impatiently.

'Shh,' Godfreys said, putting a buffed fingernail to his lips.

Sighing, Gigi slumped in her chair. She heard the chattering and murmuring of the guests punctuated by an occasional burst of laughter, the string quartet playing Mozart, and a crow squawking overhead. At a chord from the musicians, the crowd noise trickled off and Gigi turned to see an usher leading her mother from the house slowly up the aisle.

Suddenly, as loud and clear as if she were wearing headphones, she heard her mother say, 'Thank heavens Gigi is finally getting married off. I was afraid it would never happen! Of course, that Keith person isn't exactly what I would have chosen for her, being a musician and from the South, but at least he has money. Now I don't have to worry about how she's going to make it.'

What? Her mother had been concerned about her? That was news to Gigi. But wait a second – how was she hearing what her mother was thinking, anyway? Gigi looked a question at Godfreys.

'Yes, you can hear their thoughts,' he said with perfect equanimity. 'Don't worry, it's a one-way transmission. No one can hear *us*.'

'Okay, so I'm hearing my mother's thoughts,' Gigi said with

sudden understanding. 'It's so I can understand her point of view, right?'

'Yes, but perhaps more importantly so you can see that your own perception of your mother's thoughts was actually a projection of how *you* view reality.'

'Meaning that I projected what I imagined she was thinking onto her?' Gigi asked.

'Precisely. At the time of your wedding, you were convinced your mother wanted you to be a big career woman and would never forgive you. You can see now, however, that actually your mother perceived the wedding as a good thing, for her own reasons.'

Before Gigi could think about it further, the minister appeared from behind the gazebo and stood facing the crowd – which meant that Keith was about to enter, too. Gigi's heart fluttered unpleasantly as Bryce, Keith's best man, poked his head out of the farmhouse door and turned back to say something to Keith. She heard them laugh – a little drunkenly? – before they walked toward the guests. Keith's voice came at her loud and clear, the slight Southern twang yanking at her heartstrings like it always had.

'Damn, I never thought I'd be doing this,' Keith said. 'But my manager told me a wedding might help fix my image and maybe get me out of those paternity suits and of course I'd get a lot of press coverage which always helps tour sales.'

'Paternity suits!' Gigi hissed, furious. 'That snake! And he didn't want to marry me? Sales? His *manager* told him to marry me?' She clutched the pink purse with a death grip as Keith's thoughts continued.

'Still, I'm glad it's Gigi. I need her. She's good at taking care of everything so I can relax. I know I can always count on her.'

Gigi's heart softened marginally. The fact that he needed her must mean he loved her, right?

Noticing Gigi's reaction, Godfreys said, 'Remember, our point here is not to revisit old drama but to understand that everyone's "reality" has been filtered through their perception.'

Next, Gigi watched Stephanie mince down the grassy aisle in unaccustomed heels. Stephanie looked slightly giggly and tipsy, but gorgeous, and Gigi felt a pang of sadness, missing her. Then Stephanie's thoughts came through loud and clear: 'Look at Keith, what a creep. I saw him coming on to that caterer not ten minutes ago, and now he's about to profess lifetime commitment to my best friend. I'd like to punch him in his friggin' lying mouth.

'I bet Gigi's making the biggest mistake of her life, but she won't listen to anything negative about him – which is all there is to say once you get past the money. I hope I'm wrong, but I bet his "faithful commitment" won't last through the honeymoon.'

Gigi's eyes widened in shock. So even Stephanie had known about Keith! Why hadn't she said something? But she had – Gigi was just unwilling to listen. Before she could dwell on it any more, the musicians struck up the wedding march, and she gulped to see herself emerge from the back door of the house, escorted by a flushed, drunken-looking Bob. She looked beautiful, just as radiant as the papers had said, with her sweeping Vera Wang dress, rich dark hair piled on top of her head, and eyes positively glowing with love. Gigi felt a wave of nostalgia for the eager young woman with such naive trust and high hopes.

'This is my big moment! It's so powerful to have everyone here to witness my union with my soul mate,' thought Bridal Gigi as the guests rose en masse and turned to watch her progression. 'It's so incredible to be forging this lifetime bond, and it's a relief to know I'll never have to date again.'

Then she saw Keith and thought nervously, 'At least Keith *looks* fairly sober. I know they were doing shots in the kitchen, and heaven knows what else, but no one will be able to tell – will they? He promised me he'd stop drinking after the honeymoon.

And I believe him. He's not like Bob, who can't stop. I know Keith can stop anytime he wants. He'll be happier now that we're married, and he won't need to go out partying with his buddies.'

'How embarrassing and sad,' Gigi whispered to Godfreys. 'Especially knowing what Keith was thinking.'

'Again, do you see how reality is based on your point of view?' Godfreys replied. 'You perceived Keith as your soul mate – who maybe had a couple of problems you knew you could fix – and your wedding as the public expression of your undying love. But although he did see a need for you in his life, he didn't perceive you as his soul mate, and he viewed the wedding as a pragmatic and necessary step.'

'Harsh,' Gigi said softly. 'But I get it.'

'The point is, what goes on in other people's heads has nothing to do with you and everything to do with how they interpret the world through their own unique point of view,' Godfreys said. 'You spend all this time and energy wondering or projecting what other people are thinking when, in truth, their perception is purely subjective and is not based on a fixed standard of reality any more than yours is.'

'You mean it's not all about me?' Gigi asked, trying for humor.

'Exactly,' said Godfreys sternly, refusing to play along. 'A lot of people think it's all about them, but that doesn't make it true. However, as you are beginning to see, if you shift your perception, your reality also shifts. You can change your experience by changing how you look at the world.'

'That's for sure,' Gigi said. 'If I had seen Keith without the filter of my own need to prove how good I was by taking perfect care of him, I would have noticed that his drug and alcohol use was out of control, and that he was a little too interested in the women who were always throwing themselves at him. Maybe I would have noticed more if I hadn't been so smug about my ability to save him.'

'Yes, you have your hands full "saving" yourself from the

effects of the spell,' Godfreys agreed. 'In fact, it is rather arrogant to think you can "save" another person, because everyone shares the same divine heritage and needs to take responsibility to awaken in their own lives.'

'Even Keith?' Gigi asked, although she knew the answer.

'Even Keith,' said Godfreys

Without warning, Gigi felt a wave ripple through her. The world around them wobbled and melted, and she felt a sense of warm fluidity as if her body were made of hot chocolate. She closed her eyes, relishing the feeling, and when she opened them the afternoon scene had been replaced by deepening twilight. The side lawn of the farmhouse had been transformed into a glittering outdoor ballroom, and the guests were gaily eating, drinking champagne, and dancing to recordings of Keith's band pouring from the sound system. Gigi felt her heart contract painfully as she beheld herself and Keith dancing together. He whispered something in her ear and turned her over to dance with a friend of his, then walked inside.

Gigi watched her old self gazing longingly at Keith as he walked away, then laugh with fake amusement at something his friend said. Turning her back on her former self, she looked to see where Keith had gone. Through the brightly lit hall window, Gigi saw him take a small folded packet out of his pocket, cast a surreptitious look around, then dip his fingernail into the packet and hold it to his nose, inhaling.

'Cocaine at our wedding!' Gigi exclaimed in disbelief. 'He told me he had quit before we got married.'

She watched him sniff deeply, wiping the back of his hand across his dripping nose. 'I guess I should have known,' she mused. 'But I was pretty committed to not seeing anything that contradicted what I believed.'

Briefly, she felt Godfreys' hand rest on her shoulder in a comforting gesture. She smiled up at him gratefully. Then, creeping closer to the window, her vision seemed to shift and clear, and she saw things about Keith that she had never seen before. She saw the fear and pain behind Keith's eyes. She saw the loneliness and confusion of a boy whose parents had indulged his every whim – not from love, but because it was easier than providing the guidance he needed.

She saw that he was doomed to go down, and that in his heart, he knew it. All Gigi could have done for Keith was to keep him company on the way down, and to do that she would have had to go down with him.

She saw that all Keith really loved was his music, and that his most deeply held belief was: Life is painful – you have to medicate. And suffer was what he did. The coke, the alcohol and the women would only keep his pain masked for so long.

As Keith put the packet away, a breathtaking dark-skinned woman in a daringly low-cut red dress approached him, swinging her hips seductively. She was standing very close to him as they smiled and talked – too close – then suddenly they were kissing passionately. He pulled away, took her hand, and led her through a doorway.

Gigi's heart stopped for a moment. 'That idiot! So even at our wedding he couldn't keep his hands off his damn groupies.' She felt nauseated.

'Yes, and I think on some level you knew,' Godfreys said. 'But again, your filters were strong. It's like this: your brain can perceive a million tidbits of information at one time, which is too much for your mind to take in. So your mind needs to decide what to focus on.

'You focused on Keith as someone you could save, and he became your project. But you didn't see the abundant evidence that he didn't want you to save him. The question is, what was really in it for you? In other words, what was your payoff for being unwilling to see the truth?'

'That's a good question,' Gigi said. 'I guess I got to enjoy reflected glamour. And I always got to feel a little self-satisfied that I'd "saved" him. It seemed like a guarantee that he wouldn't leave me like my father had. After all, *he* was the fuck-up – 'scuse my French.'

Godfreys winked at her. 'Quite all right; I speak fluent French,' he said.

Gigi smiled at him, her sadness mingling with the conviction of a new understanding. 'I think I really get it now,' she said. 'Everyone's perception is different, and everyone has a completely different experience of the same circumstance, depending on their frame of mind, emotions and past history. Since we create our perceptions, we can also create new ones with more awareness, so we can experience the same situations in an entirely different way.'

'Bravo, my dear,' said Godfreys. 'You've got it!'

Suddenly, Gigi heard Maya's voice ringing in her ears. 'Remember, from the point of view of the energy system you call "yourself", you are seamlessly connected to what you call everything else, and all of it is alive and in constant motion. When you see life this way, you can truly know how arbitrary your perception is.'

'Yes,' breathed Gigi, her lights vibrating. In that moment she felt her connection to everyone and everything, and a swell of love and compassion swept through her. Individual perception seemed insignificant in comparison. What did matter was the connection to the light of the Divine Mystery.

She felt vibrant, filled with the energy of the lights and ready to take on anything. Suddenly she realized her feet were no longer on the ground. She was floating in the air, drifting gradually away from the wedding scene.

As she drifted, she could see everyone as both light beings and their physical selves, and it was so beautiful she wanted to cry. She was drifting up, up, into the endless nighttime sky, tumbling headlong through infinite light-filled space.

Chapter Seven

This time Gigi was ready for her landing. She sailed down into the roofless lecture hall with grace, sinking into her usual seat with crossed legs and a shake of her tousled hair. She felt fantastic. She could fly through space, look at her life and under-stand that she wrote her own script, travel back in time, and see how everything was based on a subjective perception.

Her life would never be the same! She would be able to take this knowledge into the world and create a wonderful life for herself, and share her newfound wisdom with others. She felt alive, pulsing with energy, and ready.

But wait! Hadn't Maya said there were *twelve* keystones?

'Oh no,' she moaned under her breath. *I feel so ready to go out there and apply my new learning, but I'm going to be stuck here while everyone else catches up to me. I'm sure I don't need to hear these other keystones. Haven't I already learned enough to change my life forever? I'll ask Maya to excuse me now. I'm sure she sees how well I've learned her lessons, and she'll let me go early.*

A shouted 'Whoa!' followed by a jarring *whump!* startled Gigi out of her self-congratulatory reverie. A man in a silvery-gray Stetson and frayed Levi's jacket had landed in the empty seat next to her. When he turned to her, laughing, and tipped his hat, her heart flip-flopped sickeningly.

Her new neighbor was absolutely gorgeous in a 'Calvin Klein meets the Marlboro Man' kind of way, the sort of man who looked like he was always in charge – as if he'd be equally comfortable rustling a herd of cattle, commanding a search expedition or whirling his lady around the dance floor in a confident waltz. His tanned, pleasantly weathered face set off his strong white teeth, square jaw and flashing dimples, topped by melting brown eyes that reminded her of – well, she wasn't going to think of *him* right now.

I'll hit the dance floor with you any day, Gigi thought, then blushed and looked away.

'Hey,' the man said.

Gigi took a deep breath and turned back around.

He leaned back and stared at her from under the brim of his hat, eyes narrowed. Then he emitted a long, low whistle.

'We-ell, hello there,' he drawled.

Despite herself, Gigi felt a tremor of excitement at his obvious admiration. Feigning indifference and wishing she could think of a witty comeback, she tossed her hair and said stiffly, 'I'm doing fine, thank you.'

The man grinned and stuck out a strong, tanned hand. 'Name's Buck. I'm visiting here – wherever "here" is – from New Mexico.'

Gigi took his hand, thrilling at its warmth and strength. New Mexico! So he must be a real cowboy. That would explain his tan. She'd bet he was in amazing shape from riding horses and pounding in fence stakes and whatever other manly activities he did on the ranch... and speaking of pounding... there was definite chemistry here; that was obvious.

Immediately, a warning bell went off in her head. *Watch out, girl, you're still too stuck in your old perceptions to get involved with anyone*, the voice of caution warned. But another part of herself was delighted at this unexpected encounter.

'Gigi,' she replied, willing her voice not to shake. It had been too long since she'd been face-to-face with such a juicy specimen. She could barely form a coherent sentence. 'I'm from New York – I mean I was from New York – but now I live in Blessings, Maine.'

'Well, it surely is a pleasure to meet you, Gigi from Blessings,' said Buck. 'I'm glad I decided to sit in a different seat tonight. I was up in the balcony with the Brooklyn crowd and it was a bit distracting. Hey, can I borrow my hand again? I might need it for taking notes.'

Oh, God, she was grasping his hand like it was the holy grail!

Worse, her palm was beginning to sweat. Mortified, she whisked her hand away and muttered, 'Sorry'.

Why do I have to be such a dork? Gigi moaned inwardly. *I wish I could be as sophisticated as I try to pretend I am. When it comes to men, I swear I'm still fourteen years old! That's it – I'm not going to talk to him anymore. I should just concentrate on getting Maya's attention so I can be excused from this freakish school and get on with my life!*

Abruptly, she turned to face forward and reached for her journal. But where was it? Oh, no – she must have lost it in the fog on her way to her wedding. *On the way to my wedding... how weird is that?* she thought, momentarily diverted. *I know this is all a dream, but it seems so real, and in some odd way, it all makes sense.*

Suddenly she noticed both that her journal was hovering magically in the air in front of her, pen poised to write, and that the left side of her face was burning. She slid her eyes sideways and saw that Buck was still staring at her. 'What?' she asked abruptly, unnerved.

'Oh, I just like to look at beautiful things,' Buck said easily, with a dazzling smile.

'Things? I'm a *thing* to you?' Gigi bristled, ignoring the part of her that was ridiculously flattered by his statement. Immediately, she felt sorry for being rude, but she was also frustrated with herself. Hadn't she grown up any more than this? Was she still as susceptible to male flattery as she'd been when she was a stupid teenager?

But what's wrong with enjoying a little attention? she thought. *I deserve it after all I've been through.*

To his credit, Buck looked contrite. 'Oops, sorry,' he said, studying his well-worn cowboy boots. 'I didn't mean it like that. I just think you're the prettiest thing – er, woman – I've seen in a while, and I don't get into town much. My ranch keeps me pretty busy.'

Gigi softened. He really did seem sorry, and she could tell he was one of those men who'd been brought up in old-school ways and didn't see anything wrong with showing admiration for a woman. What was wrong with that, really?

Stop it, you're such a pushover, she told herself firmly, immediately feeling defensive and thinking, *But he hasn't really done anything wrong and I should at least be polite.*

'Thanks,' she mumbled aloud. And before she had time to say anything else, Susan appeared on her scooter. Oh no, not her again. Gigi had hoped Susan might choose a different seat this time, but no such luck. Here she was, regular as clockwork.

'Regular as my period, more like,' Gigi muttered under her breath, 'and just about as pleasant.' She stifled a giggle as she realized the aptness of the metaphor. Like her period, Susan was both welcome and unwelcome. Gigi had to admit that, uncomfortable as Susan made Gigi, at least she represented some kind of normalcy in this crazy dreamtime.

Even if she was an intolerable goody-goody.

Gigi realized that for some reason, she was becoming hyper-aware of the dialogue going on in her head. *Be nice and say hello*, admonished a voice that sounded suspiciously like her mother's, while another said, *Who cares about her? She's insignificant in your reality.*

Meanwhile, Susan took in the scene with raised eyebrows and gave her usual cool hello.

'Hey, I'm Buck,' said Buck, leaning across Gigi to shake Susan's hand. She gave it to him primly and said, 'Pleased to meet you', while he flashed her the same brilliant smile he'd given Gigi. Gigi's heart shriveled. He was just a flirt, after all, and his compliments had meant nothing. God, didn't she ever learn?

Thankfully, at that point the hall went completely dark. Gigi let out a sigh of relief, but she could still feel the heat of Buck's presence next to her like a furnace. Before her eyes could adjust to the blackness, a band struck up 'Rumble' from *West Side Story*, and two rival gangs gyrated their way onstage, illuminated by spotlights and belting out the song. Gigi watched, so spellbound that she momentarily forgot about Buck. She loved musicals – especially *West Side Story*!

Just when she was really getting into it and humming along under her breath, the gangs, still belting it out, were joined by a ragtag group of rodeo clowns engaged in a riotous shouting match that quickly turned into comical pushing and shoving. Disconcerted, Gigi couldn't figure out what was going on. The clowns were very distracting. One clown landed on his behind then quickly did a back flip and landed on another's shoulders, causing the second clown to lose his balance and totter exaggeratedly. Gigi quickly became engrossed in their antics but, too soon, they were elbowed out of the way by a group of actors in a Greek tragedy, who were subsequently upstaged by a duo of opera singers enacting a dramatic death scene.

The chaos onstage was unbelievable, and Gigi covered her ears. What was this? It certainly wasn't enjoyable entertainment when these conflicting players were trying to be seen and heard all at once. She felt like her head was about to explode, and she could feel Buck and Susan shifting uncomfortably on either side of her.

Suddenly the chaotic scene froze and faded to black, and Maya's voice reverberated through the mercifully dark and silent hall.

'Welcome back, my sweet, studious, stupendous, superlative students!'

From the darkness, a clown's lisping voice echoed, 'Thweet, thtudious, thtupendous, thuperlative thtudents!'

The room filled with laugher while the spotlight bloomed to reveal Maya sitting cross-legged in midair, hands resting on her knees and eyes closed. Behind her, ghostly backlighting illuminated the still and silent cast.

Gigi settled back in her seat. She had to focus so she could find a point in the lecture where she could get Maya's attention and let her know she was ready to leave.

'Everyone, please find a comfortable position and sit quietly, breathing deeply,' Maya began. 'As you still your body, become aware of what drifts into consciousness from the corners of your mind.'

Gigi fidgeted. She hated sitting still, especially when someone told her to. *I can't believe we're doing a meditation*, she complained inwardly. *Who needs this? I'd really rather be somewhere alone where I could get to know Buck.* Finally she found a comfortable position and took a deep breath. *Get yourself under control, girl*, she thought sternly. *You are in school, after all, at least for now. You need to do your best so you can get to the top of the class. Now, concentrate!*

But she could feel Buck's arm brushing her own in the darkness, sending a pleasant shiver through her body. *He is so incredibly sexy!* raved an inner voice, while another moaned, *Oh God, I wish my hair was clean – I bet I look gross. Men don't care what's on the inside nearly as much as what's on the outside.*

Still, he seems interested, another voice chimed in. *I hope he doesn't have a girlfriend. It doesn't matter anyway; he'll need me, I can tell. I bet he's a great kisser.*

She caught herself abruptly and chastised herself. *Gigi, would you look at yourself? How can you sit here and think these things when you're supposed to be clearing your mind? And you just met him ten minutes ago!*

But she couldn't help being uncomfortably aware of sensations in parts of her body that hadn't been stimulated in way too long. *Mmm, I wonder what Buck's ranch is like*, she thought. *Maybe I should finagle an invitation to visit once we're done with this course.*

Maya's diamond-clear voice sliced through the darkness, interrupting Gigi's stream of thoughts. 'What do you discover in this silence, my dears?' she asked. 'Is it really silent in your mind, or is it, as I suspect, filled with ceaseless chatter?'

'It's like a freakin' frat party in there, Maya!' called Vinny from the balcony.

'Yeah, Animal House,' chimed in Tito.

Scattered laughter and murmurs of assent rose from the room as Maya continued serenely. 'Yes, as you noticed, Vinny and Tito, that is the tendency of the human mind. Instead of allowing you peace, your mind is filled with many different voices, similar to the noisy crowd you saw onstage a few minutes ago.

'These voices come from what I call your cast of characters – the uncontrollable mob that inhabits your mind, bouncing from one brash opinion to another, trying to hook your attention and take over the action in your script.'

Well, that's true, Gigi thought grudgingly. *I did seem to have a loud stream of thoughts and opinions going on instead of allowing stillness. Those voices in my head really do yank me around.*

With a sigh of acquiescence, she settled in to listen to the rest of the lecture, since by this point it was obvious it had something to do with her. She could always try to get Maya's attention afterward and let her know she was ready to start her job as manager of the Magical Theatre. Besides, she had to admit that things were a little more interesting around here since Marlboro Man arrived on the scene.

'Now ask yourselves, my dears: Are all these characters encouraging you to do what's best for your authentic self?' Maya asked.

Buck let out a soft groan. 'No way,' he said under his breath. 'They couldn't be. It feels like a shootout in there.'

'Exactly, Buck,' said Maya, sending a rainbow in his direction. Gigi's jaw dropped in indignation. Buck talked out of turn and got rewarded with Maya's praise, when she'd been containing her questions to avoid interrupting the group! It wasn't fair. And she could tell Buck wasn't as awakened as she was.

Or was she deluding herself? The unbidden question sent an unpleasant jolt through her.

Maybe I'm not as good a student in Remedial Angel Training as I believe I am, she thought despairingly. *Maybe I'll be here forever, repeating lessons, while someone like Buck gets to go on with his happy-go-lucky life. Why is it always so hard for me?* Then she realized she was sinking into self-pity and felt disgusted. *Stop your whining, girl*, she told herself. *You really need to get a grip!*

'You may have noticed even now that the voices have strong and often conflicting reactions to everything that goes on,' Maya continued, still sitting cross-legged but with eyes open, beaming violet light out at the crowd. 'These characters who try to control you aren't necessarily kind, wise or enlightened, and they encourage you to make decisions from a limited perspective of fear. Think about it – if you hadn't been trying so hard to appease your cast, would you have made the same decisions in life?'

Gigi sighed, thinking how she could have done things differently if she'd been able to ignore all the inhabitants of her mind that seemed to be constantly pulling her in different directions. Just as Godfreys had told her when they were reviewing her script, her characters had encouraged her to follow others' views on what she should do instead of tending to her own desires.

Maybe she wouldn't have married Keith in the first place if she hadn't had a cast member telling her she needed to prove a man wanted her, even though her father hadn't. She certainly wouldn't have wasted time messing around with losers, partying, or running track, for God's sake. And she would have dealt with her father differently. Instead of waiting for him to come back to her, she would have flown out to California and met with him face to face.

In fact, she still could.

The moment she thought it, an old, familiar voice said, *Forget it. If he had wanted to see you he would have.* Her heart clenched as she struggled to concentrate on Maya's words.

'You currently rely heavily on the input from the rabble-rousers in your head,' Maya observed. 'You even give them credit by quoting them and saying "This is what I think" – often to your detriment, I may add. Because their voices are familiar, you listen to them and take their advice out of habit.

'Yet you have mistaken familiarity for safety. A voice may sound benign because you're so used to hearing it, but does that mean you should listen to counsel that is often fear-driven and derives from past experiences rather than your present truth?'

Maya paused for effect, surveying the silent audience. 'Your people like to voice opinions that contradict one another, causing you struggle. Although this conflicting input often ends up leading you astray, you still tend to listen to the voices and give them credence. But which one is telling the truth? Which advice should you accept?'

Maya leaned forward and said in a conspiratorial tone, 'Let me tell you, my lovelies, that in all likelihood, none of those voices is giving you good advice. The secret to deciphering which voice to heed is this: Any voice that causes you to feel badly is not worth paying attention to. That is the lesson of the third keystone. Listen!'

She stood and turned toward the frozen performers behind her, brandishing a shining baton with bubbles pouring out the tip. The chorus line, clowns, actors and opera singers all jerked into motion, clasping their hands in front of them, elbows out, backs straight. At the swish of the baton, they burst into a round, singing in harmony over and over: 'Keystone 3: You are not the voices in your head.'

Gigi listened to the pleasing harmonizing of the singers, taking in the message. Could it really be that she could simply disregard the inner voices that hounded her constantly? They seemed so real, so powerful. Yet perhaps, as Maya said, they were only characters, voices formed from her experiences that did not necessarily do her any good. In fact, they did more harm than good – causing her to feel badly about herself, question her decisions, and waste energy listening to them and arguing with them.

The singers ended the round with a soft chord, and Maya

froze them again with a flourish of the bubbling baton. She turned back around, took a bow to thunderous applause, and calmly resumed her midair cross-legged position.

'So you see, my treasures, that although you will need practice to be able to stop the flow of voices, in this moment you can decide not to believe them anymore. Remember that your cast is devious and is constantly executing one "sleight of mind" after another, designed to lead you into a mire of self-doubt and confusion. Your people have a vested interest in keeping you under the Magical Theatre's spell of forgetfulness, because when you break the spell you won't need them anymore.'

Next to Gigi, Buck sighed heavily and switched from one crossed leg to another. He looked serious under his hat, his brow furrowed in thought. Gigi felt her heart swell toward him then returned her attention to the stage with effort. This was all so much to take in. Did she really have a conflicting cast of characters inside her? It made sense, but weren't they all really her? If so, how could she determine which characters to listen to?

'My angels, know that you can free yourself from the oppression of your characters and resume your rightful place as director of your own production,' Maya declared as the performers behind her began to slink offstage, one by one. 'Wake up to the fact that you don't have to direct the script of your life based on these unhelpful, fear-inspired voices that want to keep you small and limited.'

Hearing Maya's stern tone, the remaining performers rushed off, jostling one another in their hurry. 'It is essential to realize that the characters' voices do not express the true you,' Maya continued more softly, a soft light pulsating around her like a full-body halo.

'Listen carefully, my dears. You have a very special resource that will help free you from the tyranny of your voices – a wise inner sage called the "impartial observer". This serene and loving presence lives in your heart and provides you with a clear-eyed perspective of your deepest truth.

'Your impartial observer is your greatest ally,' Maya went on. 'Humans sometimes think of it as a guardian angel, but really it is an aspect of yourself that is always within you. It's here to offer you a balanced perspective. When your characters' babbling has you stressed and unable to make a decision, you can always drop into the quiet knowingness of your impartial observer, who can help you make the most loving and sensible choice.'

Gigi placed her hand on her heart and breathed in deeply. Yes, she knew it was true, because she had sensed such an impartial guiding presence at some key moments in her life. When she found Keith with the singer, for instance, through all the swirling thoughts, emotions and voices that assaulted her internally, part of her remained calm and clear-eyed.

This part of her knew how to exit the scene with dignity and make the decision to leave Keith from a place of self-love, realizing it wasn't the first time he had cheated on her – and was sure not to be the last. Of course she'd questioned this voice from time to time, and at other junctures of her life had not been able to access it through the muddled ramblings of her cast members.

'If you're wondering how to recognize the voice of your impartial observer from the babble of your cast of characters, don't worry. You can tell simply by distinguishing which voices cause you pain. Since falsehoods are always painful, any voice that causes you pain is untrue.

'So if pain is present and you experience discomfort in your body, or if you feel hurt, humiliated, confused, betrayed or angered by an inner voice – know that it is not the voice of your impartial observer but one of your misleading cast members.

'Each time a voice speaks, ask yourself, "Is this advice coming from fear or love?" Then notice what sensations the advice provokes in your body, mind and emotions. If the sensations are negative or painful, disregard the voice.

'Next, access the loving communication from your impartial

observer. To do this, open your heart and shift your awareness to the voice of wisdom bubbling up from the spring of your internal knowingness.'

Maya took a breath, inhaling the surrounding light into her heart, causing it to brighten and pulse. 'Mmm,' she said. 'It feels so good to drop into this knowingness, my dears.'

Then she added briskly, 'Your homework is to develop a relationship with your impartial observer. To do this, you'll have to wade through the strident voices of your people, paying them no heed. Your impartial observer is a lot quieter than your noisy mob of characters. In fact it does not often communicate through speech, but if you pay attention and connect with your heart, you can subtly experience this loving witness within your awareness. Best of luck, my beloveds!'

The light surrounding her heart grew brighter and brighter until Gigi had to close her eyes against its glare. When she opened them, Maya had disappeared.

'Wait!' Gigi called, springing out of her seat and waving her hands, but it was too late. Damn! She hadn't had the chance to ask Maya if she could be excused from further lessons.

Suddenly, she was aware of the curious scrutiny of her neighbors. She sat back down, tossing her hair with feigned nonchalance.

After an awkward silence, Buck cleared his throat.

'Impartial observer, huh?' he said conversationally. 'Well, Gigi, how do you think we're supposed to proceed from here? She doesn't give us real clear directions, does she?'

Gigi's heart fluttered. Surely he must find her attractive, since he'd clearly addressed her and not Susan.

'Clear as mud,' she replied dryly. 'But somehow it all seems to become apparent.'

'That's the point, really, isn't it?' Susan chimed in, stowing her journal in her briefcase. 'Maya's here to help, but really the answers are already inside us.'

Gigi rolled her eyes but, irritatingly, Buck looked interested. 'You're right, Sue, they are.'

'Susan,' corrected Susan. Her scooter arrived above her and she effortlessly leapt onto it and sped away with a quick wave.

'She's somethin' else, isn't she?' Buck said wonderingly, shaking his head. Gigi wondered if he meant that admiringly or if he, too, thought Susan was a bit of a whack job.

A palomino horse galloped out of the sky and screeched to a halt just above them, stirrups dangling.

'Hi there, fella,' Buck said to the horse with a casual grin, as if horses appearing out of thin air were an everyday occurrence. Turning to Gigi, he tipped his hat and said, 'Care for a lift?'

Gigi hesitated, unsure and suddenly painfully aware of all the noise in her mind. She wanted all the people in there to shut up! Whatever happened to privacy? Some of her people thought she should go for it, while others cautioned her against it. One voice was busy telling her that she didn't know how to ride and would look like a dork, while another assured her Buck would think her a chicken if she didn't take him up on his offer. She wanted to scream at them to be quiet, feeling more susceptible to their maneuverings than ever.

Then she remembered the impartial observer. Taking a deep breath, she focused on her heart. It was hard to maintain attention there with all the cast members shouting at her, but she kept breathing until she got a subtle vibration of comfort.

It's okay. It's my script and I can change my mind anytime I want to, she realized. Not to mention that she was still lacking her own form of transportation.

'Okay, I'll come with you,' Gigi responded to the patiently waiting Buck. He just nodded, but she could see his eyes light up at her consent.

'Here, grab a hold of the saddle horn and put your left foot in the stirrup, and I'll hoist you up,' he said, putting his hands on either side of her waist.

You should say no, since he might throw his back out from the effort, a cast member remarked snidely, while another snickered and said, *You'll be sure to fall. You should maintain your dignity.* Gigi gritted her teeth, determined to ignore their limiting advice, and stepped into the stirrup. With one sure motion he hoisted her up while she threw her leg over the saddle, and she was sitting proudly atop the palomino.

Buck said, 'I'm coming up,' and vaulted onto the horse behind her. The sheer physicality of his closeness nearly overwhelmed Gigi for a moment: his strong legs straddling her hips, his muscled arms wrapping around her, and the masculine odor of fresh air, hay and the merest hint of cologne – was it Calvin Klein?

'Grab the horn tight,' Buck said. 'Just as a warning, the going might get rough if we hit some rogue air currents. I'm gonna have to hold onto you as a precaution.'

Gigi nodded, feeling faint. At this point, he could have told her he was going to tie her up and drag her behind the horse and she would have acquiesced.

I guess it's been a while since I've been this close to a man, she thought ruefully. But before she could dwell on it further, Buck dug his heels into the horse's side, yelled, 'Gee-yup!' and they were galloping full speed out of the auditorium and into the star-filled sky, too fast for any thought but holding on and delighting in the sweep of wind in her hair.

'Uh-oh,' Buck said after what could have been five minutes or an hour; Gigi had lost all sense of time, succumbing to the bliss of leaning back against Buck's solid chest.

'What?' she asked dreamily, eyes closed against the chilly air.

'Um, I'm not exactly sure where we are,' he replied.

'Doesn't the horse know where to go?' Gigi asked doubtfully.

'Apparently not,' Buck said. 'And he seems to have lost his power to fly.'

Something in his tone made Gigi sit up straight and take a

good look around where they had landed. They were surrounded by an eerie greenish-purple light unlike anything she'd ever seen, and the ground underneath them seemed soft and swampy. In fact, the horse's feet were making sucking sounds with each step, and he seemed to be having increasing difficulty maneuvering in the deep mud. Overhead, thick vines dripped down from huge trees with trunks smooth and white like alabaster, so large she was sure ten people couldn't get their arms around them.

Suddenly Gigi was completely alert. 'Where on earth are we?' she breathed, not daring to raise her voice in the silent jungle.

'That's the problem – I'm not sure we *are* on earth,' Buck answered, trying to sound nonchalant. But Gigi heard the concern in his voice and felt panic rise in her throat threatening nausea. She swallowed but found herself unable to speak, paralyzed by fear and the sudden, urgent input of the people in her head.

Jump off the horse and run for your life!
It can't be that bad.
Stiff upper lip, my dear. Just ride it out.
Smile and look happy so he'll like you.
Hold on and pray.

Gigi put her hands to her ears. Why, oh why, had Maya called her attention to these crazies in her head? Now she couldn't ignore them, and they seemed to get louder and louder. How could she think when all the voices inside her mind were clamoring for her attention?

'Impartial observer,' she murmured, but Buck was asking her something. She removed her hands. 'Pardon? I couldn't hear you,' she said.

Buck leaned around to look at her. 'Are you all right?' he asked, and Gigi nodded reluctantly.

'I do apologize about this. I don't know what happened. One second we were galloping through space pretty as could be, and the next we got sucked into some kind of energy vortex and, well, here we are. I don't think we were traveling long enough to have reached Earth, and this certainly doesn't look familiar.'

'Not to mention that the sky is the color of a nasty bruise,' said Gigi, gazing up through the dense foliage. Immediately, it started to rain big, cold, grapelike raindrops. Gigi cringed. Talk about a bad hair day!

Buck wrinkled his brow in concern and looked around for cover. 'I sure do wish I had a saddle blanket we could use for protection from the rain,' he said. 'Never ride without one at home.' He shook his head, looking discouraged, and Gigi thought his cast of characters must be working overtime too.

Meanwhile the horse kept wandering forward, feet sinking into the goo. Gazing down at the swamp underfoot, Gigi cried, 'I know where we are! Remember what Maya said about the "mire of self-doubt and confusion?" I think this swamp is that mire. I know Maya wouldn't let us end up here unless it had something to do with our lesson.'

The thought comforted her, somehow, and she had the curious sense that Maya was watching them from afar.

'Well, maybe so,' Buck said, sounding distracted. 'But in any case, we've got to go off the path. I see an outcropping of rock over there. Maybe we can find shelter and figure out a plan.' He turned the palomino into the jungle of tangled trees. The horse reluctantly picked his way through the muck, which seemed to grow deeper with every step. Gigi chafed at their slow progress while her people once again found full voice, and the comfort she'd felt a moment ago abandoned her.

There might be snakes in here, or worse.

Yes, what if this is a planet like earth was millions of years ago, and there are dinosaurs?

Oh no, what are we going to do? I want to go home.

Relax, this has to be earth or we wouldn't be able to breathe.

Yes, and Buck knows what he's doing. He's used to finding his way on a horse. You'll be fine with him.

But even if this is earth and Buck is good with horses, we're hopelessly lost. We'll be lost here forever and never be able to find our way out. I don't want to die on a strange planet with a man I just met! No matter how *cute he is!*

Gigi tried to breathe into her heart and find the impartial observer who could help her, but she couldn't access that calm, true voice. She was too scared and disoriented.

'Hey, look – perfect!' Buck said, pointing to an enormous rock forming a sort of roof with an overhang of dark, shaggy moss.

'Yeah, perfect,' Gigi mumbled, thinking, *Perfect would be curled up on my sofa with a good glass of red wine and a* Sex and the City *rerun. This is pretty far from perfect!*

Buck expertly guided the horse underneath the outcropping, jumped off the saddle and tied the reins to a tree trunk. Relieved to be out of the rain at least, Gigi perked up slightly while she watched Buck. He really was attractive, with his wavy hair spilling over his collar and his broad shoulders straining through his jacket. Really, this was like one of those games of 'If you were trapped on a desert island...' and it was far from the worst case scenario. And she had to admit it was interesting to be somewhere totally different, where normal rules of life didn't apply – even if it was a swamp.

Buck handed her down, and her feet sunk deeply into the mushy goo. 'Eeww,' she said involuntarily, grimacing. Her spike-heeled boots would certainly now be destroyed.

'Here, climb up onto this ledge,' Buck said, jumping up onto a moss-covered shelf of rock and extending his hand. Gigi clambered up gracelessly, her useless spike heels sliding, but Buck's grip was sure and she soon found herself sitting beside him on the bed of moss, protected from the rain by the jutting rock overhead and leaning against smooth rock with her thigh smushed delightfully close to his hard, jean-clad leg.

Suddenly Gigi realized Buck had not yet let go of her hand,

and instantly the situation seemed ridiculous. Here she was, Goddess knew where, having flown through space on a palomino to land in a swamp with a cowboy from New Mexico – and now they were, of all things, holding hands! An urge to laugh started in her gut and made its way uncontrollably up to her chest. She laughed until tears sprang to her eyes, Buck looking on in wonder until he, too, was captured by the hysteria of their predicament.

They laughed together until it hurt. Then, without warning, Buck took Gigi's face in his hands, pulled her toward him, and kissed her softly on the lips. It was the most amazing kiss she'd ever experienced, and she opened her mouth to him, drinking in his salty taste, losing all sense of their bizarre surroundings, her cast of characters miraculously silent for the moment.

'Gigi, my wayward angel, are you remembering your homework assignment?' Maya's voice reverberated through Gigi's mind. Gigi jerked away from Buck and sat up straight, smoothing her hair.

'Er, yes, get to know my impartial observer,' Gigi muttered while Buck stared at her.

Ignoring the voices shouting to her to kiss him again, Gigi said, 'Look, Buck, we're supposed to be doing this homework assignment and here we are trapped on this swampy hell of a planet or whatever it is, and the racket from my cast of characters has me going nuts and I can't find my impartial observer, and Maya just spoke to me in my head to remind me to stay on task, and I have to get the homework right so I can start my new career at the Magical Theatre, and I just can't kiss you anymore right now!'

Without further ado, she burst into tears.

Buck sat stiffly, clearly uncomfortable. His hand reached out as if to stroke her hair but he retracted it quickly.

'Listen, I'm sorry,' he said contritely. 'That was my fault, and I don't want you to think for a minute that I'm the type of guy that would take advantage of a woman, you know? I just lost my head for a second 'cause I really like you.

'But you're right, we are in remedial angel training and we're supposed to be staying focused. And, I gotta tell you, my cast has been pretty loud too during this trip. And I don't know what to do either. This mire of self-doubt and confusion, as you called it, feels more like quicksand to me. I usually know just how to deal with any situation, but I can't seem to get a grip on this one.'

Gigi sniffed and wiped her nose on the back of her hand. Buck immediately pulled a checkered bandanna out of his pocket and handed it to her, and she blew her nose noisily.

'You see, I have all these two-bit characters always telling me I have to be strong, in control, gentlemanly, and be ready to save anyone or anything,' Buck said quietly. 'They drive me crazy, and are keeping me kinda saddled to all my old habits. And now, here we are in this ridiculous situation where I'm clearly not in control, and, well, the truth is my cast is going nuts firing advice at me. But I don't know which voice to listen to or which one has my best interest at heart. Probably none. So I need to get to that impartial observer fella, but I can't seem to find him.'

Buck looked down at his hands, cleared his throat, and added, 'And I also have to tell you that I've never shared anything like that before.'

Clutching the bandanna like a lifeline, Gigi felt her heart melt. She was pleasantly surprised at Buck's openness and relieved to know he was having as much conflict about this situation as she was.

'My people give me all this advice that has nothing to do with the current situation,' Buck continued. 'They base it on things I've done and old ways of being that I don't want anymore. I guess my people feel safe when they're on old familiar ground, and they want me to keep figuring stuff out from these places.'

Gigi got an instantaneous glimpse of some of his people. Obviously, his father had followed the popular, but amazingly stupid, child-rearing theory which said that the best way to teach a boy to stand on his own two feet was to knock his feet out from under him every time he tried it. She was pretty sure, though, that his mother had loved him, and showed it frequently.

Buck was determined, but not very confident. But he seemed like a loving man, and that made up for just about everything else.

'I know what it's like,' she said. 'It's like the voices keep me captive to their whining, raging, blaming and, did I mention sniping? And then, as if that's not enough, they whip me into a frenzy of panic sometimes, and then it seems impossible to make a good choice for myself. It's like they want to keep me limited and make me feel guilty if I make a new, different choice.

'So I give in and do something self-destructive, like eating a family-sized bag of M&Ms or... or... choosing someone that's going to break my heart.'

Gigi felt the familiar stabbing pain in her heart as more tears leaked out of her eyes. She waved her hand in front of her face, not wanting Buck to give her sympathy for fear she'd never be able to stop crying.

'I know what you mean,' Buck said softly. 'They want to direct the play, but their script is the pits, and ends up limiting you. I know, because mine do the same thing. They try to pretend they're on my side fighting for my best interest, but they're not.'

Gigi and Buck sat in contemplation, the silence broken only by the horse's snufflings and the steady plop-plop of raindrops.

'So here we are,' Buck said eventually. 'You, me, the horse and a huge supporting cast of our characters. And between us we haven't had one good idea of how to get off this godforsaken planet.'

Gigi sniffed juicily and blew her nose again. 'Yeah, great students we are, huh? Maybe we can meditate and try to access our impartial observers, then pool our ideas and see if we can find a way out.'

'Sounds good,' said Buck.

Gigi closed her eyes and breathed into her heart, feeling it gradually expand and grow warm, although the voices in her head wouldn't shut up.

What's Buck doing? Is he really meditating? Maybe he's just talking about this stuff to try to get you to like him so he can take advantage of you.

How could he possibly like you with your hair all stringy and your makeup smudged from crying?

He's your type, honey, you've got to go for it. Who better to be stranded on a strange planet with?

Forget Buck. You've got to get yourself out of here.

Gigi kept breathing, concentrating on letting the calm voice of the impartial observer break through the overwrought voices of her cast. But how would she know it when it arrived?

Trust, said an inner voice, and she felt her heart thrill to its vibration. *Trust yourself. Don't listen to the voices of your people. When you quiet them, answers will come to you from your inner knowing. Escaping the mire of self-doubt and confusion requires a leap of faith.*

A leap of faith... Gigi thought, opening her eyes. *Trust.* She glanced at Buck, whose eyes were still closed, then at the horse, who was unconcernedly chewing on the cabbage-sized leaves of the tree to which it was tied.

'Yes, of course,' she murmured to herself. 'The first time I traveled to Maya's lecture, I simply imagined a lifesaver and dove through it.'

She closed her eyes and pictured a lifesaver, but try as she might she could not manifest one as she had before. In any case, it would have to be a pretty big lifesaver if she and Buck and the horse all had to go through it.

Trust, reiterated her impartial observer.

At this, the cast members sent up a clamor of protest, but Gigi ignored them. Well, clearly her idea of the lifesaver wasn't working. She might as well see if Buck had any ideas. If there ever was a good time to give up control, it was now. She nudged Buck with her elbow, and his extraordinary brown eyes flew open, stunning her momentarily with their intensity.

'I've got an idea,' Buck said without preamble. 'We'll get back on the horse and visualize wings. If it could fly before, it can fly again.'

'But we can fly too,' objected Gigi, immediately forgetting her pledge to give up control. 'I flew to the first lecture without a horse. If we can visualize wings on the horse, we can do the same ourselves and we won't need the horse.'

'But we can't just leave him here,' Buck objected. 'He's a beauty, and he did carry us quite a ways. Wouldn't be right to leave him alone in this place.'

'Oh, all right,' Gigi said grudgingly. 'We'll try it your way.'

Buck helped her down from the ledge and back into the sloppy rain. They sloshed through the mud to the horse and Buck helped her up, then untied the horse and vaulted up behind her. Again she felt the thrill of his closeness, sinking back against his hard chest.

Buck gave a hopeful 'Gee-up' but the horse only sidled slowly, deeper into the jungle of trees. 'Damn,' he muttered under his breath, then said, 'Okay, Gigi, we've got to visualize big huge wings on this dang animal.'

Gigi closed her eyes tight, attempting to silence the voices who were telling her this would never work and she would be better off doing it her way. She pictured enormous white wings, Pegasus-style, beating gently and lifting them up, up, over the bruised, dripping haze and into clear, exhilarating space beyond. She visualized it so fully that when she opened her eyes she was surprised to see they were still picking their way through the swamp.

'Jeez,' Buck said, apparently having the same experience. 'I swear I thought this would work. I nearly always find a good way out of a mess. I'm sorry, Gigi.'

'It's not your fault,' Gigi said generously, though her characters loudly made it clear they didn't agree.

Suddenly the horse shied and, with a startled neigh, started to rear backward. Buck yanked on the reins and managed to turn the horse before it could dump them. Gigi held on tightly to its mane, thankful for Buck's skill. As he brought the horse around, however, she saw the cause of its panic and her stomach dropped to her ankles. They were perched on the edge of a steep precipice. Gigi willed herself to look down and beheld craggy white cliffs reaching down, down, seemingly endlessly, as far as her eyes could see.

Buck was also gazing down at the cliffs. 'Well, I guess we have to turn back,' he said. Gigi could swear his voice was shaking just slightly despite his appearance of calm. 'Maybe there's some kind of hill we can climb to get a bird's-eye view of the land and figure out a strategy.'

Gigi was about to argue that they could try it her way and visualize themselves flying, sans horse, when they heard a huge crash from the forest behind them. Gigi twisted around to look, eyes wide in alarm.

Another crash made the soggy goo beneath them tremble. Buck instinctively threw his arms tightly around her, and she had a twinge of regret that she was too frightened to enjoy the sensation. But then all thoughts left her as another crash was followed by an unearthly roar.

'Oh crap,' Buck gasped. 'We've gotta get out of here pronto.'

'But how?' Gigi shrieked in a whisper, her stomach clenched in fear. 'We're trapped between that... that monster, or whatever it is, and these cliffs.'

Buck kicked the horse. 'We'll have to ride this way along the edge,' he said. But the horse didn't budge. 'Gee-up, you stubborn animal,' Buck said fiercely, not wanting to yell and attract the attention of whatever was crashing its way toward them. But the horse stood firm.

'Oh my God,' Gigi gasped. 'Buck, I don't want to die on this stupid ugly planet, with bitten fingernails and bad hair! We have to get out of here!'

'I'm tryin',' Buck said shortly. 'Got any other ideas?'

Gigi took a deep breath into her heart, and suddenly she knew what they had to do. 'Get down,' she said.

'Down?' Buck said, not moving.

'Buck, get off this horse and help me down,' Gigi hissed.

Polite as ever, Buck did as he was asked. He swung her down and her feet sunk into the muck, making her stumble against him. She suddenly wished he would just hold her and tell her everything would be okay, but a tearing sound like a tree being uprooted shocked her into action. She grabbed Buck's hand and pulled him toward the edge of the cliff. Vertigo threatened to take over and she swayed, but Buck's hand steadied her.

'What now?' Buck whispered. 'Are you thinkin' to climb down this cliff? Because it looks pretty slick to me.'

'No, not *climb* down,' Gigi said firmly. 'We're going to jump.'

'What!' Buck jerked as if to take his hand away, but Gigi held on firmly and looked into his eyes. 'It's a leap of faith, Buck,' she said. 'We can't keep listening to our people. We can't continue doing what we've always done. That's what my inner wisdom from the impartial observer said – have faith. I know we can do this. Every leap into the unknown takes faith.'

Gigi felt her heart open, and knew she had spoken truly.

'Are you sure?' Buck asked, his eyes boring into hers.

'Yes,' Gigi said, filled with a solid sense of conviction.

'What about the horse?' Buck asked.

Gigi sighed. 'Hold onto his reins and see if he'll come with us,' she said. But just then, another jarring crash made the earth shudder and the nearest trees sway dangerously. Panicking, the horse reared up, spun, and sailed into the air. As they watched, wings sprang from its back and it soared out over the cliffs, up and up until it disappeared into the lowering sky.

'You've got to be kidding me,' Buck said. 'I can't believe that freakin' animal went and flew off without us!'

Feeling a giddy mixture of hysterical amusement and gut-wrenching fear, Gigi wasn't sure whether to laugh or cry. Possibly a good, old-fashioned scream was in order.

Before she could decide between these three enticing options, a *Jurassic Park* roar erupted behind them. Rather unnecessarily, Buck shouted, 'Oh, shit! *Jump!*'

Without waiting for further encouragement, Gigi screwed her eyes shut and pushed off, her sweaty hand still clasping Buck's. In the moment of leaping before they began to free-fall, Gigi heard her mother's voice intone its customary words of caution before any trip: *I hope you remembered to put on clean underwear in case you get in an accident.*

As far as Gigi could remember, she wasn't wearing any underwear at all.

Chapter Eight

Gigi landed with a soft thump on what felt like a dense mattress and tried to screw up the courage to open her eyes. Was she dead? Injured? Was a man-eating monster looming over them? Was she in some sort of undead limbo? Something made her want to cough. Dust. She opened her eyes but could see only blackness. Where was she?

Gradually she became aware of Buck's hand still clutched in hers and, as her eyes adjusted, she realized they were lying side by side on a pile of something soft like clothes and pillows – a very dusty pile – in a dark room filled with strangely shaped shadows. Furniture? Artwork? She couldn't tell, but the most important thing was that no matter where they were, they had escaped the horrible swampy planet. And best of all, she seemed to still have all her clothes on. Contrary to her mother's belief, clean underwear was apparently not the key to survival.

More to the point: her impartial observer had been right, and the plan had worked! They were alive!

Or... at least *she* was alive. Suddenly she realized that Buck hadn't moved at all. She shook her hand free and bent over him. No sound. His hat lay on his chest. She shoved it aside and put her head to his chest but could feel no motion of breath.

Panicked thoughts assailed her. *Oh God, I've killed him. Now I've really done it! I knew it was too good to be true. I always mess everything up. Buck listened to my harebrained scheme to jump, and now he's...* A dry sob escaped her throat. *Oh, Buck, why? Why am I so impulsive? Who am I to think I have all the answers? I should be the one who's dead.*

Then Buck's chest gave a great heave and he spluttered, struggling to rise to his elbows. He stared at her through the gloom for a moment, uncomprehending – then smiled, dimples flashing. Arrested mid-sob, Gigi felt her heart fill with joy. She couldn't speak, the gratitude too great for words. 'Are you okay?' she asked hurriedly to cover her embarrassing surge of emotion.

'I believe so,' Buck said haltingly, wincing and slowly lowering himself back down. 'Got the wind knocked out of me, is all.'

'I'm so sorry,' Gigi said contritely. 'It's all my fault. I'm so glad you're not dead, because I can live with a lot of things but not killing someone.'

Gigi felt Buck's eyes on her. She lay down beside him so she didn't have to meet them. *She* wasn't feeling so hot either after their tumultuous journey, come to think of it. And here she was, lying next to a very attractive and possibly injured man in an unspecified dark and gloomy storage room, having just escaped a terrible monster in a really strange swamp that was possibly located in some unknown dimension of outer space.

How did she manage to get herself into these situations? Why couldn't she just be normal, even-keeled, and handle her life with grace instead of finding herself constantly in awkward places? Hadn't she learned *anything* in Remedial Angel Training?

'Gigi,' Buck said huskily, still breathing with effort. 'Listen to me. This wasn't your fault. Hell, girl, you saved us! It should have been me who saved us, not you. I'm the man, and it's my job to save us. I'm the one who blew it here, not you. I should have found a way to get us off that dang planet right away instead of wandering around like some sort of city idiot.'

'Oh, Buck, that is so kind of you to say, but really, I'm the one who said we should jump, and now you're in pain. Believe me, this is so typical of my life; I always screw things up.' Buck must think she was a real piece of work. So much for making a good impression. He probably regretted kissing her. He probably couldn't wait to get as far away from her as possible.

'Well, join the club, because I seem to be pretty good at making a mess of things too,' he said. 'I mean, look at us, lying here in some strange dark place not knowing where we are, and

I can't even get up because my ribs are killing me.'

Suddenly a loud whirring noise invaded the dark room. Gigi involuntarily grasped Buck's arm and asked in alarm, 'What is *that?*'

Before he could answer, the ceiling was illuminated with a square of wavering light and an old-fashioned countdown of black-and-white numbers. Four, three, two... and a grainy image of Maya's face appeared before their startled eyes. Over the whirring of the invisible film projector, her warm tones greeted them.

'Hello, sweeties. How are you feeling?' Maya asked.

'Can she hear us?' Gigi asked Buck, who managed a shrug. 'We're okay,' said Gigi loudly, feeling foolish. 'A little the worse for wear, but... Can you tell me where we are?'

'Of course, Gigi. You are in the props room in the Magical Theatre.' The room was suddenly infused with rose-colored light. Curiously, Gigi looked around. It was strange – many of the objects in the room seemed familiar. For example, that stuffed panda on the shelf in the corner looked like the one her father had given her before he left.

She got up creakily, stretching her sore joints, and went to look. Yes, the panda was missing one eye and had a Kool-Aid stain on its stomach. It was hers! She reached for it, but her hand went right through it and she couldn't pick it up.

'Buck, it's all my stuff from my past, but it's only an illusion,' she said wonderingly.

'Really? Must be because you were the one who told us to jump. We jumped into a storeroom of your past,' Buck theorized, painfully pushing himself up to a half-sitting position.

Gigi took in the rest of the room at a glance. The shelves were untidily heaped with mounds of schoolbooks, boxes of costume jewelry, and jumbles of magazines, well-worn cassettes and toys. 'Junk,' Gigi whispered to herself. Along the opposite wall rested painted backdrops: her childhood bedroom, her college dorm room, the living room of her Fifth Avenue apartment. She drifted toward them but was brought up short by Maya's voice.

'Gigi, I do understand that you are interested in these remnants of your past, but I must bring your attention back to the present. Rest assured you will have a chance to revisit the past again later, but for now please join Buck for today's lesson. We'll be having a distance class since it appears you are unable to make today's lecture.'

Gigi flopped back down next to Buck on what she now saw was the queen-size bed she'd bought at a yard sale when she first moved out on her own, topped by a well worn array of her old blankets and pillows. Recognizing a pillow encased in a shabby Cinderella pillowcase, she rested her head on it and leaned back to watch Maya on the ceiling.

'So, my valiant students, you have become acquainted with your impartial observer,' Maya began. She chuckled softly, her eyes beaming at Gigi. 'Yes, you now recognize that wise voice that supports the truth of you, once you can single out its heartfelt understanding from the conflicting input of your cast of characters. And Gigi, don't doubt that voice's wisdom. You, my dear, did a beautiful job back there in the *mire* of self-doubt and confusion.'

'So that *was* where we were!' Gigi blurted.

'Indeed, a perfect set design even if I do say so myself,' continued Maya. 'And by listening to your impartial observer, you were able to extract yourself from the mire and get yourself and Buck back on track. Buck, you also did a lovely job of listening to your impartial observer, who told you to listen to Gigi and follow her suggestion despite your cast's opinion that as the man *you* needed to be the one to save both of you.'

Gigi beamed. *I knew I was going to get to the top of the class*, she thought smugly. 'But it would have been better if Buck hadn't been hurt,' she blurted aloud.

Maya's face turned solemn. 'Gigi, you just made my next

point, which is that, as you've surely noticed by now, your impartial observer is sometimes overpowered by a nasty little cast member called the "critic".'

'No kidding,' Buck muttered.

'Yeah,' Gigi agreed. Then she noticed she was still holding on to Buck's arm. Embarrassed, she took her hand away.

Maya sighed and continued. 'Yes, the tyrannical critic, whose voice all too often dominates the others. The critic poses the biggest obstacle to accessing the impartial observer.

'Unfortunately, this inner judge is the voice you listen to the most. But, my dear— the critic is not on your side. He sizes up your every word, decision and action, making him difficult to ignore. And he has you suspecting you are fundamentally flawed, does he not?'

Gigi felt as if Maya were looking into the depths of her soul, as if she could hear the constant stream of self-criticism in Gigi's head.

'Like most souls under the spell of the Magical Theatre, you probably spend precious time and energy trying to please your critic,' Maya said. 'You try and try, don't you, my darlings? Look.'

Maya's face gave way to a slow montage of scenes. Gigi gasped to see past moments in her own life: herself standing in front of a full-length mirror, anxiously peering at her reflection and turning to look at the size of her behind; pulling a cheese soufflé out of the oven and swearing in frustration when the puffy, perfect-looking concoction fell as she placed it on the counter; anxiously bent over the computer at her office desk with the wall clock behind her reading 10:30 p.m.; locking herself in the bathroom at a music industry party, crying because she was sure she'd humiliated herself in front of everyone after having one too many margaritas; hating talking to her distant mother on the telephone while castigating herself for not calling more often.

Gigi closed her eyes, unable to watch any more scenes of herself trying so hard to please that voice inside her that told her she'd never be good enough, smart enough, accomplished enough, pretty enough, thin enough, hardworking enough, loved enough. And how humiliating to have Buck see these pathetic scenes too! What would he think of her now?

'There goes your critic right now, trying to make you feel badly for being human,' Maya said calmly. Gigi's eyes flew open. How could Maya read her thoughts through a film projector? 'Have you noticed that trying to please your judge doesn't work? Instead, it only becomes more and more difficult. Remember the goalposts of perfection Godfreys told you about when you were reviewing your life with him? Those standards that constantly advance farther and farther away even as you strive to reach them? Well, it's the critic who places them there and keeps moving them, so that every time you fail to reach these impossible standards of what you *perceive* as perfection, the critic hands out perverse punishments, keeping you from being happy and satisfied. Isn't it so, my pets?'

Another montage replaced Maya's face on the ceiling, this time with a scene from Buck's life. Buck groaned as they watched him falling off a rodeo bull over and over and getting up seriously bruised yet trying one more time; coming home after a disastrous date and drinking half a bottle of whiskey; going over his ranch accounts and holding his head in his hands; and standing stiffly at his father's funeral, paralyzed by the critic's rantings.

'Now, you need to make sure you understand this, so I'll recap. Your critic demands a perfection that is always just out of reach. The moment you achieve one step on the road to the critic's idea of excellence, the goal magically moves farther away and you're no closer to reaching it. It's like walking on a treadmill – you don't actually get anywhere. This is because your critic believes that self-criticism leads to self-improvement. But really, if you could improve yourself by berating yourself constantly, wouldn't you already have broken the enchantment? 'Yeah, if castigating myself made me a better person, I should be a saint by now,' Gigi said through the thickness in her throat that threatened tears.

'Me, too – I'd be the first cowboy saint,' Buck said with a wry smile, and Gigi grinned as she savored the intimacy of his humor.

'But really, Maya,' Gigi said slowly. 'How can we improve ourselves if we don't set high standards and strive to achieve them?'

'Yeah, I think if I didn't do that, I'd just become a slacker,' Buck admitted, squeezing Gigi's hand. 'My dad always told me I was good for nothing, and I guess even though he's dead I'm still trying to prove him wrong. But dang, it's hard.'

'Ah,' Maya said softly. 'So, my beloveds, you are buying into the enchantment, believing in your imperfection, no? What if, instead, you took the stance that you are already whole, even perfect, just the way you are?'

'But I'm *far* from perfect!' Gigi objected. 'I'm impulsive. Sometimes I make stupid decisions. I can't maintain a relationship no matter how hard I try – look at what happened with Keith.

'My hips are too big and my nose tilts sideways, and I eat too much chocolate. I can't make my father love me enough to even call or visit, and I don't pay enough attention to my mother. I like to spend money on myself, and I don't do as much volunteer work as I know I could. I get cranky sometimes. I never went on to get my master's degree like I planned, and now I've lost my job.' Gigi took a breath and concluded, 'I am *so* not perfect.'

'Mmm, very good, Gigi,' Maya said.

'Very *good*?' Gigi snorted.

'Yes, very good. You anticipated my next request, which is to make a list of your critic's accusations. It could take all day, couldn't it? Your critic knows just what is "wrong" with you and can articulate it beautifully.

'Isn't it sad that you've spent so much time and energy

making black marks against yourself to perpetuate the image of yourself as flawed? Yet you think if only you berate yourself enough, all day long every day, you'll get better. It's tragic, my dears, simply tragic! But,' she continued cryptically, 'perhaps with a bit of practice you will learn to place your focus elsewhere so the critic is not able to hook your attention so easily.'

Gigi felt Maya's love flowing into her heart, and simultaneously recognized the agony that her critic's accusations produced. She felt tears form unbidden and course down her cheeks, dripping down her neck.

Just then, the projector made a sputtering noise and the picture flickered then went dark, leaving the rose tinged light filling the air.

'Gosh, that was some intense stuff,' Gigi sniffed. I wish there was some chocolate around here. I could use a little self-medication.'

'Well, Ms. Gigi, the doctor is in,' Buck said with a light laugh. I just happen to have a source sitting on the nightstand over here.' Buck turned and slid toward her with a soft grunt of pain, doing his best to balance a box of truffles on his outstretched hand. Gigi squealed with delight as Buck set the new found treasures down between them. Carefully, and almost in slow motion, he lifted one of the decadent morsels to her lips.

'OMG, that is amazing,' Gigi uttered in pure pleasure. 'Now you,' Gigi said, quickly looking over the choices and selecting another piece of the chocolate. She took a deep breath as if to steady herself and then, locking her eyes to his, moved closer and leisurely placed the truffle in Buck's open mouth. They took turns feeding each other the sweet delights while giggling out loud. They were finally beginning to relax.

Buck became mesmerized by Gigi's joyful abandon. He found it charming to the point of excitement. Instantly, she sensed the change in his mood. A pleasant ache flickered in her solar plexus and caught her off guard. She was thrilled and yet inwardly embarrassed by her sudden yearning for Buck. As if by magic, her self-pity, along with her cast and critic, were all swept away on the wind of this budding desire. When she realized Buck's breathing was ragged and quick, over the rapid thump-thump of her own heart, the ache in her stomach turned into a familiar and pleasing warmth that spread through her entire being. She could feel his warm breath on her face. It smelled like chocolate now, sweet and enticing.

Without a word, Buck picked up the box of chocolates and returned it to the nightstand. Then reached over, pulling Gigi toward him. As her heartbeat quickened, he tenderly lifted her chocolate-covered fingers to his lips and unhurriedly licked off the sugary remnants of their exquisite indulgence. Placing his hand behind her neck, he moved her head slowly toward his face. Gigi closed her eyes in surrender as his lips sought hers in the soft glow of the dimly lit room. As their lips touched ever so tentatively, she could swear she felt a long-absent spark reignite deep inside her. Lovingly Buck's lips caressed hers, and with infinite care she licked the smeared confection off with the tip of her tongue. She savored the sweet essence in an attempt to make this delicious moment last just a little longer.

Sighing softly, Buck wrapped his arms tightly around her and pulled her impossibly close. His kisses grew more urgent, more passionate. Gigi let herself be overcome, parting her lips to allow his tongue to tenderly explore her mouth. Sinking into the pure pleasure of their embrace, he grasped her tighter as she thrilled to a shiver of excitement that ran through his entire body. Tentatively she smoothed her palms down the plank of his back, resting them just above his belt. Although longing to continue her exploration, she felt suddenly shy. Sensing her hesitation, Buck pulled away a fraction and gently murmured, 'Gigi, you're so beautiful, so sexy, I don't want to stop, but I can – I mean I will – I mean I need to know what you're feeling...We've just been through a lot and I need to know what you want...'

Gigi wanted to peel off her top, her jeans, her very skin and meld with him—flesh on flesh, soul to soul. She wanted to share everything with him, to feel his pleasure as her own, to merge and float into the infinite as one. She'd never felt so alive as she felt here, in the middle of nowhere, in the endless dreamtime. She felt secure at last, just the two of them in their own universe, in the safe cocoon of dusty blankets. With her entire body longing for union, Buck took her breath away when, for a moment, he leisurely traced a line of kisses down her jaw. In the stillness, her unleashed desire moved Gigi beyond the fires of time. She let the boundaries between them dissolve, and for an instant they were disembodied, shimmering lights dancing together in the vast universe.

Feeling Buck's heart pounding against hers, Gigi wanted this ecstasy to last forever. But their moment was already over. Abruptly, Buck pulled away and winced in excruciating pain. 'Da-amn,' he drawled, reluctantly interrupting the spell and sending them both into a fit of giggles. 'Ouch,' he added, readjusting his position and grasping his ribs, which only made them laugh harder. 'Nothing like a near-death experience to kick up some passion.' 'That's for sure,' Gigi said lightheartedly, masking her sudden fear. Did he mean that it was only their circumstances that made him want her? Would he really choose her, disheveled as she was after their muddy interlude on Planet Swamp, clearly insecure and an emotional mess?

With a jolt and a hiss, the projector's whirring began again, a flickering image appearing on the ceiling. Gigi panicked. *Oh no, here comes Maya and my critic is having a field day,* Gigi thought. *What is wrong with me? I've just had some of THE most extraordinary experiences a girl can have with a very desirable man, and I can't even give up the critic for one second. I'll never be able to stop. Aargh, I'm hopeless!*

'I hope you're not regretting what happened,' Buck whispered. 'It's my fault; I just lost control. I should have realized you're in a vulnerable state now. I feel terrible.'

Oh great, all the emotions he could choose and he felt terrible--she'd made him feel terrible.

Maya's voice beamed toward them from overhead. 'I apologize for the interruption, my angels. I was called to attend to some important playing. I trust you made good use of the time.' Her knowing laugh filled stuffy room with the refreshing scent of roses.

Gigi cringed inwardly with embarrassment. She was mortified by the thought that Maya knew what they'd been doing. Had she been watching them? It was worse than the time her eighth-grade teacher had caught her making out in the custodian's closet during study hall. Oh, why couldn't she have controlled herself?

'So, did anything come up with regard to our little discussion earlier?' Maya asked.

'Yes,' Gigi replied reluctantly, at the same time that Buck said, 'Sure did.'

'Oh – you go,' Gigi said.

'No, please, you first,' Buck insisted.

'Okay.' Gigi hesitated, clearing her throat. 'Well, I'd actually managed to give the critic the slip for a little bit, but then the second my attention was not focused on something' — she looked for Buck's reaction out the corner of her eye—'he was back like a bad penny. I know I shouldn't judge myself; I mean I've read enough self-help books to fill the New York Public Library. And what you said Maya made perfect sense. I am *so* well acquainted with the critic, but even when I managed to get a moments reprieve, the second he returned I felt icky again. I feel icky now. I don't know how to break the cycle.'

'Yeah, I know what you mean,' Buck added quickly. Something in his voice made Gigi glance over at him, and in the light of the projector she saw his face working as if he were trying not to cry. She wanted to reach out and touch him but stopped herself as he continued. 'It's like the critic criticizing the critic, if you get my drift. Like you've reached enough awareness in life to know on some level you shouldn't be criticizing yourself. Then when you do, you feel bad for doing it and criticize yourself for *that*. Am I making any sense?'

'Perfect sense, my dear,' Maya's voice said from the ceiling. 'But you *can* see how nonsensical it all is, can't you? In the twisted logic of your human experience, it makes sense. But coming from your angelic heart, you know it makes no sense at all.'

'Yes!' Gigi blurted out. 'That's partly what makes it so painful— being aware that it makes no sense but being unable to stop myself.'

'Precisely,' said Maya. 'But I have good news for you, my sweet. Today you have the opportunity to empower yourself by refusing to accept the critic's opinions.'

Gigi's heart leapt. 'You mean it??'

'Of course I do, my angel. Write down that list of your critic's accusations we discussed earlier then read over the critic's statements, engaging the help of the impartial observer to discover the truth. You'll know what is untrue because it will cause you pain or discomfort.

'The moment you drop into awareness of the impartial observer, the critic's statements begin to lose their power over you. That's because your impartial observer always comes from your heart and is therefore more powerful than the critic, who is fueled by fear.

Allow the inner wisdom of your impartial observer to offer you clarity on the critic's allegations. Armed with this new insight, you can refute the critic's vague accusations from a place of your deepest knowing.'

Buck cleared his throat and said hesitantly, 'But what if we find out the critic is right? I mean, what if I really am an underachiever who will never be a successful rancher like the critic says? What if I really am unfit to have a deep relationship with a woman? What if deep down I'm just a no-good slacker like my dad always predicted?'

'Ah, my poor suffering angels,' Maya breathed, infusing the room again with pink, rose-scented light. Gigi breathed it in, feeling her heart expand as Maya continued. 'There is no need to be afraid. The truth can never hurt you. Remember, you are beings of exquisite perfection. It is actually your blind acceptance of the critic's judgments that causes your suffering.

'When the answers arise from the stillness of your heart, you will learn that you are far greater than you ever dreamed. The critic wants to keep you small, but the truth is that you are a unique and splendid facet of the Divine Mystery.'

Gigi felt her fears calm and dared to look at Buck again. He was staring at the ceiling reverently, both hands on his heart.

A muffled voice in the background of the film said something to Maya. She turned and conversed with its invisible owner then turned back to the camera and said, 'I must leave you in a moment, for I have much play to attend to. Listen carefully to the rest of this lesson. I ask you to be on the alert for the critic's persistent comments. Your critic is an ingrained presence, and his comments won't just stop because you want them to. Your task is to notice the critic's stings and immediately administer the antidote.'

Across the bottom of the screen, like yellow subtitles, appeared the words: 'Keystone 4: Self-love silences the critic.'

'Yes, the antidote to the pain of self-criticism is the healing power of self-love. Here's how it works: When the critic says something mean-spirited or disempowering, allow yourself to notice that you are judging yourself.

'Next, instead of piling up punishments by judging yourself for judging, interrupt the process. This is the fun part, my dears! It's pointless to argue with the critic, because the stream of criticisms is never-ending. Giving the critic attention will only take you down the all-too-familiar road to self-condemnation. To prevent yourself from following this road, nourish yourself with love. Sing, laugh, dance, listen to great music, recite nonsense poetry, spell words backwards – anything you enjoy that will help jolt you out of the well-worn ruts made by the critic's judgments.

'Now don't just think about doing something new – *do* it, because this interruption is the antidote of self-love in action. It's a way of substituting kindness for self-battering. When you focus completely on something positive, or something loving' she said with an uncharacteristic smirk, or even something ridiculous, there's no room in your mind for critical thoughts. Let this loving action become a new habit you apply each and every time the critic rears his ugly head. In this way, you can cast off the chains of self-accusation and rejoice in the freedom of self-acceptance. Every time you substitute self-love for self-criticism, you open new vistas for your increasingly expansive role in the Magical Theatre.'

The muffled voice from the background again caught Maya's attention, and she said hurriedly, 'I must twirl on soon, my dears – the stars and planets need me to choreograph a dance.

'Quickly, let me tell you the second part of your homework: as you take that list of accusations your critic has made against you and bring it to the attention of the impartial observer, have faith. The impartial observer has a deep knowingness of your true worth and can easily refute the critic's nonsense.

'Oh, I really must fly. Please take this keystone to heart, and remember, I love you.'

'But...' Gigi felt the now-familiar sensation of confusion and abandonment that hit her every time Maya took her leave. What was she supposed to do now? How would they get out of here? What was she going to do about Buck? The picture went dark, but the room was still infused with a cotton candy pink light.

Buck struggled to sit up and propped himself against a pile of dusty pillows. Feeling self-conscious, Gigi sat up too.

'So,' she said uncomfortably, avoiding Buck's eyes. She had no idea how to act around him now that Maya was gone. Had their passion been a fleeting moment born of extraordinary circumstances or was there something more? She didn't know how he felt. Was he judging her?

'It's not others' dreaded judgments of you, but your *own* criticisms that cause you pain,' Maya's voice whispered in her mind. 'No one can hurt you without your consent, sweet angel.'

Gigi breathed in the words, sensing their power. It was true – she was better at hurting herself than anyone else, even Buck, could ever be.

'Yet if Buck told you that you weren't attractive enough for him, it would cut you to the quick, am I right, beloved?' Maya's voice whispered as if in answer to Gigi's thoughts. 'And why is that? Because that is one of your own criticisms about yourself, so you believe it to be true. Your critic would jump on the bandwagon and hound you with judgments about your looks. If you didn't believe it, the critic wouldn't be able to hold your attention.'

Gigi sighed, closing her eyes in fatigue. This was all so much more complicated than she'd realized.

'And yet so beautifully simple,' Maya murmured. 'Once you get in the habit of replacing self-criticism with self-love, nothing anyone says or does can hurt you.'

A touch on her knee caused Gigi's eyes to fly open and look directly into Buck's. The room's pink light seemed to pulse with energy as they stared at each other without speaking. Slowly Gigi placed her hand on top of Buck's. 'I'm not sure what to do now,' she said softly. 'I've never been in a situation like this before.'

'You can say that again,' Buck agreed huskily, his eyes filled with emotion. 'Frankly – and it's hard for me to admit this – I don't know how to proceed.'

Gigi nodded. 'I guess we should do the homework – you know, write our lists.'

'I didn't mean about our assignment,' Buck said. 'I mean about you and me. I feel like I took advantage of you, but I have to admit I enjoyed it.'

'Took advantage of me because... because it was just a momentary interest?' Gigi asked fearfully, not really wanting to hear his answer.

"See? You never could get your timing right," her critic chastised her. She breathed into her heart, calling on her impartial observer to lend her a loving perspective while she awaited his answer.

Buck shook his head. 'No, that's not what I meant. Damn, I never was any good at expressing my feelings. Oh, that was my critic talking, wasn't it?' Gigi gave him a wan smile, only too aware of her own critic's strident commentary. 'What I'm trying to say is, I know we haven't known each other very long, but I am really attracted to you,' Buck said. 'I knew there was something different about you the first time I laid eyes on you at the lecture. You're beautiful, and you have depth. You're the kind of woman I never thought would be interested in me.'

Filled with relief at his words, Gigi asked, 'Why wouldn't I be interested in you?'

'A hick like me? Not cultured or educated enough, kinda rough around the edges, don't know much about art or which fork to use at a fancy dinner.'

'Sounds like you're already doing your homework,' Gigi remarked dryly.

Buck grinned. 'Yeah, I guess that's the beginning of my list of criticisms. But don't worry, there's plenty more where that came from.'

'Well, maybe it's time to write down our lists and let the impartial observer refute them,' Gigi said, glad for the momentary distraction from the intensity of her emotions.

'Wait, you didn't tell me how *you* feel,' Buck objected.

Gigi bit her lip. She didn't want to reveal to Buck how much she cared about him, the sense of connection she felt between them, or how he seemed like the man she'd been looking for her whole life – the man she'd thought Keith was.

But she couldn't risk that kind of disappointment again, could she? Her cast members were engaging in a frenzy of debate about what to say.

'I, um, I really like you too,' she muttered finally, instigating an immediate barrage of judgments from her critic, who ridiculed her adolescent choice of words.

But Buck just nodded, seeming satisfied, and said, 'Now, where in the universe do you imagine our journals have got to?'

'Good point,' said Gigi, thrilled to focus on the mundane for a moment. 'I have no idea.'

'Maybe I can find something to write with at least,' Buck offered, putting on his cowboy hat and pulling himself to standing with a grimace of pain.

'Are you okay?' Gigi asked, jumping to her feet and ignoring the cast member who asked derisively why he had to put on his hat to get up.

'Yeah, just bruised some ribs, I think,' Buck said. 'And my ankle's a little sore. No big deal.' He lurched toward the shelves along the wall, Gigi watching him in concern. He didn't look okay to her. Maybe he'd broken a rib. And he was limping; he could have sprained his ankle or torn a ligament.

'Buck?' Gigi ventured. 'Um, I'm not sure you should be walking on that. Why don't you let me look for pens and paper?'

'I'm fine,' Buck said curtly, grasping on to a shelf for support. Just then, Gigi heard a whistling noise from above. Looking up, she saw two books hurtling down at them.

'Watch out!' she cried, but it was too late. One after the other, the books bonked Buck on the head then bounced off. He reeled, lost his grip on the shelves and slid to the floor.

Before she knew what had happened, Gigi was kneeling at his side. 'Buck! Are you okay?' She took his face in hers. His eyes were closed and he was slumped over. Had he been knocked unconscious?

His eyelids fluttered and he gazed at her with an unfocused look. 'Wha' happen?' he slurred with effort.

'I don't exactly know. Two books flew down from nowhere and hit you in the head,' Gigi answered, trying to repress a bubbling of hysterical laughter. Suddenly the whole situation seemed intensely humorous. Fighting against the shaking in her diaphragm, she reached for the books now lying nearby. When she saw what they were, she gave in to irrepressible giggles.

'Wha' funny?' Buck asked.

'They're... they're...' Gigi doubled over with laughter, then wiping away tears controlled herself enough to say, 'They're our journals!' The sound of her quavering voice sent her into another fit of hysteria.

Buck gave a hiccup of laughter then grabbed his ribs, wincing. 'At least I had my hat on,' he murmured, increasing Gigi's mirth.

'That damn hat probably saved you from a concussion,' she said.

'It's a good hat,' Buck said with an attempt at dignity. 'Or at least it *was*.'

He held it up to show the dents in the crown and the bent brim. Then he gave in, joining her in uncontrollable laughter. They laughed until they cried and Buck was doubled over in pain.

Sprawled out on the floor, Gigi wiped her eyes and said, 'So, are you ready to admit you could use some help now?'

'Yes,' Buck said sheepishly. 'I think I wrenched my ankle some more on my way to the floor. And I guess I should have someone look at these ribs.'

'Good. The first thing will be to figure out how to get help,' said Gigi, taking control. She got up and made her way through the cluttered room, distracted by all the objects from her lifetime production in the Magical Theatre. They seemed pitifully shabby and useless.

Gigi's gaze was torn from her old clock radio by the clanging of a door opening in the far wall. Standing in the brightly illuminated doorway was Godfreys, wearing green hospital scrubs and busily pulling on latex gloves, a white sterile mask dangling around his neck.

'Hello, my dear,' he said briskly to a slack-jawed Gigi. 'And where's the patient?'

Unable to speak, Gigi pointed weakly in Buck's direction. Godfreys stepped into the room, followed by two orderlies with a stretcher. They picked their way through the dim clutter to Buck, where Godfreys knelt and asked him questions, took his pulse, shone a light in his eyes, pulled off his boots and palpated his ankle, and performed other medical duties with typical precision.

'Mmm, yes, we'll need X-rays. Probably one or two cracked ribs and, from the size of his ankle, I'd say a nasty sprain. Up you go, then.'

The orderlies helped Buck onto the stretcher and lifted him effortlessly, then maneuvered their way out the door with Godfreys following, a satisfied look on his face.

'Um, Godfreys?' Gigi asked, arresting him with a hand on his arm.

'That's *Dr.* Godfreys,' he said, pointing to his name tag.

'Yes. Er, I wasn't aware you were a doctor,' Gigi stammered.

'I'm whatever Maya needs me to be,' Godfreys said enigmatically.

'Well, that's great! I mean, Buck is really hurt and I'm glad you're here,' Gigi said. 'But can you tell me where you're taking him and what I should do?'

'Why, to the emergency room, of course,' Godfreys said. 'And perhaps you could gather up your journals – you both still need to finish your homework, although I see you've already started a good mental list –and you can wait in the green room.'

'The green room?' Gigi asked, feeling slightly out of her depth at this unexpected turn of events.

'Yes, the waiting room, you know,' Godfreys said, turning to leave.

'Hold on! Do you mean like a green room that's the waiting room in a theater, or a literal green waiting room in a hospital?' Gigi asked desperately.

'Why, your Magical Theatre's green room, of course,' replied Godfreys, checking his watch. 'I must hurry off to attend to my patient.'

'But where is it?' Gigi plucked at his scrubs, unwilling to be left alone in this shadowy storeroom.

'Really, you should know, since it's your own production,' said Godfreys impatiently. 'Gigi, I haven't time for more of your rather redundant questions. I'm on a schedule.' And he let himself out the door through which he'd come.

Before it swung shut, Gigi caught a glimpse of a bustling hospital corridor, white floor gleaming and nurses busily wheeling patients through the halls. The door closed with a click of finality, and when Gigi tried to push it open it wouldn't budge.

She was alone in the dim room, and the rose-colored light was fading quickly. She felt trapped in the close space and betrayed by Godfreys. He was supposed to help her, not shut her out!

Well, no good bemoaning that now. She had to find the green room door. The problem was, she was sure she hadn't seen any such exit. Sweeping up the journals, which were vibrating as if furious writing was going on within, she picked her way through the room. The shadows had taken on a menacing quality, there was no green room door in sight and her cast members were having a field day offering her conflicting advice. Then her critic chimed in, castigating her for again getting into a ridiculous situation.

Increasingly panicked, Gigi rushed from one side of the room to another, stumbling over her old rocking chair and an ancient plaid La-Z-Boy from her first post-college apartment. When she knocked over a set wall, she screamed in fright then stopped and stood still, a hand over her rapidly beating heart.

'Impartial observer,' Maya's voice breathed in her ear, leaving a trail of warm, rose-scented air. 'Find the peace in your heart, and you will find the door you seek.'

Gigi breathed deeply, closing her eyes and trying to shut out the damaging voices of her cast and critic. But they were too loud; she couldn't silence them. Then she remembered Maya's advice: To keep yourself from going down the road of self-condemnation, there is only one thing to do— STOP! To prevent those voices from starting up again, powerfully occupy your mind with positive thoughts and then do something loving for yourself.

The words to Gigi's favorite song from *The Sound of Music* suddenly popped into her head and, feeling foolish but determined, she forced herself to sing them in a dry, squeaky voice. 'Doe, a deer, a female deer... Ray, a drop of golden sun...'

As she sang, her voice got stronger and she noticed that the cluttered storeroom had remarkably good acoustics. 'Me, a name I call myself, Far, a long, long way to run...' she warbled.

Now her feet wanted in on the action, so in her finest Ginger Rogers style she danced--as best she could in her mud-caked spiked heels-- over to the nightstand to grab a last truffle. As she continued to shuffle and sing, spewing bits of chocolate she realized she was no longer afraid and the voices of her cast and critic had disappeared. Then she remembered that not only did her perception create her reality, but she had the ability to write her own script.

Still singing, clutching the vibrating journals, she danced her way across the room. And she wasn't too surprised to see the door that had led to the hospital now sported a glowing neon sign that read: 'Green Room: Actors and Guests Only'.

Belting out 'Doe, doe, doe, doe,' she pushed the door open with a flourish.

Chapter Nine

Gigi closed her journal and, hand to heart, breathed in a new sense of well-being. She had finished the homework the journal had started for her by writing down the list of her self-judgments. Armed with courage after her recent experiences and buoyed by the comforting atmosphere of the green room with its petal soft beige leather sofas and potted palms, she had read each of the critic's painful statements.

Then she had turned each one over to the impartial observer, who had refuted the criticisms and countered the condemnations with the deeper truth of her being. Her heart now felt warm and soft, and her breathing seemed easier.

I think I'm really beginning to get this, she thought, looking around at the attractive décor of the green room and enjoying the rare sensation of inner peace that came from loving and trusting herself. Her cast and critic were silent, her perspective was aligned, and she now knew that she really could write her own script. She also recognized that there were more lessons to be learned and sensed a willingness in herself that she had never before fully embraced.

She closed her eyes and sensed the relaxation in her body, intoning a few 'Oms' to add to the good vibrations. Couldn't hurt, right?

In mid-Om, Buck's dazzling smile drifted into her mind and her heart which fluttered excitedly. She hoped he was doing all right. It was kind of strange to be in this limbo-like room not knowing what was happening to the man she'd had a passionate make out session with not an hour ago. But she was getting pretty used to strangeness. In fact, it was entirely possible that far more than an hour had passed since their lusty encounter (the memory of which caused a melting rush of warmth to surge through her like a wave).

'Focus, Gigi,' she whispered. It seemed important to ascertain how much time had passed. What if hours had gone by and Buck was wondering where she was, angry that she wasn't at his bedside? No, she would not listen to the cast member who told her she ought to be a good girlfriend by being with him through this. After all, she wasn't exactly his girlfriend.

And Godfreys had seemed like he knew what he was doing. Confusing as he could be at times, his presence tended to inspire confidence. Oh – but Buck would need his journal!

Suddenly it seemed of vital importance that she get it to him. How else could he do his homework and be prepared for the next keystone? Plus, she really wanted to see him and make sure he was okay. And maybe kiss him again. And feel him pressed up against her with his arms wrapped tightly around her body. And his lips caressing her throat, her... Mmm...

Reluctantly, Gigi wrenched herself away from a budding fantasy starring Buck, realizing there was a pressing question: Why did she feel so compelled to go to him now? Was it her insecure cast members who wanted to see what she could do to help Buck? Was it really in her best interest? She breathed into her heart to consult her impartial observer, but couldn't get past the wall of voices to find a clear idea to follow.

I'll find a way to see him, she decided. *After all, if I could find my way off that marshy planet and discover a green room door that previously did not exist, I can certainly figure out how to get to the hospital.*

'Ask me,' said a voice. Gigi whipped around but couldn't see anything.

'Over here,' said the voice. It had a hollow metallic quality, as if coming from inside a heating vent. Gigi looked around the edges of the room, seeing no such vent.

'The mirror, hel-*lo*,' said the voice.

The mirror? Feeling ridiculous, Gigi walked over to a large oval mirror set in an elaborate wrought-iron frame. She looked in it and saw her own reflection, hair disheveled and makeup completely worn off except for the flakes of waterproof mascara migrating down her cheeks. Ignoring her critic's remarks about her appearance, she examined the mirror for a microphone or speaker that would explain its tinny voice.

'Well, go ahead,' it said impatiently, startling her. 'Aren't you going to ask me a question?'

Okay, the mirror really was talking to her. But she didn't particularly want to talk back to it, even if no one was here to see her. *I mean, I have to maintain some semblance of sanity, don't I?* she thought doubtfully.

'Who are you trying to impress?' the mirror asked, as if it had heard her question. 'That crowd in your head? That big boss judge? Or someone who's not even here, like... Rancher Boy?'

Gigi's reflection wavered and seemed to melt then reassemble into a scene of a hospital room. Startled, she took an involuntary step back.

'Scaredy cat. Aren't you curious?' the mirror taunted. 'Come on, take a closer look.'

Gigi stepped close and saw Buck sitting up on the edge of his hospital bed. He looked pretty good, even in one of those awful green thigh-length hospital gowns. A young red-haired nurse handed him a pair of crutches and he hoisted himself up, grimacing.

'So do I get to leave now?' he asked.

'Yes, as soon as the doctor gives your discharge. Looks like your cracked ribs just have to heal; there's not much we can do. And stay off that ankle. It's a bad sprain. You need to take it easy, now, understand. No strenuous activity for a while.'

'Define "strenuous",' Buck said with a wicked grin.

Oh my God, he's flirting with her, Gigi realized, and felt a swift pang of jealousy.

'No activities that raise your heart rate,' the nurse simpered, holding eye contact several seconds too long. Naturally, not being dead, she was taken by Buck's charm.

A doctor in a white jacket strode in, consulting a chart, and the nurse turned briskly and began straightening the bed.

'Well, you're very lucky,' said the doctor in crisply accented tones, and Gigi recognized Godfreys. 'Nothing serious, and you didn't have a concussion. So you are free to go. Do you have a ride?'

'Oh, I should be there to drive him,' Gigi moaned, momentarily forgetting that she was transportation challenged. 'How is he going to get out of there without me?'

But Buck was nodding. 'Yeah, I've got a ride,' he said, glancing toward the nurse. 'Got some things I need to take care of. I do appreciate your help, Doc. And I promise to take it easy.' Gigi thought she saw him wink at the nurse, whose face flushed a pretty shade of pink.

The scene faded, and Gigi stood stunned in disbelief, her stomach churning. What did this all mean? If the scene was real and not the product of her overheated imagination, Buck was checking out of the hospital; that was clear. And he had some sort of ride. But with whom? Was the redheaded nurse going to drive him? What was the business he had to attend to?

And how could he leave without a thought for her, with whom he'd gone through so much? She was the one who'd gotten them out of the scrape he had led them into on Planet Swamp, and she was the one who'd insisted he needed medical care. Not to mention everything else that had happened between them... and now he was just leaving her like it all meant nothing. Leaving, like every other man she'd ever had in her life.

Well, why was she surprised? That's what men did, wasn't it – left her? Why would she expect it to be any different this time?

Feeling weak, Gigi slumped onto a nearby loveseat. She was truly alone, and her sense of well-being was pretty well shot. Why did she have to go through this over and over again? Why did she let herself care about men who would only abandon her? And what was she going to do now? Overwhelmed with self-pity, she gave in to tears.

'Here, my beloved,' said a rich, comforting voice, and Gigi looked around to see Maya seated next to her, holding out a rose-scented lace hankie. Too miserable to be startled or self-conscious, Gigi took it and blew her nose into it noisily.

'There, my dear,' Maya said. 'Now tell me what's the matter.'

'Don't you already know?' Gigi said crankily. 'You seem to know pretty much everything.'

Maya threw her head back and laughed, and Gigi stared in astonishment as a silver-and-gold butterfly flew out of her mouth and landed on Maya's outstretched, beautifully manicured hand. Trembling, it delicately opened and closed its iridescent wings.

'See this butterfly?' Maya asked reverently. 'This gorgeous creature is perfect just as it is, wouldn't you agree?'

'Yes,' Gigi breathed, mesmerized by its beauty.

'And like this butterfly, everything in the universe is also perfect just the way it is, am I right?' Maya asked rhetorically. 'Even if – like the butterfly, who can't see the color of its own wings – it can't admire its own beauty?'

'Well, that's what you've been teaching us,' Gigi said, sniffling. 'I think I'm starting to get it, but it's pretty hard to hold onto that idea when things keep happening that make me lose sight of it.'

'Mmm, yes,' Maya said, releasing the butterfly with a gentle shake of her hand. It fluttered through the room in a graceful dance. 'Like Buck leaving the hospital without sending word to you.'

Gigi nodded miserably.

'And his leaving made you feel abandoned, yes?'

'Yeah,' Gigi mumbled.

'*No!!!*' Maya thundered, startling Gigi and causing the butterfly to disappear in a sudden chilly whirlwind. Shivering, Gigi hugged her knees to her chest and eyed Maya warily. This goddess, or whatever she was, definitely had the potential to be scary.

'Um, what do you mean?' Gigi asked timidly, without meeting Maya's laser-like eyes.

'Listen carefully, my angel,' Maya said, her voice resuming its normal tone. 'No one can *make you feel* anything. No one but you can hurt you. You're hurting *yourself.* Remember our little discussion about that with regard to the critic? Well, double its importance right now, because we are going to talk about what has been ruling your life until this point.'

'It's about time!' a hollow voice chimed in.

'Please hold your tongue, Magic Mirror,' Maya replied. 'We will have need of your services again later. Meanwhile, do try to keep your opinions to yourself.'

'Fine,' said the mirror sulkily, and its reflection went dark.

'I apologize for the interruption,' Maya said, waving her hand in the mirror's direction. 'So. You need to know that there are some persistent pests that have been holding you prisoner in an earthly melodrama of your own creating. They have been keeping you in patterns of thinking you have no control over your life, and letting people and circumstances "make you feel" certain ways.

'These pests have kept you in a little box, not living up to your potential. They have trapped you in a cycle of reaction rather than positive action. They have a stranglehold on your life in the Magical Theatre, and until you release yourself from their bondage you will not be able to find happiness or peace.'

The room had definitely gotten colder, and dark clouds hovered at the ceiling. Maya's words had put a pall over everything. Gigi hugged her knees tighter. What were these things that had her in bondage? She'd really like to know, because she was sick and tired of feeling bad.

'These things that run your life are your *beliefs*,' Maya said with a new tenderness.

Gigi shivered. The room was growing eerily dark and silent. Suddenly she noticed that dark shapes were peeling off from the ominous low clouds, and her stomach contracted when she recognized bat-like figures flitting menacingly about the room, emitting low screeching sounds. She hunched over, afraid one would land in her hair.

'Yes, your beliefs,' Maya continued. 'Your beliefs are your convictions about who you are and how life should unfold. Unbeknownst to you, these beliefs have been controlling your life, directing your every action in the Magical Theatre. Some of them are as insidious as termites gnawing invisibly on support beams – constantly eating away at your self-confidence and limiting your options.'

Gigi cleared her throat, keeping an eye on the threatening-looking bats. 'Do you mean beliefs like about the meaning of life, or, um, recycling?'

'Well, the meaning of life would be an overarching belief. But a belief about recycling might feel neutral to you. It's the fear-based beliefs that hurt you that we're concerned with here. You have many kinds of fearful beliefs that run your life – beliefs that are formed by childhood experiences, social conditioning and your responses to others' actions. Listen, my sweet, here are some examples.'

A bat swooped down and hovered just in front of Gigi's face. She gave an involuntary scream. She'd always been a little afraid of bats since reading *Dracula* as a teenager. She stared in horror as the bat opened its fanged mouth and said in a half-scream, half-whisper, 'You'll never be attractive enough!' Then it dove down and nipped her scalp.

'AARGH!' Gigi screamed, covering her head with her hands. She drew her fingers away to see if there was blood, but they were clean.

Gigi whimpered, her throat suddenly dry although her underarms were slick with cold sweat. To her relief, the bat swept off. She turned to Maya in indignation, but just then another bat swooped down to hover in front of her. She cringed as it shrieked, 'You need to make a lot of money to be successful!' Then it bit her on the shoulder.

'What the...?' Gigi yelled. She was getting mad, now. 'Maya, help me! Please stop these disgusting flying rats from biting me!'

Maya said calmly, 'I can't stop them – only you can. They're your beliefs, not mine.'

Before Gigi could argue, another bat swept toward her. She tried frantically to protect her face and head while it screeched, 'You'll never be happy until you find true love!' Fast as lightning, it dove down and seized the tip of her finger.

Gigi frantically shook her finger, flinging the bat across the room. Nauseated, she stuck the finger in her mouth and tasted blood. Before she could plead with Maya again, a group of bats descended all at once, and she cowered, whimpering.

'Leave me alone!' she cried, but they swarmed around her, screeching a cacophony of accusations:

'You're selfish if you spend money on things you want!'

'You need to work hard at self-improvement in order to be a good person.'

'You have to try to be super perfect.'

'No one will love you the way you are!'

'It's not safe to say what you're thinking.'

Despite her efforts to fight them off, each bat took a nip somewhere on her body until she was covered with welts.

Cringing, Gigi cried, 'Maya, please call them off! I think I'm starting to understand.' She was sure she couldn't handle another hideous pronouncement. It was as if the bats were articulating all the hurtful thoughts that had kept her on an emotional yo-yo for as long as she could remember. Just then, an albino bat swooped down and stared at her with its bulging red eyes. It hovered for a moment before screaming, 'YOU'LL ALWAYS BE ALONE!' Then with an unearthly wail, it bit her squarely on the nose before flying off.

'Ow!' Gigi howled then grasped her nose and buried her head in her knees, shaking. This was awful.

'Do you see how hurtful your fearful beliefs are?' Maya asked. 'Just like these bats screaming horrible things at you and biting you, these beliefs cause you pain and leave you feeling wounded. The pain is your first clue that a belief is based on fear and therefore false.'

Gigi was sucking air and letting out pitiful little sobs. The agony of having her own hurtful beliefs thrown in her face felt unbearable. Had she really lived for thirty-five years shackled by such negative statements? How could she have survived under such a burden? It was a miracle she hadn't ended up in a loony bin.

'The false beliefs sound harsh and ridiculous, do they not, my treasure?' Maya asked softly. 'And they cause you great suffering.'

Head still buried, all too aware of the throbbing bat bites all over her, Gigi said faintly, 'Yes, I just don't understand where they all came from.'

'It is simple.' Maya continued with great tenderness. 'You created your beliefs out of your perception of past events, and then forgot you created them. You have used them to guide you in the world and also projected your understanding onto others, assuming your beliefs were the hallmark of reality. Perhaps now you can see that even your projection can't pass a lie detector test since it only really exists in your imagination. So let me ask, do you know *intellectually* that these beliefs are untrue?'

'I guess. Yes.'

'You do! And yet you've been letting them control your life?'

Gigi nodded, grimacing.

Maya's voice softened. 'You're not alone, my dear. Every person in the Magical Theatre does this. It's one of the great paradoxes of life on earth. You can know intellectually that something is true or untrue, but it is what you fundamentally believe that runs your life – even if your beliefs go against what you know to be true.'

'Jesus,' Gigi said. 'You're right.'

'I'm not the beloved Jesus,' Maya replied primly, 'but I *am* right. Now, this paradox also explains why even though you intellectually know you should be able to view yourself as lovable, you persist in believing that you are not perfect enough to deserve love.'

'It's true,' Gigi said, gulping back tears. 'But if knowledge doesn't help, how *can* I override these beliefs?' Daring to look up, she saw with relief that the bats were gone and she could again see the ceiling through breaks in the clouds. The painful throbbing was fading, and when she looked at her arms and hands, she saw that the bites were disappearing.

'Ah, I'm so glad you asked,' Maya said, clapping her hands. Immediately sunshine flooded the room and a waterfall appeared in the corner, splashing gaily into a pool suspended above the floor. A rainbow danced in its droplets.

Maya smiled in delight at her creation. 'Waterfalls and rainbows are two of my specialties. Isn't it beautiful?'

'Lovely,' Gigi agreed, feeling her constricted breathing loosen in the moist, flower-scented air.

'So, my love, simply awakening to the beliefs that direct your actions will help you overcome your automatic responses to events. And I have a little system that will help you do this.' Maya giggled gleefully. 'I call it LIQUID.'

'Liquid?' Gigi asked in confusion. Clearly the waterfall had something to do with this, but she couldn't see the connection between water and her beliefs.

'Yes. It's an acronym, my treasure. Listen carefully. You can free yourself from the grip of your false beliefs by practicing LIQUID.'

Shimmering droplets danced out of the waterfall to form the

acronym:

Listen

Identify

Question

Intuit

Decide

'Yes, my dear. This is what you have to do: *Listen* to the thoughts voiced by your cast of characters to locate the belief at the core of your discomfort. *Identify* the belief as carefully, thoroughly and honestly as you can, using the impeccable clarity of your impartial observer. *Question* its validity by looking at it through the eyes of the impartial observer to see the truth – is it a projection or is it real? *Intuit* what it would be like to live the rest of your life with the belief, then intuit what it would be like without it. Finally, *Decide* if you want this belief impacting your experience of life. If you don't, make a conscious, willful commitment to begin to release it. Of course, it will take time to let it go completely.'

The water droplets shivered and fell back into the waterfall. Gigi was glad to see her faithful journal hovering above the coffee table taking rapid notes, since she wasn't sure she could remember all this.

Maya followed her glance and beamed her eyes at the journal. It immediately closed with a final-sounding snap then disappeared in a shower of raindrops.

'My journal!' Gigi cried.

'You don't need it anymore,' said Maya. 'As you release your false beliefs and shift your perception to reflect the truth of your magnificence, you no longer need to record the lessons. Intellectual knowledge is not going to help you awaken. You need to take action.'

Gigi felt panicky. How was she going to take action if she couldn't remember everything? There was so much information...

'Trust in your ability to learn and grow,' said Maya. She touched Gigi briefly on the crown of her head, and Gigi felt an immediate sense of well-being and confidence.

'And now, my dear, I leave it up to you to take it from here,' Maya added briskly, suddenly businesslike. 'I have more rainbows to paint and, as always, spectacular sunsets to direct. I really must vanish. In parting, I offer you this keystone.' She waved a finger at the waterfall, which contracted until it was as thin as a faucet then writhed in the air to spell out the words: 'Keystone 5: Free yourself from false beliefs.'

When Gigi turned back to Maya, she was gone, but her voice lingered in the air, light as a breath as it whispered, 'Start with your projection about Buck – the belief that is even now constricting your heart...'

The waterfall vanished just as suddenly, leaving only a light mist in its wake.

Alone again, Gigi thought, that familiar feeling of abandonment tugging at her heart. *It's just like that white bat said: I'm always alone. Buck's left me, and Maya has left me. And here I am again all by myself, not knowing what to do next or how to get out of here.*

She felt self-pity threatening to blossom into a mushroom cloud all around her, and just in time took herself in hand. *Okay, that's a belief. It's not true, just something my cast of characters invented to explain why certain things happen. I guess that's the belief I'm supposed to address with LIQUID.*

'No, Air-for-Brains,' a tinny voice piped up. 'There's another one that came first – one you have to release to get yourself out of this holding cell.'

'Holding cell?' Gigi was offended. The Magic Mirror sure knew how to make things sound unpleasant. 'This is the green room.'

'Yeah, yeah, whatever,' the mirror said sarcastically. 'Call it what you want, but you can't leave here, can you? Not until you get this belief out of your system. And who knows how long *that* will take. You're beginning to set a new standard for remedial, if you catch my drift.'

Gigi bit back a cutting remark. She needed the mirror's help and, much as she'd like to smash it and risk the seven years of bad luck, it was pretty clear that wouldn't be the wisest course of action. She took a deep breath, crossed her fingers behind her back to counter the lies she was about to tell, and forced herself to ask deferentially, 'Mirror, in your all-knowingness, could you please help me identify the belief so I can release it?'

'Certainly,' said the mirror smugly. 'Approach.'

Gigi went over and looked in. At first there was nothing but swirling darkness, then shapes started to appear. She gasped. There she was at age eight, a year and a half after her father had left. He'd called her a few times and had sent her a present at Christmas. And a couple of weeks before, he and her mother had had a long, secretive phone conversation after which her mother emerged from her room, red-eyed and stern.

'Your father is coming to get you for a visit,' she'd said in a flat voice. 'He wants to take you to Disneyland.'

Gigi tried to contain her joy for her mother's sake, but inside she was dancing. Her father was finally coming for her the way he'd promised he would! And she knew that once he saw her, he would never be able to give her up again.

She could start a new life far away from dull Maryland and her increasingly strict mother, in glamorous, exciting California. She would be friends with the daughters and sons of movie stars and go swimming in their gigantic pools. She would gorge herself on the avocados that would grow on a tree right outside her bedroom window. And she would go to the beach every day and learn to surf and send pictures back to her friends at home who would swoon with envy.

Gigi walked on air for the next two weeks. Nothing could faze her, not even the razzing of the popular and mean Judy Jowers.

When Judy whispered, 'Gross!' as Gigi walked past her desk, Gigi just smiled benignly and hugged her California vision close to her heart. Even the constant rain and slush didn't bother her like it usually did, because she knew she'd soon be living in the land of endless sunshine.

And this was the day her father was coming. He had driven cross-country and was due to arrive in the afternoon. Gigi was up at six o'clock in the morning, repacking her small flowered suitcase for the umpteenth time. The day seemed to go by achingly slowly, as if every minute were an hour.

She occupied her thoughts with fabulous daydreams. She could already imagine cruising down the highway in her dad's new car (he'd said it was a Mercedes), laughing at his constant stream of hilarious stories about the idiosyncrasies of his rich and famous clients.

Two o'clock was the appointed hour of her father's arrival. She sat on her bed looking out the window, because she had a view all the way to the street corner from there. She waited and waited. Three o'clock, three-thirty, four o'clock. 'He must have hit traffic,' her mother said without conviction. But when dinnertime came and there was still no sign, she said she had a headache and retired to her bedroom.

Gigi hugged her knees, refusing to leave her bed in case she missed seeing his car turn up the street. She sat there until it got dark, then finally fell asleep. The next morning her father called. 'I'm sorry, sweetie,' he said, his voice sounding regretful. 'I just couldn't make it. I thought I could, but it just didn't work out.'

Gigi's despair was so deep she could barely speak. 'Don't you want to see me, Daddy?' she asked, using her little-girl name for him.

'Of course I do, Princess. But I just couldn't get away.'

'But you'll still come, won't you?' Gigi asked.

He hesitated. 'Sure, I'll call you,' he said vaguely.

'Great!' Gigi said with false enthusiasm, not wanting him to know her heart was breaking. 'And then I can stay with you and go to junior high in California, right? And I can be friends with all the rich kids and play in their pools and go to the beach and go to Disneyland every day and...'

'Whoa, slow down, pardner,' her dad said, his voice curiously hollow. 'I never said anything about living here. You have to stay with your mom. She needs you.'

'Don't *you* need me, Daddy?' Gigi asked in a small voice.

'Sure, Princess,' he said. 'But I just can't have you move out here with me. I'm sorry. That's just how it is. Someday you'll understand.'

Gigi let the phone slide from her hand and dangle from the cord, swinging back and forth. She could hear her father's voice saying, 'Gigi? Princess?' She walked away, leaving the phone swinging, and went back to her room where she curled up, dry-eyed, on her bed. The scene froze and began to dim.

'It was at that moment that you solidified the belief that any man you loved would abandon you,' the mirror intoned, startling Gigi back to the present.

Gigi closed her eyes and breathed, listening for the belief. As she thought it, it appeared simultaneously on the mirror as if written in lipstick: *Men will always leave me.* The pain of that belief stabbed like a knife in her heart, telling her she was right on. She then had projected the belief onto Buck, firmly believing he had abandoned her, but what proof did she have? He might even be coming to look for her. Yet she'd bought into abandonment hook, line and sinker due to that debilitating belief.

'So let's go through the remaining steps of LIQUID,' said the mirror in a bored tone. 'I suppose you don't remember them, so I'll help you. You've already done the first two: listened for the belief and intuited that it is bad for you. Now question its validity. Once and for all, is it absolutely true that men you love will abandon you?'

Gigi put her hand on her heart to access her impartial observer. It sure seemed true, but was it really true? Just because her father had left and Keith had cheated on her, did that mean all men would do the same? Her impartial observer told her no. It didn't make sense to project decisions onto the future based on what had happened in the past.

'Um, I guess it's not true,' Gigi said slowly.

'Finally! So you get that it's pretty stupid to believe all men will leave you just because a couple of morons messed up,' the mirror agreed in its inimitable fashion. 'Now decide if you want this untrue belief governing your thoughts and actions.'

'No!' Gigi shouted, startling herself with her vehemence. Suddenly she saw that not only had she let that stupid belief run her life, but sometimes she chose irresponsible men so she could feel right about her point of view.

'Well, duh,' said the mirror. 'So now, you can release this belief and be free to live without it. Thank the stars!'

Then the mirror belted out its best Sting impression: 'If you love somebody, set them free...'

'But how do I release it?' Gigi interrupted, whereupon the mirror shut up in a huff. 'I mean, I've lived with it for so long. It doesn't seem like it will just go away because I want it to.'

'Remember, you are a spark of the divine light,' Maya's voice breathed in her ear. 'Now focus your awareness on your attachment to being right about the belief and release your attachment. Next, consciously choose not to let the belief rule you anymore. Then select a life-affirming belief to replace the old one. Then practice, practice, practice what you want to master.'

'Okay,' said Gigi, feeling suddenly empowered. Using her sleeve, she wiped the lipsticked words off the mirror with a flourish. Feeling ten pounds lighter, she twirled around and said, 'Ta-da!'

To her surprise, the mirror erupted in thunderous applause. She bowed, blushing, then performed an impromptu tap dance, showering dried mud all over the tile floor. She could do this! She could live without this awful feeling of doom every time she met a man! So Buck had left the hospital without her. So what? The truth was, his actions probably had nothing at all to do with her. He had his own beliefs to deal with.

Suddenly Gigi stopped in mid-twirl. A shiny set of elevator doors had appeared in the wall opposite the mirror, topped by an illuminated upward arrow. As she stared, the arrow flashed and the elevator 'pinged', announcing its arrival. The doors slid open to reveal a plush interior occupied by a hotel bellhop dressed in a maroon suit and cap.

'Going up, my dear?' the bellman inquired in a familiar British accent, and Gigi nearly laughed when she recognized Godfreys. So – she was ready to move on, and Godfreys was to be her guide once again.

'Certainly,' she said with as much dignity as she could muster despite her flushed cheeks, disheveled hair, muddy boots and filthy clothes. With what she dubiously hoped was an air of refined elegance, she swept into the elevator.

Chapter Ten

Godfreys punched a button and the elevator silently shot upward. Soft music played, but it wasn't typical elevator music. It had a haunting quality that tugged at Gigi's heart, and she felt herself getting a little emotional. Again!

'It's the music of the spheres,' Godfreys said. 'Beautiful, isn't it?'

'The music of the spheres? You mean the celestial sounds stars and planets supposedly make?' Gigi asked skeptically.

'Indeed,' said Godfreys. He flipped a switch on the control panel, and the walls of the elevator seemed to disappear. Gigi gasped to see that they were speeding through space, passing stars so fast that they looked like streaks of light. Instinctively she grasped the railing along the sides of the elevator.

'It's all right,' said Godfreys, dropping his formal manner and patting her arm in a fatherly gesture. 'The walls are made of specially treated glass. You're perfectly safe.'

Perfectly safe was hardly how Gigi would describe this moment, or any others she'd experienced recently. But she managed a weak smile at Godfreys and, taking a deep breath, reminded herself that she was in the dreamtime and could travel through space all she wanted without fear.

After a few minutes, the elevator slowed and came to an abrupt stop with the 'ping' that indicated arrival at the selected destination. Gigi stood up straighter, mentally preparing herself for whatever she was to encounter next.

'After you, my dear,' Godfreys said, stepping aside.

Determined not to reveal her trepidation, Gigi marched forward into... another jungle? A scene from her past?

No – apparently, she had landed in a large walk-in closet.

A closet? She'd traveled through space to wind up in someone's *closet*? Granted, it was a very nice closet. In fact, it was approximately the size of her entire post-divorce apartment and was beautifully organized and outfitted with all the shelving, mirrors and plush accoutrements that she'd seen on TV shows about celebrity homes. It was illuminated with invisible, flattering lighting and boasted an enormous three-way mirror.

But it was still a closet! She'd been expecting something a little more, well, exotic.

'Darlings, you made it!' crowed a cheerful male voice. While Gigi looked around, confused, an impeccably groomed man stepped directly out of the three-way mirror and walked toward her, arms thrown open in welcome.

He looked familiar. That perfectly mussed and moussed blond hair, the pink-tinted eyeglasses that matched the silk handkerchief peeking out from the pocket of his impeccably tailored Italian suit...

'Oh my, you *have* been in Remedial Angel Training,' he said, grasping her arms and twirling her around for his scrutiny. 'But never mind, plenty of time to fix you up. Besides, I hear you have a few more possibly hair-raising adventures to get through before you're finished.' He tittered, releasing her arms and covering his mouth daintily with a manicured hand.

Omigod! Gigi stepped back instinctively. This was the man who had stolen her possessions on the train to Blessings! She looked around wildly for Godfreys and was relieved to see him standing at the doorway. The elevator doors had disappeared, leaving a paneled wood door in their place, and in front of them Godfreys stood perfectly composed, as always, with an amused look on his face.

'Godfreys, what is this guy doing here?' Gigi asked, trying not to sound hysterical. 'He's the one who stole my bags from the train!'

The man put his hands on his hips and said in a hurt voice, 'I'm not just some guy. I'm Mitchell, the wardrobe mistress.'

'Mitchell is one of the angels who assist with Remedial Angel

Training – the one I mentioned at your wedding,' Godfreys clarified. 'We call on him for all our fashion needs.' He indicated his own bellman uniform.

Gigi scowled at Mitchell. 'How dare you act so flippant with me when you know you stole everything I had? And I don't appreciate that pink dress you put me in at the wedding, either.'

Batting his eyelashes in annoyance, Mitchell replied, 'You didn't need your stuff anymore. And that dress was to keep you humble. Besides, what would *you* have picked to wear for the wedding, Miss. — who put the R in —Remedial?'

Gigi had to admit that, given her current sartorial state, Mitchell had a point about her fashion choices. 'But it wasn't up to you to decide what to do with my stuff,' she insisted. 'You shouldn't have taken my things.'

'Do you miss them?' he asked, arching a perfectly waxed eyebrow.

'Well, yes, of course,' Gigi said, but even as she spoke she was unsure. *Did* she miss her clothes, her makeup and all the trappings of everyday life? Granted, she didn't look her best, but she realized that somehow this no longer bothered her. More important concerns had overtaken her in this strange dreamtime existence.

Mitchell swept out one arm dramatically. 'Well, there they are if you want them.' Gigi peered at a shelf and, with a jolt, saw her suitcase with her Kate Spade bag perched primly on top. Could she really give up her reliance on makeup and clothes to make her feel good about herself? Could she have been wrong all these years about how they helped her feel better? But what would that mean – that she had been living a lie?

Godfreys came up behind her and placed his hand on her shoulder. 'It's all right to admit you've been wrong,' he said quietly.

'Heaven forbid!' Mitchell put in, with another annoying titter. Gigi was beginning to like him even less than before, if that was possible.

Godfreys steered Gigi to the mirror. 'Take a look at yourself. Who would you say you are right now?'

'Um, I don't know,' Gigi muttered. 'I'm just me, I guess. I mean, I've been too busy learning the keystones to try and be anything else.'

'Ah, very good,' Godfreys said. 'So perhaps you have dropped your mask for a time.'

'My mask?' Gigi asked. 'What do you mean? I don't wear a mask.'

'Don't you?' Godfreys said. 'Haven't you felt a strong need to be right about things?'

'Well, yeah,' Gigi said. 'But doesn't everyone?'

'Perhaps,' said Godfreys. 'And that is partly what makes it so hard to be human in the Magical Theatre. That mask you wear, the mask of needing to be right, keeps you distanced from your authentic self.'

Gigi shook her head, confused. 'I guess I don't quite get it. What's wrong with being right?'

'Good question!' Mitchell trilled from the corner, where he was pushing buttons that made the hanging clothes circle into the room like at a dry cleaner's.

'Gee, thanks, Mitch,' Gigi said sarcastically.

The clothes stopped circling abruptly. 'It's Mitchell, thank you very much,' he said.

'Oh, sorry, Michelle,' Gigi rejoined mischievously.

'Honestly, Godfreys, the people you bring me,' Mitchell said petulantly. 'I swear I'm going to quit this job.'

'And go back to earth duty?' Godfreys asked with a hint of a smile. 'Why don't you get some outfits ready while I explain the mask to Gigi.'

Mitchell saluted and began sorting through the hanging clothes. They looked like a mishmash of outfits from different eras, and as Gigi peered at them from across the room, they appeared distinctly familiar.

'It's like this,' said Godfreys to Gigi's reflection. 'Generally, humans feel a strong need to be right. They think if they're wrong, something terrible will happen. That's sometimes referred to as "losing face". You are familiar with this notion, are you not?'

Gigi nodded. She could identify all too well with the need to avoid the humiliation that accompanies being publicly wrong about something.

'However, there are dangerous consequences to this need to be right. Putting on a mask of righteousness blocks your access to your authentic self. In other words, by protecting yourself from appearing to be wrong, you are also masking who you really are. This keeps you deeply under the spell of forgetfulness and entrenched in the belief that you're imperfect.'

'Ta-da!' Mitchell crowed, dancing up behind them holding an outfit hanging from a silk-covered hanger. 'This is fabulous. It's so... *vintage*, isn't it?'

Gigi's jaw dropped as she saw the outfit Mitchell was holding, rendering her unable to come up with a snappy reply to Mitchell's obvious dig about her age. 'That's my pep squad uniform from my freshman year of high school!' she said finally. She'd know it anywhere: the green-and-white miniskirt, the white sweater with a huge navy 'H' on the front, the pom-poms.

Immediately a cheer reverberated through her mind: 'Hornets are the best in town, Hornets gonna get on down. Hornets gonna turn around and SCORE! Get down.'

Mitchell waved the uniform at her and she realized he wanted her to put it on. 'Oh, hell no,' Gigi said. But when she turned back to the mirror she saw she was already wearing it.

'Here's one mask you wore in adolescence,' Godfreys said as Gigi grimaced at the image of herself as a perky-on-the-outside teen. (Not to mention that her thighs didn't look quite as cute in the short skirt as they once had, and the poor sweater was stretched to maximum capacity.) 'Clearly it is uncomfortable for you to remember this mask. Can you tell me why that is?'

'Well, partly because I look ridiculous,' Gigi said. 'But seriously… because this wasn't *me*. I hated football and couldn't stand the competitive bitchiness of the other girls on the squad. But I felt like I had to join to fit in. In junior high I had my place in the pecking order. I was the funny one so everyone kind of left me alone and didn't pick on me. But it wasn't that way in high school. I knew I had to try harder to fit in.'

'So just being yourself wasn't enough,' Godfreys said. 'Even in junior high, you had to wear the mask of the "class clown" to give yourself a sense of belonging. Then in high school, your mask shifted to show team spirit.'

Gigi snorted, and Mitchell let out another guffaw. Gigi glared at him in the mirror but he seemed oblivious.

'So you needed to be seen as "right" in the eyes of your peers,' Godfreys said. 'You needed to fit in and be accepted.'

'Of course,' Gigi said. 'If I hadn't, life would have been horrendous. Teenagers can be really mean to the kids who don't fit in.'

'What really would have happened if you were somehow wrong – if you didn't fit in?' Godfreys probed.

'I don't know,' Gigi said slowly. 'Some kids who were truly being themselves seemed oblivious to the taunts of the others. I always kind of envied them.'

'Mmm,' Godfreys said. 'Mitchell, I think we're ready for the next costume.'

In a flash, Mitchell was brandishing another hanger and, before Gigi could say 'No way', she was wearing a different outfit. Immediately she recognized the flowered dress she'd worn for her high school graduation. Her mother had picked it out for her and even though it was ridiculously girly and prissy, she'd worn it to please her.

Gigi groaned. 'I hated this dress.'

'Thank Goddess,' Mitchell said. 'If you'd said it was your favorite, I might have had to quit after all.'

'Why did you wear it, then?' Godfreys asked, ignoring Mitchell.

'Because my mom wanted me to,' Gigi replied. 'I guess she had this image of me as a "good" girl, and I didn't want to spoil it for her. Not that I wasn't good, but I would much rather have worn something more hip, like the other girls did.'

'So it was important to both be cool to your friends, and be a good girl for your mother,' Godfreys said. 'And either way, you were wearing a mask to look right in their eyes.'

'I guess so,' Gigi admitted. 'And of course it wasn't just clothes, either.'

'Certainly not,' Godfreys said. 'The clothes are simply an outward symbol of what you would do to please others and not be seen as wrong.'

Suddenly Gigi realized the hideous flowered dress was melting into an ever-changing array of outfits: her band uniform, her track suit, her college cap and gown, a leather miniskirt and tube top she'd worn when she first met Keith, the string bikini she'd bought to please him even though she felt stupid in it, a tailored business suit for work. Her hair and makeup changed with each outfit. Finally the display settled on her in a pair of tight jeans and a leopard-print top, with bright lipstick and big hair.

'Rock star wife,' Gigi said, biting her lip.

'Goodness,' Mitchell said, eyes wide in mock horror.

'Shut up, Mitch,' Gigi said, but her heart wasn't in it. This getup stimulated uncomfortable memories. She'd tried so hard to be the wife she thought Keith wanted. She remembered wearing this at one of Keith's outrageous parties at their condo. She'd been so tired that Friday night after a long week at work and had wanted nothing more than to sink into the sofa and watch bland TV. But Keith had called and told her he was bringing some friends home, and as usual she'd given up her own plans to throw together a dinner party.

'And as usual, you turned a blind eye to Keith's drug use in your home,' Godfreys said. 'You put on the mask of cool, tolerant wife so you'd fit in with his crowd.'

'Yeah, and I even got a bonus when I got to be right later about the fact that all men would leave me,' Gigi said, realizing how the mask she'd worn had supported her beliefs.

'Exactly,' Godfreys agreed. 'Remember when we talked about selective evidence gathering?'

'Yep,' Gigi said. 'Supporting my beliefs by seeing only what makes them true. Choosing the rotten fruit even though there's a lot of ripe fruit in the orchard, then saying, "See? All the fruit in my life is rotten."'

'Excellent summation,' Godfreys said. 'And wearing your mask of righteousness allowed you to continue your selective evidence gathering – using a certain angle of perception to see what you wanted to see and justify your beliefs. That way, even when presented with a different point of view, you could choose evidence that proved you were right.'

Gigi pondered this new angle on an old theme. 'So to get rid of the masks I've worn, I have to admit I'm wrong?'

'Bingo!' shouted Mitchell from behind her.

'You're really getting on my nerves, Mitch,' Gigi said, whirling on him. 'I'm working through some deep stuff here, and your little sarcastic comments don't help.'

Mitchell looked hurt. 'Sor-*ree*! Just trying to have a little fun. Someone's got to lighten it up in here. It's not like you're the first misguided angel I've worked with, you know. You're all the same, really. Caught up in your earthly desire to prove yourselves right and seeing only what supports your rusty old thinking, even when it obviously makes you miserable!'

Gigi bit back a sharp retort. He was right. She was the one who'd been wrong, painful as it was to admit it to herself. But she sure wasn't going to admit it to him.

'Yes, my dear,' Godfreys said. 'To embrace any kind of spiritual practice or inner growth, you have to give up your attachment to being right. This allows you to arrive at the point of admitting you were wrong about how you perceived reality. Once you do this, the possibilities are endless.'

A warm, rose-scented breeze wafted into the room, and Gigi turned back to the three-way mirror to behold Maya's reflection. Her rich coffee-bean skin shone with tinges of bronze and her violet eyes gleamed in triplicate as she smiled radiantly at Gigi. 'Yes, Gigi dear, you are getting it! You are seeing that by wearing a mask of needing to be right, you have placed the responsibility for your emotional well-being outside yourself.

'True, not playing the self-importance game may temporarily cause you to lose the superficial trappings of others' acceptance or approval. Yet is it not a far greater loss to hide your splendor behind a false mask?'

Gigi nodded, feeling the excitement of discovery building inside her. Could she really throw caution to the winds and be herself, not caring what others thought?

'Yes, yes!' Maya said, laughing. 'You can create a fabulous new production in the Magical Theatre simply by removing your mask and opening to the possibility that *you have been wrong about many things, including the truth of your very being*. And what a refreshing revelation!'

Gigi noticed suddenly that inscribed on the golden headband encircling Maya's forehead – larger than life in the mirror – were the words: 'Keystone 6: Sacrifice your mask to save your soul.'

Gigi imagined a stiff, grinning mask falling from her face to reveal the soft flesh beneath. So she might have been wrong. So what? No lightning bolts had struck her down. She could be wrong and still be okay. More than okay – she could be herself!

'Maya, it seems relatively easy to think about being myself here in the dreamtime, but how can I be sure to follow through when I get back to waking life?' Gigi asked. She had a feeling that it would be all too simple to fall back into her people-pleasing persona when confronted with the 'reality' she was accustomed to.

'To remove the mask, first call on your impartial observer to let you know when you are attached to being right,' Maya said. 'You may feel annoyed, for example, when someone challenges your point of view.'

'Oh no, not Gigi,' said Mitchell from his corner. Gigi shot him an apologetic look.

Maya continued, 'When paying close attention to your impartial observer, you may realize you have inadvertently attached your sense of well-being to conditions beyond your control. For example, you can't control whether or not someone agrees with you, accepts you or approves of you. You *can*, however, hold tight to your happiness by focusing on your heartfelt connection to life.'

Gigi thought about how many times her heart had been touched during this strange dreamtime adventure and how good it felt to be connected to her heart. In contrast, it felt awful to be in the place of defending her righteous position as she had with Mitchell.

'Once you've identified instances when you are attached to being right, you can remove your mask by learning to hold the position of *no position*,' Maya said. 'When someone disagrees with you, allow your impartial observer to witness the situation without trying to change it. Very soon you will see that your happiness was not placed in jeopardy simply because someone thought you were wrong. In fact, it doesn't really matter at all, does it?'

'No,' agreed Gigi.

'Sheesh,' muttered Mitchell.

'As you release your attachment to your opinion and accept that *there is nothing to defend*, your mask will fall away. In your new position of no position, it has nothing to adhere to. Then from your new, unmasked position center stage, you can begin living life as the real you.'

'Cool!' Gigi exclaimed with a little hop, then immediately felt silly. Automatically, she glanced at Godfreys and Mitchell to see if they noticed her geeky outburst – then caught herself, realizing that if she was going to drop her mask she would have to risk looking silly sometimes. It felt good to be excited, and her impartial observer wasn't attached to what the others thought.

'Of course, being yourself doesn't mean you won't mess up every now and then,' Maya cautioned. 'But you need to know that mistakes are actually an important part of life in the Magical Theatre. If you didn't make mistakes, how would you know what doesn't work? When you blunder, naturally, your cast of characters will raise their voices to let you know what an idiot you are. But when you're living from the truth of you, their comments won't faze you because you'll know you have traded in your mask for a far greater prize – intimacy with your soul's expression.'

'So mistakes are good?' Gigi asked hopefully. 'Because if there's one thing I can be sure of, it's that I'll make lots of them.'

Maya chuckled, violet eyes twinkling. 'You and everyone else in the Magical Theatre, my sweet.' And before Gigi could respond, her image shimmered and evaporated.

Gigi felt that now-familiar mix of exhaustion and exhilaration that came with absorbing Maya's keystones. It was thrilling to imagine truly being herself without attachment to being right. How would she have handled things differently in the past if she'd been able to drop her mask? For one, she could have told her father just what she thought of his abandoning her and sticking her with all these issues about men.

'Ah, be careful,' Godfreys said, shaking his finger at her. 'It's that kind of thinking that keeps you wearing the mask of the victim. Your victim needs to be right about being abandoned. But what if you could be wrong about being a victim?'

Gigi's mind resisted the idea, but her impartial observer knew Godfreys had a point. 'So feeling victimized by my father's abandonment is part of my mask?'

'Yes,' Godfreys confirmed.

'I don't know... I don't feel like a victim,' Gigi said. 'I feel like a survivor.'

'Flip side of the same coin,' Mitchell put in.

'We'll discuss the victim aspect more later,' Godfreys said, seeing that Gigi didn't quite buy his explanation yet. 'Just allow the idea to begin shifting your perspective a bit. Entertain the thought that you might have been wearing the mask of the victim.'

'Okay,' Gigi said, but she wasn't convinced.

'Meanwhile, think about how your life could have been different if you hadn't been wearing the mask of righteousness,' Godfreys prompted.

For one, she would have stuck to her guns about studying what she wanted in school instead of trying to please her mom and stepdad. She would have dumped Keith the second she found him snorting coke in the bathroom or not coming home at night.

She would have dumped Keith! She'd never thought anything of the kind before. She'd always blamed him for the divorce and imagined that if it weren't for his blatant infidelity they could have lived happily ever after.

But that wasn't true! If she'd been true to herself instead of madly trying to defend her choices and look important in the eyes of the world, she would have dropped him like a hot potato. She could have admitted that she'd made a mistake in choosing him.

And maybe she would even have given sweet Steven from the drama festival a chance. He probably would have treated her like a queen, and never had an affair with women *or* cocaine.

'So if I'd been willing to admit I'd been wrong about Keith, I could have saved myself a lot of heartache,' Gigi murmured.

'And if you could admit you'd been wrong about me, you could save *me* a lot of heartache,' said Mitchell.

Gigi smiled gently at his hurt tone. 'You're right, Mitchell,' she said. 'I was wrong about you. I had you pegged as a thief and a liar, but really you were just doing your job and trying to help me. I apologize.' And as she spoke, she felt a weight lifting from her heart. It felt great to admit she'd been wrong! Much better than holding onto resentment and righteousness.

'Apology accepted,' said Mitchell with a wide grin. 'Now, darling, I really think we ought to get you into something more appropriate.'

Gigi realized she was still wearing the 'rock star wife' getup and agreed heartily that she needed a change. Expecting Mitchell to return her mud-stained jeans and spike heels, she was surprised to see him advancing with a bright blue flight suit and sturdy boots.

'Don't you have anything a little more, er, feminine?' Gigi asked hopefully.

Mitchell laughed. 'Of course, darling, if you'd like to wear an evening gown to go skydiving.'

'Ha ha,' Gigi said feebly, sure he must be kidding. She turned to Godfreys, who was again wearing his signature amused expression. She noticed with trepidation that his bellman uniform had been replaced by a khaki flight suit, boots and a helmet.

Gigi was instantly catapulted into an unwelcome memory. Lily, an acquaintance of hers in college, had asked her to go skydiving with a group of students from their dorm to blow off steam before finals. Gigi was not in the habit of taking unnecessary physical risks, but she'd agreed to go because Lily was captain of the girls' soccer team and very popular. Gigi didn't want Lily to think she was a wimp, and she wanted to be friends with her.

'Another mask,' Gigi muttered to herself.

At the last minute, however, Gigi had found herself swamped with studying and a project to raise her grade in physics class. Reluctantly deciding that good grades were more important than social bonding, she'd told Lily she couldn't go. That evening, devastating news had ricocheted across campus: Lily's chute had gotten tangled, and although she'd survived the fall, she had a huge number of broken bones. The horror of it had kept Gigi awake for nights on end. She'd vowed never to do anything as stupid as skydiving in her whole life.

But wait – she was in the dreamtime, and she'd been flying through space freely for a while. 'I get it,' Gigi said to Godfreys. 'We're just going to play at skydiving, right? Because in the dreamtime, we can't get hurt.'

Godfreys cleared his throat. 'Er, actually the skydiving will be very real,' he said. 'Somewhere over Kansas, I believe. Or maybe it's Tibet – I can't remember. But the location is of no consequence. The point is to address your worst earthly fears.'

'Oh, no,' Gigi said, backing away. 'No way. I am not going skydiving. And there is absolutely no way you are going to get me to put on that hideous suit.' But it was already on her, and the boots were lacing themselves up against her will.

'Godfreys,' Gigi pleaded, 'how many times have I said I'd never take stupid risks like skydiving? You must know how I feel about it. It's ridiculous to risk your life for a few minutes' thrill.'

Godfreys inclined his head and said, 'Remember, my friend, be willing to be wrong.'

'But this isn't any ordinary situation!' Gigi argued. 'I get that mistakes are okay, but one mistake while skydiving could be fatal!'

'Relax, it'll be fine,' said Mitchell easily, plunking a helmet on her head and tucking in stray strands of hair. 'You'll have fun. Trust me.'

'Trust *you*?' Gigi shrieked, but Mitchell ignored her, instead taking her shoulders and marching her over to the paneled wood door. Godfreys was already there, pushing the elevator button. Gigi could barely hear the whir of the elevator over the screaming of her cast members, who were berating her for getting herself into this situation and mocking her for being a coward.

'Release into your inner knowing,' said Maya's voice inside her helmet. 'Allow yourself, unmasked and center stage, to discover what makes the real "you" shine. It may be different than you think. When you feel afraid, connect with your impartial observer.'

Gigi breathed deeply, focusing on the sensation of being maskless. What was the worst that could happen? This was a dream, after all, no matter how real it felt.

The elevator pinged, the doors slid open, and Mitchell propelled Gigi inside.

Chapter Eleven

Gigi's stomach dropped as the elevator began a rapid descent. At least this time she was prepared when the walls fell away to reveal stars streaking past in the opposite direction.

She concentrated on the haunting music of the spheres as she tried to calm her breathing. But her thoughts ran rampant, her cast of characters having a field day. She couldn't believe Godfreys was taking her skydiving. Maybe it was just a setup to test her, and they wouldn't end up going, after all.

Hope spiraled as she gazed at the stars. Maybe if she wished on a star she could get herself out of this? But they were going too fast to focus on any single star. She closed her eyes anyway in an effort to send a wish out into the universe.

It was no use. All she could picture was herself tumbling out of an airplane, free-falling from 20,000 feet. Her parachute wasn't opening. Oh God, she was going to hurtle to earth and splatter on the pavement. Or be impaled on a branch. Or slam into the ocean going seventy miles an hour. Or...

The elevator slid to a stop.

'Ah, here we are,' said Godfreys, self-satisfied as always. Gigi shot him a look as the doors opened noiselessly. She stalked past him into a large concrete-and-steel structure filled with small airplanes. The strong aroma of motor oil assailed her nostrils. A hangar! So it was true – she *was* going skydiving. Her heart shriveled into a tiny nut and her breath came in shallow gasps.

'This way,' directed Godfreys briskly, leading her around a row of planes into the center of the hangar. Seated on brightly colored mats clumped around one of the planes was a small group of students, all in blue flight suits, helmets at their sides.

'Have a seat,' Godfreys instructed. Gigi plunked down on the nearest mat gratefully, her legs weak with fear. Godfreys proceeded to the front of the group and hoisted himself up to sit on the airplane's wing facing them, boot-clad feet dangling.

'Welcome to skydiving school,' Godfreys said. 'Since there are so many of you in Remedial Angel Training and we can only take a limited number on any plane, we've divided this segment into groups. You are the Blue Group, and I'll be your instructor.'

Immediately, one of the student's hands shot up, and Gigi recognized Susan, looking as cool and composed as ever with a jaunty white scarf tied around her neck, the blue of the uniform contrasting beautifully with her raven hair. Well, this was no surprise. Of course Ms. Smarty-pants would have to be in her group so she could lord it over Gigi with her intimate knowledge of rocket science and consummate skydiving skill – perfected, no doubt, while serving selflessly with a foreign aid group dropping food and medical supplies for the needy. God.

'Yes, Susan?' Godfreys said.

'Are we sorted into groups by skill level?' she asked. 'Because although I've never gone skydiving before, I have gone hang gliding and was told I have a lot of potential. I just want to make sure I'm in the right group.'

Well, at least she hadn't trained as an astronaut. But that didn't make her any less annoying.

Here we go again, thought Gigi, filled with the bitter mix of disdain and inferiority that Susan seemed uniquely able to bring out in her. Her critic instantly began tongue-lashing her for not looking as cute as Susan in her flight suit, and not having any experience in the air – then launched into criticizing her for being critical.

Oh, gosh, honey, I hear you, but I've learned you're not helping, Gigi responded inwardly, delighted to note that she was unfazed by the critic's words. They no longer had the power to make her feel miserable. Instead, much to her surprise, she identified a belief that she wasn't coordinated enough to take physical risks safely.

Probably stems all the way back to dodge ball in elementary school, when I was always the butt of the boys' torture, she mused. Then, proud of herself for knowing what to do, she performed a quick session of LIQUID to challenge the belief.

When she was done, she took herself in hand. Since it was obvious she was going to go skydiving regardless of her opinion, she might as well adopt the perspective that this would be a good learning experience instead of a disaster.

'Excellent, my sweet,' Maya's voice breathed in her ear. 'And don't forget to drop your mask of being right about how people shouldn't take part in unnecessarily dangerous activities. Now be sure to listen and absorb this next keystone. You are well on your way to awakening, but you still have lessons to learn.'

Distracted, Gigi realized she'd missed Godfreys' reply to Susan, but from the woman's disgruntled expression, she gathered that it hadn't been to her liking.

'Now we shall begin,' Godfreys said. 'Today's skydiving lesson will take you on a journey into the present.'

The present? Gigi wrinkled her brow in confusion.

'Let me explain,' said Godfreys. 'First, ponder this question: If you are not your mask, your beliefs, your critic, your cast of characters or your script – then who are you?'

Susan's hand shot into the air but Godfreys ignored it. In the sudden silence, Gigi thought about the question. Who was she? An assemblage of cells? The culmination of her amassed experiences? Her past lives? Her perceptions? No, she was much more than any of those things. Maya had said she was an angel, but she sure didn't feel like one. At least not at the moment.

As if in answer to her thoughts, Godfreys continued, 'To find your authenticity, you need only remember the truth of who you are in a "now" moment. This means taking emotional responsibility for your experience of life in the present time. Because when all is said and done, the moment is all there is.'

He looked around at the students to see if his message was sinking in.

Gigi took the opportunity to really look at them for the first time. A couple of the students looked vaguely familiar from Maya's lectures. And the man in the front row at the far side of the group, with his back to her, wearing a cowboy hat with his flight suit – it couldn't be – it had to be – was it Buck?

Her heart raced and she felt blood pulsing at her temples. Just then he turned his head and she saw his unmistakable chiseled profile underneath his Stetson. A rush of warmth suffused her and she began to quiver, remembering his touch..

As if he could feel her staring at him, Buck suddenly twisted around to look behind him, and their eyes locked. His face lit up with a smile, and he gave her a little wave. Gigi's heart leapt. She felt their connection as strongly as ever. Hope flared in her like a greedy flame.

Maybe it could still work. She'd gotten over her belief that all men would abandon her – hadn't she? And her critic had started to lose its power. She had dropped her mask. Wasn't she ready to meet him head-on again? If only she had on a fabulous sexy outfit and wasn't wearing this unflattering flight suit, and if only they weren't in this horrid skydiving class... She was sure that if they could be alone, sparks would fly even hotter than before.

Godfreys cleared his throat loudly, looking from Buck to Gigi, and Buck snapped back toward the front. Gigi blushed as the students all turned to look at her. Susan gave her usual tight smile, which Gigi worked hard not to interpret as supercilious.

'As I was saying, class, the now moment is where you can connect your awareness to the present so you can make conscious choices,' Godfreys said pointedly.

'If you are not in the now moment, chances are you're making fear-based decisions that stem from past experiences that likely have very little to do with what is really happening. That's why we've chosen skydiving as the activity to illustrate being in the moment. You will need to be completely present, operating neither from projections into the future nor from fears based on the past.'

'But that sounds impossible!' Gigi blurted. 'Sorry, forgot to raise my hand. But seeing as we each have a whole lifetime of experiences behind us, how is it possible not to choose based on experience? And isn't it only natural and healthy to make projections about potential outcomes?'

'Excellent points, Gigi,' Godfreys said, favoring her with a smile. Out of the corner of her eye, Gigi saw Susan shoot her a look, which she ignored as Godfreys continued. 'Humans under the enchantment of the Magical Theatre do tend to make choices based on past experiences or future projections. But this keeps you in a cycle of action and reaction.

'You respond based on what you think you know, so it keeps you repeating the same mistakes and generating the same outcomes. To change this, you must come fully present into the only moment truly available to you – *now*. Your future is automatically determined by what you do in the present. If you want to influence the future, consciously choose your action in the current moment. Remember, *it is the only one available to you*.'

'So our choices in the past have just been reactions based on our tired old experiences?' asked a man with a familiar Brooklyn accent. It had to be Vinny, but he was much more serious and subdued. He must have really been having some awakening experiences in Remedial Angel Training.

'Yes, Vinny, you've got it,' said Godfreys encouragingly.

'I can understand not acting based on the past, but isn't focusing on the future a good thing?' asked Susan. 'How would we ever accomplish anything if we didn't look ahead?'

'Yeah, I gotta have hope,' chimed in Vinny.

'I can see it's time for me to introduce the imps,' Godfreys said, and before Gigi had time to wonder what on earth he was talking about, three tiny old-fashioned planes zipped into the hangar, twirling and racing above the class. After a stunning show of aerial skill, the planes formed a triangle and hovered near Godfreys.

From the open cockpit of each plane, Gigi beheld a visor-clad creature with pointed ears and soft tufts of hair sticking out the sides of miniature leather helmets. One of the creatures was covered in green fur, one in yellow, and one in red, but other than that they looked exactly alike. They waved at the students with webbed paws, their wide grins revealing an abundance of sharp white teeth.

'These are the three imps who *imp*ede – pun intended – your progress,' Godfreys explained. 'They look friendly, but they can create a lot of mischief. Their names are Hope' – the green imp revved his plane into motion and wrote the word 'Hope' in the air – 'Potential' – the yellow imp followed suit and skywrote his name – 'and Wishful Thinking.' The red imp wrote his name with a flourish then all three returned to their formation above head.

'This tricky triad will tempt you to look longingly into the future and miss out on the treasures available to you in the moment,' Godfreys said, ignoring the jeers and insults the three pilots began yelling at him.

'Hope may seem positive because it claims to lend you an optimistic viewpoint. Yet it can act as a sedative, luring you away from taking action and pulling you into the inertia of procrastination. Potential promises that you'll find happiness just as soon as a circumstance shifts or a person changes – even though you have no control over these external possibilities. And Wishful Thinking traps you in a cycle of expecting different results from similar circumstances.

'All three are unhelpful at best, and destructive at worst. Beware of their false promises, and banish them when they buzz around you.' Godfreys made his hand into a gun shape and pretended to shoot the imps. Laughing maniacally, they executed simultaneous loop-de-loops and zoomed out the way they'd come.

Gigi sighed. Godfreys was right, of course. Hope, potential

and wishful thinking had kept her longing for her father and married to a man who wasn't good for her. Hope had helped her justify her inaction, potential had taken over the moment and shifted her focus to a future possibility, and wishful thinking had distanced her from making good decisions.

But having just the moment to go on, after relying on past and future to make choices, felt like walking a tightrope across a canyon and suddenly realizing there was no rope there, after all. Could she really trust the moment?

She took a deep breath, inhaling the pungent scent of motor oil that permeated the hangar, and willed herself to just be there, sitting on the spongy mat in a state of listening and waiting. It felt pretty good, actually, and she realized with surprise that her fear of skydiving had abated.

Godfreys jumped to the ground and said briskly, 'Just now, it's the moment to practice your jumps.' Gigi's newfound courage nearly failed her, but she reminded herself to simply be present as she rose and helped the other students stack the mats on top of each other beneath the open side of the plane.

She noticed Godfreys helping Buck to his feet and handing him a pair of crutches. She'd completely forgotten Buck's injuries. How was he going to skydive? And didn't he have to take off his ever-present Stetson and don a helmet like everyone else?

She sent him a questioning look as he limped toward her, and he grinned. 'I'm going to be the co-pilot,' he said.

'You know how to fly?' Gigi asked, surprised.

'Not really,' Buck admitted. 'That's my part of the test. To just perform in the moment and not lose my lunch or anything.'

'Lose your lunch?' Gigi repeated.

'I'm afraid of flying,' Buck said, avoiding her eyes. 'Had a bad experience on a small plane once. So looks like this is my chance to make a new choice.'

He didn't look all that thrilled about it, but Gigi had no time to respond. Godfreys was handing out parachutes and explaining how they worked. She became completely absorbed in learning how to put it on and pull the cord in case it didn't open (best not to think about that), then practicing jumping out of the plane. It wasn't as bad as she'd thought, but of course she was only falling four or five feet.

'Moment, moment, moment,' she sang to herself, a comforting mantra that kept her present. Shockingly, she didn't even care when Susan got complimented on her jump. Learning to stay in the moment took a surprising amount of her attention. She had no time to feel jealous.

Before she knew it, Gigi found herself strapped into the bench in the back of the plane with the other students, all in nervous states varying from excitement to downright terror. Gigi tried not to think about which end of the spectrum she belonged to, repeating her mantra endlessly and focusing on the small details of the moment instead of thinking ahead to what could well be her doom. No use worrying over what couldn't be changed, right? Godfreys sat nearest the cockpit, helping Buck get situated. Though a touch pale, Buck still looked damn sexy in the co-pilot seat – hot enough to make Gigi wriggle in her tight flight suit.

'Hey, who's gonna fly this rig?' asked Vinny, who was looking rather green around the gills.

'I am, of course,' trilled Maya, appearing with a *poof!* in the captain's seat in full flight regalia. She turned around to look at them and waved casually. 'Hello, my dears! Sorry I'm late. I've been so busy with all the flight groups – I have to bounce from one to another. But this is my favorite part. I wouldn't miss it for the world! Or even for a double rainbow.'

She then turned her attention to the controls, and Gigi focused on breathing and not panicking. But a sudden commotion in the cockpit drew her away from her meditation.

She looked up to see Buck frantically trying to unbuckle his seatbelt as he ripped the earphones off his head. 'I can't do this!'

he said urgently, managing to undo the buckle. He lunged for the door, but the handle wouldn't give.

Maya said calmly from the pilot's seat, 'Buck, stop. Now take a deep breath and talk to me.'

Buck slumped over, not looking at her. Gigi could see that he was sweating profusely. Her heart went out to him, and she sent him a silent prayer of encouragement. She could identify only too well with his struggle.

Maya silently beamed violet light at Buck until he admitted, 'I'm afraid to fly.'

'Yes, I know, my love,' Maya said soothingly. 'And you're not alone. Everyone on this plane is experiencing some level of fear right now – aren't you, my darling angels?'

'Yes!' everyone shouted through their helmets.

'You can do it, buddy!' yelled Vinny.

'Yes, you can,' Maya agreed. 'And do you know how you can do it, no matter how much resistance you're experiencing?'

'No,' said Buck. 'I feel like I'm gonna be sick. I'd better get out.'

'You're not going to be sick,' Maya said firmly. 'Now listen to me, my dear – and all of you, too,' she added, twisting around to beam her gaze on the others. 'This is a valuable practice for all of you.'

She returned her attention to Buck. 'Remember today's lesson – being present in the moment?'

'Yeah,' Buck muttered with a notable lack of enthusiasm.

'My sweet, I know you have a history with flying that produces a reaction in you, and that reaction causes you to behave in a certain way – namely, avoiding air travel. But you have the chance to change that behavior now.'

'Can't I change it later?' Buck asked. 'I've at least sat in the cockpit – that's more than I've done in years. Maybe next time I'll be able to make it down the runway.'

The red imp suddenly buzzed into the airplane, laughing

madly, and traced three circles around Buck's head. Buck batted at the imp, but he just let out an exuberant whoop and zoomed back out the open passenger door.

'Wasn't that Wishful Thinking?' Susan called from the rear of the plane.

'It was, indeed,' Maya replied, chuckling. Then her voice softened. 'Remember, my treasure, if you want to create a different outcome, you're going to have to choose a new response based on the moment. Even if you postpone flying, your opportunity will still show up as *now*. The future is based on what you decide in this instant. Fear is a projection into the future. If it shows up, just let it flow through you. When it has no future projection to hook onto, it will simply disappear.'

'Okay, I get it,' said Buck, sitting up a little straighter. 'So if I want to change this wimpy behavior, I have to do something different in this moment – not think about what I'll do differently later, or what could happen when we're airborne, or what happened that time in Montana.'

'Yes, that's it, my dear. And you must also refrain from judging it,' Maya cautioned. 'It's your critic who sees the situation as wimpy. In the moment, it simply is what it is.'

Buck nodded and sat back in his seat. Gigi could feel waves of concentration emanating from him. After a few minutes in which the plane was absolutely silent, Buck nodded and refastened his seatbelt. He craned around to give the others a thumbs-up before repositioning his headset.

'Ready?' Maya said.

'Ready,' he replied.

Gigi's relief for Buck lasted only as long as it took for the plane to taxi out of the hangar.

Omigod, it's real, she thought in a sudden fit of panic as they emerged onto the runway, a thin strip of tarmac suspended in space. This was no pretend airplane. They really were going to take off and she really was going to be forced to jump out into thin air.

Well, I jumped off the cliff with Buck and survived, right? Gigi rationalized inwardly. *But I didn't have so much time to think about it then. And I felt more confident, because my impartial observer had told me to take a leap of faith. This, on the other hand, seems more like… a leap of sheer stupidity.*

In fact, now seemed like a good time to quiet her people and drop into the knowingness of the impartial observer. Gigi breathed, hand on heart, and immediately felt calmer.

'Moment, moment, moment.' She repeated her mantra as the plane gathered speed and took off into the starry sky. Looking around at the others sitting stoically in the cabin with her, she saw reflections of her own mixture of fear and resolve. She had a sudden rush of compassion for them, even Susan. They were all in the same boat, or rather plane, after all. In here, they were leveled. All there was, was now – now – now – and now.

The sky outside the plane lightened into a bright pale blue, and when Gigi peered out of the open door, she saw a bland landscape of cornfields and straight roads that looked like Kansas or Iowa. The ground looked very far away.

Breathe, she told herself. *You're in the plane right now – you're safe.* But her momentary serenity was shattered when Godfreys stood up and shouted over the drone of the motor, 'All right, everyone, who wants to go first?'

The students looked at one another but nobody volunteered.

'Then we'll go in seating order,' Godfreys said, looking at Gigi. She realized with a shock that she was first in line. No use wishing it otherwise; she'd already met that imp. The only thing to do was get up. At least she'd get this whole shebang over with soon and know if she was going to end up dead or alive.

Unbuckling her seatbelt, she grabbed onto the strap above and forced her shaky legs to stand. Suddenly, she was far from being in the moment. She was in the future – and it didn't look so great. All she could see was a slow-motion film of herself free-falling to her doom.

Dimly she realized that Buck was giving her another thumbs-up from the cockpit, and that he was a little pale around the mouth. She saw in his eyes that he was struggling with not being able to help her – his critic was obviously berating him for not being more in control.

She wiggled a finger at him admonishingly, and he grinned.

Godfreys motioned Gigi forward until she was standing at the edge of the plane. She closed her eyes. If she looked down, she'd never be able to do it.

Right now, I'm standing at the edge of the plane, she thought, and that helped her. Here she was. She was not falling. She was fine.

Godfreys gave her an encouraging pat on the back. 'Heave ho!' he yelled – then gave her a gigantic push.

She was falling, falling, her heart was stopping; she would tumble to her death! Her mind whirled. Would her whole life flash before her eyes? But there was still so much more to do! Then with an abrupt jerk, her precipitous descent grew slow and gentle. She looked up to see the parachute ballooning above her like a giant mushroom. She took a deep breath and looked down.

The landscape looked different than it had from the airplane – more dramatic. In fact, as she watched, the bland prairie was metamorphosing into a vast wilderness of dense forest punctuated by sharp, rocky outcroppings and steep caverns.

Oh, shit, Gigi thought wildly. *Toto, we're not in Kansas anymore! This place is starting to look dangerous. What will happen when I land? I'll be in the middle of nowhere, and nobody will know where I am! I'll starve to death or be eaten by wild boar! Wait, wild boar don't eat people, do they? What about mountain lions, or grizzlies?*

Suddenly her attention was arrested by a strange cloud formation just below her. The clouds seemed to be shape-shifting into letters that spelled out a message.

Yes, there it was! It read: 'Keystone 7: Be present in the heart of now.'

Smiling in spite of her fear, Gigi realized Maya was still with her. 'Now, now, now,' she chanted softly as she descended slowly through the clouds and got another view of the landscape. It was actually rather pleasant to be bobbing through the air, and the view was spectacular. Actually, she realized, she was enjoying herself. In the moment, there was nothing to be afraid of.

Wow, I didn't see that *coming,* she thought with a fierce surge of joy. *I never thought I'd actually have fun doing this.*

'That's why it is so important to be present rather than rehashing the past or imagining the future,' Maya said, close to her ear.

Used to hearing Maya's disembodied voice by now, Gigi just nodded her head in agreement. But then out of the corner of her eye, she saw something flying alongside her. It was a majestic golden eagle.

As she watched, it soared around her then paused, regarding her with a piercing, violet-colored eye. It let out a shriek that sounded a lot like a laugh, then flew off.

Miracles happen in the moment, Gigi thought, awed, then wondered if that insight came from Maya or from herself. In any case, it sounded true, because if miracles did happen, the only time they could be recognized was in the moment.

The thought relaxed Gigi as she continued drifting down toward the mountainous countryside below. Willing herself to be present, she deflected the fearful questions that kept drifting into her mind: *Where will I land? What will happen to me? How will the others find me?*

'The future is being determined by your current decisions and always shows up as NOW, since there is no other time that exists,' Maya's voice breathed in her mind.

'It's okay to be afraid, because feeling fearful emotions is natural in certain circumstances. Where you get into trouble is in your resistance to the fear. You don't want to experience the uncomfortable emotion, so you impede its flow and it gets trapped inside you. When you drop your resistance, the emotion can move right through and out of you. In the heart of the moment, let your resistance free-fall and simply feel what you're feeling.

'Now that you know the truth about your resistance, the moment of transformation is yours for the taking. You can either resist, or go with the flow. It's your choice: fear or happiness.'

The choice was obvious.

'Okay,' Gigi whispered as the treetops grew larger and larger, the mountainous crags more and more menacing. *I'm in the moment and I'm feeling fear and I'm not going to let it steal my happiness. It's okay to feel fear, too, because I know when my emotions are flowing naturally, they don't have to affect what I decide to do.-*

Chanting her mantra 'Now, now, now', Gigi swayed downward toward the dense forest.

Chapter Twelve

When the treetops were so close they began to snag at her sturdily booted feet, Gigi realized she no longer felt afraid. She was completely focused on maneuvering her parachute so that she could get to a small clearing she'd seen earlier.

On the way down, she'd had plenty of time to practice dropping into the heart of the moment. Occasionally one of her people would crow, *I'm in the moment – cool!* to be immediately followed by the stern voice of the critic who said sourly, *If you're outside it enough to say you're in it, you're not in it.* Then a pulse of fear would shiver through her as another voice said, *Oh, shit – I'm a long way from the Village. How the hell am I going to get out of here?*

Her only thought was how to tug on her parachute cords just right to guide herself through the trees. She couldn't afford to get tangled in their grasping branches, or she might never be able to untangle herself. Out of sheer necessity, the voices were silenced, and there was no room for anything but the present.

To her immense relief, the trees dropped off abruptly and the clearing emerged, a circle of green intersected by long late-afternoon shadows. The soft-looking grass was dotted with yellow and white wildflowers, and she could hear the burbling of a nearby stream. Apparently it was spring here instead of fall – wherever 'here' was. It all looked very inviting, like a scene from a Disney film. She half-expected to hear the warbling of Snow White drifting through the loamy air.

Now she just had to get this overgrown umbrella to land in the middle of the clearing.

Luckily she was drifting down slowly, and she'd figured out how to steer the parachute. Easy enough: pull the right toggle, turn right; pull the left toggle, turn left. She was doing it – the soft-looking grass of the clearing was approaching...

To her delight, she vividly recalled Godfreys' instructions on how to fall into a parachute landing. Land on the balls of the feet and roll on the downwind side. Calf, thigh, bottom – and she was down, rolling along the ground with the parachute gently mushrooming then collapsing on top of her.

Gigi gratefully disengaged herself from the parachute and removed her helmet. It felt delightful to be free of gear and on solid ground. She splayed out on the soft grass, taking a deep, delicious breath. Then gripped by a sudden, powerful thirst, she heaved herself up and headed to the stream on rubbery legs, licking her dry lips in anticipation of the cool water. She leaned down to drink, but just before her lips touched the burbling surface, a warning bell went off in her head. Was she stupid? She could get giardia, the intestinal parasite that wreaked havoc from drinking unfiltered water.

'I don't care,' she said defiantly. 'Besides, it's the dreamtime. Giardia only exists in real time.' She cupped her hands and scooped up a deep, refreshing drink. If there were any bacteria in there, she sure couldn't taste them. Then she splashed water on her face and ran her hands through her matted hair.

Sitting back on her haunches, she realized she had no idea what to do next. She was pretty sure she wasn't going to be met by a limo with a fully stocked bar and a change of clothes. A brief review of her situation did nothing to lighten her mood. She was alone in a strange wilderness, the sun was getting lower by the second, and she had no idea what to do or in which direction to head. In this moment, sure, she was okay, but what happened when the sun set? She didn't even know if she was on earth or what creatures might be already checking her out as a possible meal.

When she was a child, her mother had always told her, 'If you get lost or separated from me, just stay where you are and I'll find you.' But that advice didn't seem to apply in this situation, because no one was around to find her. She assumed that Maya had an eye on her, but she couldn't feel her presence anywhere. Maybe some of the other students would land here too, but she hadn't seen any of them on her way down.

The landscape had changed, after all, and perhaps each of them was landing in their own private world. That seemed like something Maya would dream up.

I have only myself to count on, Gigi thought. Immediately, cold fear gripped her, but she knew enough now to let it pass through her as she breathed into her heart to connect with her impartial observer.

Take it one step at a time, said her inner wisdom. *Stay in the moment. Remember all the lessons you've learned, and don't be a victim. Now is your chance to put your emerging awareness to the test.*

Gigi took a deep, centering breath and opened her eyes. She froze.

She was looking directly into the amber eyes of a huge mountain lion, who was just lifting his head from drinking on the opposite side of the stream.

Crap, Gigi thought wildly, willing herself to move. But her muscles would not obey, and she remained frozen on the ground. Then without warning, her fight-or-flight reaction kicked in and she was up and running, heart knocking against her ribs as she sprinted across the clearing. Spotting a huge old oak, she took refuge behind it, scanning upward for footholds in case she had to climb. But lions were just over sized house cats —they could climb, too, right? Well, all she could do right now was wait and see. She didn't dare peek around, but she didn't hear anything.

'Very good,' said the tree in a deep, hoarse voice.

Gigi jumped back and stared at the rugged trunk.

'Did you notice how fear triggered the sensible reaction of running away from physical harm?' the tree went on calmly. Its voice seemed to be emanating from a nearby knothole, and although its timbre was low, its tone sounded suspiciously like

Maya's.

'Don't worry, the lion isn't real. It was an illusion produced to help you learn about the nature of fear. You conquered fear while skydiving by staying in the moment, and you can do that anytime. But there are some situations where fear is healthy and appropriate – such as when you are confronted with the possibility of physical harm.'

'Oh,' was all Gigi could manage, adrenaline still pumping through her.

'The feeling of fear was included in the design of the Magical Theatre to protect you from physical harm,' the Maya tree continued. 'Unfortunately, humans began paying too much attention to fear in situations where it is not useful. Fear of a mountainlion is appropriate; fear of the future is not. Do you see?'

'I see,' said Gigi, glad her pulse was finally slowing. 'We project fear onto situations where it only impedes us instead of helping us.'

'Yes!' barked the tree. 'Please keep that in mind as you continue your training. Every time you start to be influenced by fear of future events, you can stop and ask yourself if there is any real and present danger and use that answer to guide you.'

'Okay,' said Gigi, gathering the courage to step out from behind the tree. 'Thanks,' she added, feeling slightly foolish. She could swear the tree swayed a little in response. Shaking her head, she walked gingerly back to the stream.

Illusion kitty was gone.

'This way!' called a familiar voice, and she caught a glimpse of Godfreys through the trees. He seemed to be gesturing her to cross the stream. Gigi hopped as fast as she could from rock to slippery rock, then jumped onto the opposite bank. Finding the entrance to a narrow, twisting path, she began to follow it hurriedly, hoping she'd find Godfreys up ahead.

When he wasn't anywhere to be seen, she broke into a run,

tripping over roots and dodging tree branches that seemed to reach gnarled fingers out to grab her. The forest grew denser and darker. It was just like that scary scene in *Snow White* when she runs away from her evil stepmother and all the trees come alive and threaten her. That scene had given Gigi nightmares as a child. Maybe she was trapped in her own nightmare! The trees were evil – she could feel it! They secretly wanted to tear her to pieces.

Just as Gigi felt fear's iron grip start to paralyze her, Maya's recent words drifted through her memory. She forced herself to slow and stop in the middle of the dark path.

Okay, I need to get a hold of myself, she thought. I am not in immediate danger – not that I know of, anyway. So there is nothing to be afraid of in this moment. Plus, I've learned seven of Maya's keystones, so I certainly have the understanding to guide me out of here. She mentally reviewed the keystones: script, perspective, cast, critic, beliefs, mask, moment.

And surely this experience was meant to help her learn another lesson. So all she had to do was use what she'd learned, and she would get to the next keystone.

Walking forward with renewed confidence, Gigi chanted the keystones in her head and thought about each one as she moved through the now marginally less frightening forest. *No problem*, she thought. *I can do this. I'm not scared… not* real *scared, anyway.*

After what seemed like a long time but could have been only a few minutes, Gigi was relieved to see a clearing ahead in the rapidly dimming light. A babbling brook ran through it. She hastened forward, thinking she could sure use another drink of water. But when she reached the stream, she stopped short in disbelief. This was the same stream she'd drunk from before! And in the clearing beyond, she could see her discarded parachute lying limply on the ground. She had gone in a circle!

A circle – how cliché, she groaned inwardly. *Don't all lost people wind up going around in circles?* Hadn't her knowledge of the keystones taught her anything? Clearly she was just as lost and clueless as she'd ever been. She had failed, and now she'd never get out of here.

Dragging her feet, Gigi knelt beside the stream and drank some more of the cool, clear water. As she drank, she saw her reflection in its depths melt and shift, revealing Maya's smiling face.

'Maya!' Gigi called, reaching out to her, but her hand encountered only water. The ripples she generated dissipated Maya's image, and despair stabbed her heart.

'I'm right here, my dear,' said Maya's voice, and Gigi looked up to see her sitting, siren-like, on a mossy log in the center of the stream. Her mass of braids was decorated with weeds and her dress was waterlogged.

Gigi let out a sob of relief. 'Maya, I'm so glad to see you,' she said, her voice catching. 'I thought I had it all figured out, but I was only going in circles. I don't know how to get out of here.'

'Good, my sweet. Admitting you don't know is the first step,' Maya said merrily. 'Thinking you know everything on your spiritual path is a trap that will keep you tracing the same old circle that has worn a tired groove in your psyche. But true knowing is wisdom, and wisdom comes from experience.

'Knowledge can be gained by studying, but is not the same as experiencing, which takes time and considerable patience to acquire. If you hurry blindly, you may develop a tendency to misinterpret knowledge as wisdom – thus skipping the practical work you must undertake to ascend the spiral.'

'Ascend the spiral? What spiral?' Gigi asked, confused.

'The spiral of self-awareness,' Maya said. 'You see, the circle you walk in everyday life keeps you in the same old rut, repeating the same old choices over and over. When you assume conscious responsibility for your experience of life, the circular rut you've created opens and transforms into an ascending spiral.

'When you move up this spiral with ever-increasing

awareness, it leads you gradually toward your awakening from the enchantment.'

'Really? But I thought I was already on that path,' Gigi said.

'It is a slow process,' Maya said enigmatically. 'You must realize that as you begin to reclaim your true nature, the main ingredient you will need is patience.'

'Ick,' said Gigi. 'Patience has never been one of my virtues.'

'Ah, that is why you need to cultivate it. Your journey along the spiral of self-awareness will not be a fast trip, but the important thing is that you have begun.'

'Begun! But I've been working on myself since I first went to a therapist when I was in college,' Gigi objected. 'Surely I am already ascending. I can't be stuck in the same rut I was then.'

'Indeed you have, my love. And if you recall, that therapist focused your work on the impossible task of creating consensus among your cast of characters. In attempting to do this, you went in circles for so long that you wore a deep rut in your psyche. This was actually a good thing, because you got a chance to learn firsthand that that approach wasn't going to work for you. Then you were free to release that option and look for what came next.'

'Wow, I never looked at it that way,' Gigi mused. 'So that was part of my spiral?'

'Yes, and it was just as essential as every other part,' Maya replied. 'That experience illustrates how the spiral is characterized by stages. You cannot advance to one stage before "getting" or mastering the previous one. And you may have to circle around to land at the same stage numerous times. But each time you'll be higher on the spiral and will be able to see the same view from a different vantage point. Now get comfortable and listen carefully, my sweet, and I'll explain more about the spiral.'

Gigi leaned back against a tree trunk and willed herself to simply listen, silencing the critic, who was shouting at her that she should have had this figured out by now.

'Here's how the spiral works, my love,' began Maya. 'Let's say you want to free yourself from the harshness of your emotions – because they can be harsh, can't they? – and learn to live in a state of loving compassion.'

'That sounds like a good goal,' Gigi said. 'If I could free myself from being yanked around by my emotional reality every ten seconds, I might actually be able to make a change in the world.'

Maya smiled. 'Indeed, my sweet. So on this quest for compassion, initially you might read self-help books and attend workshops, study psychology, and memorize information that would allow you to don the disguise of a master. This disguise would allow you to *act as if* you were compassionate, and others might see you that way, reinforcing your belief that you'd mastered compassion and freed yourself from the grip of your emotions.

'This technique may temporarily fool you into thinking you've achieved your goal – but in truth you are trying to leap over the necessary stages in the spiral because you have not resolved your internal experience. So ultimately, you find you need to start your trip through the spiral all over again.'

Gigi felt the truth of Maya's words even as she resisted them. She wanted to think that awakening could happen quickly, but in her heart she knew it had to be a gradual, step-by-step process.

Maya continued. 'The first stage on the spiral, then, is to walk through the torturous fires of shame and judgment and find the simple truth of where you are on your life's path. Acknowledging this truth will provide you the grace of awareness necessary to propel your journey of self-discovery. Perhaps, my dear, the truth right now is that although you long to live from love, you don't feel loving much of the time and your heart is often closed to yourself and others.'

'That's for sure,' Gigi agreed.

'Good. Your acknowledgment brings your awareness into

alignment with your inner truth. Then you can progress to the next stage of self-mastery – identifying the emotional reactions that thwart your ability to open your heart and taking a clear-eyed look at the hold they have over you.

'Then you're ready for the next stage – the stage you were working on during your jump – accepting your emotions so they can flow easily instead of getting stuck or keeping you in reaction. In this stage, you can discover that letting your emotions flow is less uncomfortable than avoiding or indulging them.'

Gigi nodded, thinking of all the times when she'd tried hard not to feel something or had gone the opposite direction, wallowing in the emotion until it overtook her whole life.

Suddenly chilled in the gathering darkness, she shivered. Maya pointed her weed-strewn wand at the bank of the river, and a bonfire appeared nearby, shooting out rainbow-colored sparks. Gigi gratefully warmed her hands, heartened by its cheerful crackling.

Illuminated by the fire's multicolored glow, Maya went on. 'When you reach the next turn of the spiral you consciously begin to make choices that align with your heart. In doing this, you use LIQUID to identify and release the fear-based false beliefs that originally spawned your emotions. Then you replace these beliefs with wisdom from your impartial observer.

'Finally, you achieve the level of awareness necessary to rewrite those parts of your script that trigger negative emotions. From this vantage point, you are able to witness that your movement through the spiral, while sometimes unpleasant, was essential and has freed you from unconscious reaction. You are now able to live from a place of unconditional love and compassion.'

Gigi nodded. 'I think I understand. Much as I'd like it to, self-awareness doesn't occur all at once. In fact – although I hate to admit it – even though I've thought of myself as a very aware person, until recently I can see I have been going around in circles.'

'True,' Maya agreed.

'So I have to slow down and allow each stage of awareness to build the foundation for the next,' Gigi continued.

'Yes!' Maya said excitedly, standing up on her log and performing a graceful pirouette. 'And you can spend as long as you need to in each stage. You'll know you're ready to advance when you truly *experience* your new wisdom rather than just knowing it intellectually.'

Gigi felt excitement building inside her. She knew she'd been in a rut before attending Remedial Angel Training. She could see that although she might have advanced in small ways along the spiral, she'd been basically tracing and retracing her steps for a long time. She couldn't wait to embark on the journey with her new understanding.

The fire suddenly darkened, and Maya appeared in front of it, looming over Gigi like a phantom. 'But beware of your impatience, my sweet,' she intoned, her shadow casting Gigi into darkness. 'Impatience, especially when coupled with fear, can create detours that seriously delay your progress.'

Gigi nodded wordlessly.

Maya returned to her log and the fire blazed cheerfully once again. 'Remember that each step along the spiral path provides additional strength necessary to break the spell of forgetfulness,' Maya said. 'You must have compassion for yourself as you bravely walk your spiral. Use your awareness to notice what you are doing as you move through your life. Without judgment, see if what you are doing is congruent with your ascent up the spiral. I realize that this constant vigilance can feel exhausting at times, but remember: With each step you are drawing closer to the truth of *you* as an essential aspect of the Divine Mystery.'

And with that, she dove into the stream and disappeared. Instantly, the fire was extinguished, leaving only smoldering embers in its place. Violet-colored smoke curled upward to spell out a message: 'Keystone 8: Patience is the fastest way to the authentic self.'

Gigi's pulse fluttered wildly in her ears as she realized she was alone in the dark woods, armed only with the keystones. She wished Buck were here. She was sure his solid, capable presence would comfort her now. Not to mention his warm hands and oh-so-tender lips. Where was he? Had he landed the plane successfully?

Gigi's cast members called out conflicting advice as she searched her mind for options for what to do next. Should she find a safe place to settle in for the night, or strike out on the path again? But what if it just led her in the same circle? Were there really wild animals in the woods?

Calling on the wisdom of her impartial observer, Gigi willed herself to re-enter the moment. 'The present moment is all there is,' she muttered to herself. She took a deep breath, feeling her feet on the ground and looking at the silent forest around her. Really, there was nothing scary in the moment. *Nothing except my cast members, coming up with wild scenarios and panicky decisions,* she realized. In the moment, she was simply standing in the woods.

Gigi let go of all thoughts and just stood there, listening to the rushing of the stream and feeling the cool night air on her face. And in that moment, she knew what she had to do. She had to follow the path again, but this time with intent and awareness. She would be patient and notice what she was doing without judgment, gently bringing herself back to center whenever she needed to.

'I can count on myself,' she said aloud with dawning confidence. 'I'm sure that when I'm not stumbling toward an imagined outcome like last time when I was trying to find Godfreys (who was probably just a vision egging me on), the path will expand into a spiral.' And however long it took, that spiral would lead her where she wanted to go.

But where *did* she want to go?

A great horned owl hooted from a nearby tree, startling her. She looked up and saw its eyes glowing violet in the darkness. 'Travel into the heart of your authenticity,' hooted the owl. 'You cannot know what is going to happen. Simply put one foot in front of the other.' Then it flew off.

'Okay,' said Gigi. She stood, squared her shoulders, and walked slowly and deliberately toward the path.

Chapter Thirteen

Focusing on placing one foot in front of the other and staying present in the moment, Gigi followed the path through the woods once more. This time she did not stumble or trip since she was aware of her surroundings. Her senses seemed heightened, and even though it was dark she had no trouble seeing.

After a while, she realized that the path was not circling back around to the stream as it had done previously, but taking a turn uphill.

I'm on the spiral! she crowed inwardly, with a surge of excitement.

It felt good to stride along the gradual upward slope, sensing her feet as they struck the ground and listening to her slightly labored breathing. Occasional sounds from the forest prompted her cast to begin creating scenarios, but she left them behind as she continued forward in the present. The moment a thought would form, it was gone. It felt wonderfully refreshing to be free of plaguing voices and simply *be*.

After what could have been one hour or three – Gigi's sense of time had altered since she was not tracking every minute in her mind –she saw a clearing and realized she'd arrived at a rock outcropping. Stepping out onto it, she looked out over an endless sea of trees, tipped with silver from the light of a rising moon. It was so beautiful that it made her want to cry. Realizing her legs were tired, she sank onto a boulder to enjoy the view.

As if her body's stillness had prompted thoughts to re-enter her mind, Gigi was suddenly assailed with longing for Buck. She wished he were here with her. What was he doing right now? Did he miss her? And honestly, did it even matter?

She knew she was approaching the end of the Remedial Angel Training course, and what would happen after that? She and Buck would presumably go back to their separate realities on different parts of the continent – if he really existed in waking life – and she'd be alone again.

Alone! The word tugged her down into murky thoughts of a dark future. Suddenly she felt exhausted and unable to maintain her handle on the present. She tried to drop into the moment again but was powerless against the surge of negative thoughts that overtook her. Giving in to fear and despair, she began to cry in deep, heaving sobs. Alone, alone, alone – she was destined to walk this path alone, forever!

Suddenly desperate to get out of this lonely wilderness, she bolted back onto the path and started running, half-blinded by tears. Branches tore at her hair, and roots reached out to trip her as she ran, but she didn't care. Dimly, her impartial observer noted that she had fallen out of awareness and was turning against herself, but she couldn't seem to stop.

Finally, out of breath, throat sore from sobbing, and eyes nearly swollen shut, she slowed and looked for a place to rest. Eventually, she stumbled upon a large, mossy tree stump and sank onto it gratefully. Somehow, sitting on the stump comforted her enough to bring her back into the present, a process which happened naturally and gradually, as if her pupils were coming back into focus after being dilated.

'Whew,' Gigi sighed. 'That was intense. Okay, this is my opportunity to notice that I have stepped off my upward spiral and, without judgment, get back on the path of the keystones.' Saying that gave her a welcome feeling of empowerment, and she gave a little involuntary hop on the stump.

The stump emitted a loud groan.

Gigi froze, the hair on her neck standing up. Was there something hiding in the stump? Quickly, she drew her legs up and hugged her knees. Perhaps this was an animal's lair. But when the sound came again, she realized it was the creaking of old wood. In fact, the stump seemed to be sinking downward. Before she could leap off, the trunk completely gave way beneath her.

She was tumbling backward! She flung out her arms for support, but instead of hitting the ground as she'd expected, she kept falling, down, down, down. Wind whooshed in her ears and her limbs flailed, reaching only emptiness.

She landed on her rear end with a spine-jarring thump. Blackness surrounded her. Where was she? It felt like she'd fallen a long way. She struggled to catch her breath and wished she were somewhere else, anywhere but here. Maybe if she just willed away the darkness, she'd find herself somewhere more welcoming. Like a rat-infested alley on a deserted waterfront, for instance. Or in a junkyard, facing a rabid Doberman.

When she dared to look up, she found her eyes had adjusted to the gloom. She appeared to be in some sort of underground cave. Ghostly light filtered down from the moon above, illuminating eerie shapes and dark shadowed corners. Gigi felt frozen to the spot. This place was creepy. Maybe the fall had killed her and she was in the underworld. The chilly, dank air assailed her nostrils and made her shiver in cold and fright. All knowledge of being safe in the moment seemed to have fled.

Forcing her shaking legs to unfold, she stood. The light came from a large circular opening in the high ceiling of the cavern, partially obscured by fallen logs and debris. She looked up at it wistfully. That must be where she'd fallen from. It seemed very far away. She had no idea how she was going to get out of here. Giving in once again to despair, she sank to the ground and curled up in a fetal position.

A rustling sound shocked her upright. Where was it coming from? Due to the cavern's strange acoustics, she realized the sound could be right beside her – *oh God, please don't let it be a snake* – or quite far away. She listened with all her being and realized that it was echoing off the chamber walls from a distance, and it was approaching.

She could now hear distinct footsteps and a rasping sound

like someone or something breathing heavily. It was impossible to tell which direction the sounds were coming from or how far away they were. She looked around wildly for a weapon and spotted the dark form of what must be a large rock. After giving it a tentative kick to make sure it wasn't alive, she heaved it upward and crouched, ready to throw it at whatever grisly being was headed toward her.

Orange light appeared as the being approached through what must be a tunnel at the opposite end of the cavern. The light threw wavering shadows over everything and revealed glistening stalactites and stalagmites dripping with moisture.

Somewhere in Gigi's panicked mind, she registered that the cavern was really quite beautiful. But what was this glowing being? Was it a dragon breathing fire? An ogre brandishing a torch? Was it the specter of death arriving to take her away, spiriting her to the other side?

Worse. It was Susan. Gigi let out a hysterical laugh and dropped the stone, narrowly missing her toes. Susan squeaked in fright, jumped, and dropped the flashlight she'd been carrying. It rolled toward Gigi as she stood rooted to the spot on rubbery legs, and stopped halfway between them.

'Gigi?' Susan asked, voice quivery.

'Yeah, it's me,' Gigi answered, her voice sounding equally weak. She tottered over to the flashlight and set it on its end so the beam lit up the cavern. She was shocked to see Susan's unkempt appearance. She looked like she'd had as rough a time of it as Gigi had. Her hair was caked with mud and stuck out from her head at wild angles, her mascara was smudged under her eyes, her lips were chapped, and her flight suit was stained and torn.

Gigi had to admit to herself that she was glad to see Susan. Of course, she would have preferred to run into Buck or even Vinny, but the mere presence of another person was instantly comforting. Perhaps she wasn't dead, after all, and maybe between the two of them they could find a way out of here.

'So,' Gigi said, not knowing where to begin.

Susan ran a hand through her hair, and Gigi noticed a long, nasty-looking cut on her arm. Before she could ask about it, Susan asked in an overly casual tone, 'How did you get here?'

'I fell down a hole,' said Gigi. 'How about you? Are you okay?'

'Just taking a little detour,' said Susan, tossing her head in her accustomed disdainful gesture. 'I'm doing very well, thank you.'

So that's how it's going to be, thought Gigi. *Even though we might be the last two people alive, we're not going to be honest with each other.* Fine. Damned if she'd let Susan see how upset she'd been.

'Well, it's sure swell to run into you,' Gigi said aloud. 'I hope you've been getting as much out of the keystones as I have. The skydiving was really terrific, wasn't it?'

'Absolutely,' Susan said. 'I had the greatest time. It was completely exhilarating.'

'Did you land in the forest?' Gigi asked. 'Because that was really the best part of all. I've always had such an affinity for nature, you know, and it was so powerful to be one with the elements.'

'Yes, I landed in the forest, too,' said Susan. 'I have a lot of experience hiking and camping, so it didn't scare me at all. And of course I already knew about the spiral, because I've studied so much psychology.'

Gigi gave her a fake smile. 'But it's good to be reminded that advancement takes time, isn't it? And that we can't move forward simply on the strength of our intellectual knowledge. I mean, you have to really experience every stage to be able to move ahead.'

Susan gave a tight-lipped smile. 'Naturally.'

An awkward silence descended during which Gigi was acutely aware of the strangeness of their situation. To break the tension, she asked, 'How did you come across a flashlight?'

'It was in my pack,' Susan said, looking askance at Gigi. 'Didn't you have one in your pack, too?'

Gigi had no idea what pack Susan was talking about.

'The backpack that was attached to the parachute pack,' Susan clarified.

'Oh, of course I did!' Gigi said with what she hoped sounded like a careless laugh. 'But I had to leave the pack behind when the bear started chasing me. I had to run as fast as I could without extra weight.'

'You had to run from a bear?' Susan asked.

'Yeah, but it was no big deal. I used to be a track champ in high school,' said Gigi.

'I had a little run-in with a cougar, myself,' said Susan, holding up her injured arm. 'But I hit it on the head with the flashlight, and it ran away.'

'Stop right there,' commanded a male voice. Susan and Gigi froze while the voice echoed around and around the chamber.

Gigi's heart sank. What now? Was this cave the lair of a psycho killer who was going to drag them into his underground den filled with bones of dead women and make them watch while he hacked bits of them off and ate the flesh?

Laughter resounded as a figure came into view. 'Gigi, my dear, you really do have the most astonishing imagination,' said a familiar British voice.

'Godfreys,' Gigi breathed, knees weak with gratitude as she beheld his trim figure clad in mountain climbing gear and carrying a stout walking stick.

'I knew you'd come,' said Susan, trying unsuccessfully to cover her relief with her usual superciliousness. 'Great. Tell us how we can get out of here.'

Godfreys raised an eyebrow. 'I'll tell you what you need to do, but it is up to each of you to make your own way out,' he replied.

Gigi sighed, heavy with the feeling that this was not going to be easy.

'Have a seat,' Godfreys said, gesturing with his arm. Three large rocks appeared in a circle around the flashlight, and they each settled on one.

'Now, my dear girls, it is time to introduce Maya's next keystone,' said Godfreys. 'The first part of the lesson has to do with candor.'

Gigi winced. Did Godfreys know that she'd just been fibbing up a storm?

'First, let me ask you a question,' Godfreys said. 'When you speak do you reflect your true thoughts and feelings all of the time?'

'Of course not,' said Susan stiffly. 'They're private.'

'No,' admitted Gigi.

'Most of the time?' Godfreys asked.

They both shook their heads.

'Some of the time?'

'Maybe,' said Gigi, and Susan nodded in agreement.

'So you tell the truth of what you are thinking and feeling every now and then,' Godfreys said. 'Now why do you suppose that is? After all, other living entities on earth express themselves authentically, do they not? Trees don't apologize for their falling leaves in autumn or their bare branches in winter. Dogs do not pretend to be nice to other dogs or people whom they perceive as a threat. Rabbits nibble on vegetable gardens even though it makes the owners angry. So why do humans, who consider themselves so evolved, avoid expressing their truth?'

'Because we have a societal agreement to say pleasant things and not make others uncomfortable,' said Gigi.

'And because we're afraid that if we say what we really think or feel, we'll expose ourselves to judgment or censure,' added Susan.

'Mmm, yes,' agreed Godfreys. 'You both seem well aware of reasons not to speak with candor. And you demonstrated that marvelously just before I arrived, did you not?'

They nodded reluctantly, exchanging a swift embarrassed glance.

'And yet not speaking candidly causes you to suffer, doesn't it?' Godfreys asked. 'When you are untrue to yourself, you feel uncomfortable on many levels. Physically, you might experience a tightening of the throat or a constriction in your heart. Emotionally, you may feel sad or angry because you have abandoned yourself. Mentally, you know you are not being true to yourself. And spiritually, it decreases your awareness of yourself as part of the Divine Mystery.'

'I see that,' said Gigi softly, looking at her boots. 'But it's scary to share what I'm thinking, 'cause it isn't always what the other person wants to hear.'

'Regardless, it may be what you need to express,' said Godfreys. 'Using your voice truthfully allows you to drop your mask and express yourself on deeper and deeper levels, no matter what others think.'

'And that's precisely what we were *not* doing before you arrived,' Susan concluded. 'Right, Gigi?'

'Right,' Gigi said. Their eyes connected and they smiled ruefully at each other.

'Precisely,' agreed Godfreys. 'And telling the truth will allow you to find your way out of the cave. So I suggest you begin now.' With a soft grunt, he hoisted himself up with his walking stick and used it to write with moonbeams in the air: 'Keystone 9: Use your voice to speak the truth.'

The wisps of moonbeams hovered in the air as Godfreys walked away.

'Wait!' called Gigi, but he had already disappeared into the shadows.

Gigi and Susan eyed each other warily.

'All right, it's truth time, I guess,' said Susan finally.

'Guess so,' said Gigi, unwilling to begin. Could she really tell Susan how scared she'd been in the forest? Worse, could she actually voice what she thought of her?

Susan cleared her throat. 'Well, if I'm going to be truthful, I have to admit I was crazy scared of skydiving,' she said.

Gigi giggled. 'Me too!'

'And landing alone in the forest didn't really improve my spirits,' Susan added. 'I lied about being good at hiking and camping. I'm more of a city girl at heart.'

'Yeah, me too. I like well-groomed parks with paved walking trails,' said Gigi. 'And I didn't run away from a bear. I just didn't realize there were supplies in the pack so I didn't bring it with me. I guess there was no cougar, either, was there?'

'Actually, that part was true,' said Susan.

'No way,' said Gigi, not believing her. 'Come on, we're supposed to tell the truth.'

'That *is* the truth,' Susan insisted. 'I can't help it if you don't believe me. And I don't care.'

'Yes, you do,' Gigi said. 'You care so much about what others think that you can hardly stand it.'

'What do you mean by that?' asked Susan, bristling.

'Oh, come on, Susan,' said Gigi. 'That know-it-all attitude has to be a cover-up for feeling inferior. With all your so-called psychological expertise, you must realize that.'

'Fine, I admit I do use my intelligence as a shield at times,' said Susan. 'But at least I'm not a total loser. You think you're so smart and attractive, but you've obviously had no idea how to make good choices for yourself. I could tell how insecure you were the moment I met you.'

Gigi felt rage building inside her. How dare Susan make assumptions about her? 'You have no idea about my life!' she shouted. 'Here's the truth – I can't stand you! You're a stuck-up, pompous, supercilious, mean-spirited smarty-pants! You might be book smart, but you're an emotional infant. I knew that the moment I met *you*!'

This was easier than Gigi had thought it would be. It felt great to unburden the feelings she'd held in about Susan for so long.

Susan looked like she was about to explode. 'You think you're so evolved, Gigi, but you're a pathetic little...'

'Enough!'

A puff of pink smoke swirled in the beam of the flashlight, filling the cavern with the scent of roses. When it cleared, Maya was sitting, cool as a cucumber, on the rock Godfreys had recently vacated.

'Enough, my sweets,' she said. 'It's clear that you have both begun to express the truth of your feelings, but you need to hear about the rest of the process.'

Gigi's heart was pounding, and she took a few breaths to calm herself. Susan was still looking daggers at her, but she ignored her and focused on Maya, whose violet eyes seemed to glow in the semi-darkness.

'First, tell me what that felt like,' she said.

'It felt pretty good,' said Gigi. 'It was powerful to finally express myself to Susan.'

'Powerful, yes,' said Susan. 'But I have a lot more to say.'

Gigi shot her a look.

'So by accessing your anger, you both felt powerful,' Maya clarified.

They nodded.

'Understood. And yet being angry uses an excessive amount of energy, does it not?' Maya asked. 'After a while, anger saps your authenticity and distances you from the truth of your being. And that's far from powerful. So now it's time to look at what is beneath the anger – to go deeper.'

Gigi wasn't sure what Maya meant by going deeper, but she definitely agreed that getting riled up in order to express herself might not be a habit she wanted to get into.

'You see, my dears, when people first begin to express the truth after living from a state of repression, it is common for the truth to come out in an abrasive way – and in fact you often pridefully boast that you are going to confront someone,' Maya said. 'Obviously, you two have strong judgments – and possibly even projections – about each other. You've been holding in these thoughts for the sake of politeness, and to continue appearing to be the good girls you want to be.

'But as I mentioned, expressing your feelings angrily may ultimately hurt you rather than help you. True communication must come from the heart.'

Gigi sat in silent contemplation, feeling the truth of Maya's words.

'Now, tell me this, my dears: What do you think it would feel like to be truthful and responsible about your expression and not hurt someone else?' Maya asked.

'Better,' muttered Gigi, although she had trouble imagining speaking to Susan from her heart.

'I know this may take time,' Maya said gently. 'It is all part of the spiral of self-awareness. Right now, you have ascended to the first stage of candor by opening your throats to let the truth come out.

'However, as you noticed, your unused voices were ragged and rough. As you ascend along the spiral of learning to speak your truth, you will discover how to express yourself in a more measured manner. Part of the reason you were so strident in voicing your truth just now was that you felt defensive because you were afraid.

'As you ascend the spiral, you will learn to let go of fear and stop justifying your actions. Remember that fear only serves you when you are in immediate physical danger.'

'Like when the cougar pounced on me,' said Susan.

'Yes. But fear has no place in your authentic expression. Once you let go of it, you will no longer need to defend yourself, and you will stop blaming anyone – including yourself – for how you experience the world. You will be able to express your integrity easily, regardless of your concern for the opinions and expectations of others. Doesn't that sound delightful, my doves?'

They nodded, their anger finally deflated.

'It is essential to keep in mind that you cannot control the reactions of others, only the way you express yourself,' Maya added. 'You must take responsibility for the words you speak by delivering your honest messages from a place of kindness.'

Maya looked from Susan to Gigi with a gentle smile. 'Now, my dears, I ask you to access the place of heartfelt truth inside you. Take charge of your expression and let it flow from your heart. Advance to the next stage on the spiral of candor.'

Poof! She disappeared as suddenly as she had come.

The two women again sat alone, eyeing each other warily.

'Maybe we should take a little private time to access our heartfelt truth,' Gigi suggested after a while.

'Sure, that sounds like a good idea,' Susan agreed hastily.

They hurried off into separate areas, relieved to have a minute to themselves. Gigi concentrated on returning to the present moment and imagined her heart glowing with love. She let the glow slide up her throat and pictured it emanating from her mouth in the form of truthful words. When she felt calm and centered, she returned to her boulder. Soon Susan joined her, and their eyes met in understanding.

'Gigi, I apologize for the harsh words I said to you,' Susan began. 'Although they expressed my judgments truthfully – and possibly my projections about you as well – they were not likely the *truth*. Of course I don't know much about your history, and I made assumptions.

'To be honest, I disliked you because I felt intimidated by you. You seemed like the sort of carefree, fun person I'd like to be. And instead of voicing that, I treated you coolly and put on a mask of superiority.'

Gigi realized her mouth had fallen open and closed it with a snap. Susan had been intimidated by her? Unbelievable!

'Thanks, Susan,' she said softly. She took her time in

responding, imagining each word glowing with the light of truth. 'It's refreshing to hear your truthful words, especially because they mirror my own experience. I felt completely intimidated by you and decided you were just the kind of person I couldn't stand. I treated you badly and had mean thoughts about you. But the truth is I felt badly about myself, so I blamed you for being the kind of person I wanted to be.'

'Wow,' said Susan.

'Yeah,' agreed Gigi.

'Jeeze,' said Susan.

'Uh-huh,' added Gigi.

They broke out into giggles. Gigi felt giddy with the relief of expressing herself and the delight of knowing the truth about Susan's experience. They were exactly the same! It was amazing.

'I think we should become friends,' Gigi added, surprising herself.

'Me, too,' Susan agreed. She stuck out her hand, then changed her mind and went over to envelop Gigi in an awkward side hug.

'I didn't really have a rash,' Gigi said. 'So you don't have to worry about catching it.'

'I knew you didn't,' Susan rejoined with a grin.

Feeling suddenly shy, Gigi stood up and brushed off her flight suit. 'So now maybe we can work together to find a way out of this place, huh?' she said.

'Yes, please, let's get out of here,' Susan agreed quickly. 'I think that's what Godfreys must have meant when he said telling the truth would allow us to find a way out.'

'Funny, I always think of *avoiding* the truth as a way out,' Gigi said. 'But I'm sure the truth can lead us in the right direction.'

Businesslike, Susan took up the flashlight. 'Okay, since there is only one light, I propose that we stick together.'

'Never divide your search party,' Gigi intoned pompously.

Susan giggled. It was really good to hear her laugh. Gigi had wondered before if she was even capable of giggling.

'Let's go this way,' Susan said, beaming the flashlight along the stalactites and stalagmites and pointing it to an opening in the far corner.

Gigi felt an immediate reaction in her body, like a fist closing around her stomach. From nowhere, dread assailed her. She was certain her true intuition was telling her not to go that way. But, sure of herself, Susan was already picking her way along the rock-strewn cavern toward the opening.

'Um, Susan, I'm not sure this is the way to go,' called Gigi, stumbling after her in the semi-darkness.

Susan stopped, turning the flashlight on Gigi. 'Really? Why not?' she asked.

Gigi gulped. She didn't want to mess up their newfound friendship, but the feeling of dread was growing stronger. Remembering the inner prompting that got her and Buck off the marshy planet, she knew she had to listen to her body's warning.

'I just have a bad feeling about it,' she explained.

Susan cocked her head quizzically. 'Maybe you're just afraid because it's an unknown,' she suggested.

'Maybe,' Gigi agreed half-heartedly.

'Logically, it's the best way to go,' Susan went on. 'I came from the tunnel at the other side of the cavern, and I know that at the end of it is a high, slippery wall. I doubt we could climb it. And as far as I know, there's no other way in or out.'

'Except the hole at the top,' Gigi said.

'Well, yes, but there's no way to get out through that,' Susan said. 'I understand your trepidation, but I really think we should go this way.'

'Okay,' Gigi said, giving in. Susan's reasoning was, of course, impeccable, and her own objection was based on nothing but a feeling. She walked just behind Susan, following her steps so she wouldn't trip.

When they reached the tunnel opening, an acrid smell assailed them. Gigi's dread increased until she felt like she could barely breathe. She couldn't go through with this, no matter how much she wanted to placate Susan.

'Coming?' Susan asked, pausing at the entrance.

'No,' Gigi said. And the moment she said it, the fist squeezing her innards eased and she felt a joyful lightness.

'Congratulations, my dear!' trilled Maya's voice. 'You just learned the next component of candor: how to truthfully say that small but powerful word, "No!"'

Gigi looked around but couldn't see Maya anywhere, though her voice sounded close by. Then, robes swirling, she emerged from the tunnel, nearly bumping into Susan who was standing at the entrance.

Maya laughed at their confused expressions and said, 'Let me explain. Your cast of characters – those troublemakers! – often encourage you to say yes even if agreeing might cause you to suffer. They have a lot of reasons for you to agree against your better judgment – fitting in, not wanting to upset someone, looking like a good girl, and so on.

'But the courage to say "no", voiced from an honest awareness of what is right for you, aligns you with the truth in your heart. On the other hand, every time your mouth says yes even though your heart is screaming no, you sacrifice a precious bit of your authenticity.'

'So saying no is a good thing?' Gigi asked. She'd never thought about it that way before.

'It can be,' said Maya. 'When, as you just did, the "no" is an authentic reflection of your truth.'

'I've sometimes gone the other way and said no automatically when yes would have been a better choice,' said Susan.

'That's because "no" became a defense for you,' said Maya. 'Saying yes was scary for you because you'd have to reveal a part of yourself. As my dear colleague Mitchell would say, it's the flip side of the same coin.'

'It's definitely going to take some practice to learn truthful no-saying,' reflected Gigi. 'I've been the quintessential yes-woman, even to the point of risking my integrity.'

'And your health,' added Maya. 'You worked yourself to the bone because you didn't want to look bad by saying no at work, at home, or with your friends. And you couldn't even let yourself off the hook with strangers. Remember the old woman on the train when you were on your way to Blessings?'

'The cranky old bat who fell into me, then made me go get water for her so I missed my chance to tell the conductor my bags had been stolen?' Gigi asked.

'Yes, her,' Maya said. 'Or, rather, me.'

Gigi gasped. Those violet eyes... Oh no, she'd just called Maya a cranky old bat! But Maya's eyes were twinkling with mirth.

'So you set me up,' Gigi said, shaking her head.

'I did, my dear. And can you see now how that was a situation where you could have said no in order to take care of your own needs?'

'But I was too stuck in trying to prove to her, or rather you, that I wasn't one of those good-for-nothing youngsters,' Gigi said, slapping her forehead. 'Wow.'

'So just out of curiosity, what made you not want to go this way?' Susan asked, gesturing at the tunnel.

'Just a feeling,' said Gigi, then realized she could tell the truth. 'Actually, I had a bad experience in a tunnel once. When I approached this tunnel, I felt kind of like I was having a panic attack. I sensed danger. And the truth is I couldn't tell if it was a reaction to the past or a real gift of intuition.'

'*Is* there danger in there?' Susan asked Maya.

'That doesn't matter,' Maya answered. 'What is important is that Gigi got past her fear of saying no and was willing to trust her instincts.' She turned to Gigi.

'Later, as you ascend the spiral of candor, you can learn to distinguish between dread based on real intuition or relevant facts and dread that stems from past experiences.'

'So the dread from past experiences might hold me back if I let it?' Gigi asked.

'Yes, my dear. It's like walking in the woods and seeing a bear. The bear frightens you, but you associate your fear with the woods, so every time you walk in the woods you are still afraid. You associate the feeling of fear with the woods itself, and it can last long after the actual memory has faded.'

'Kind of like a Pavlovian response,' murmured Susan.

'You mean like an automatic emotional reaction?' Gigi asked.

'Precisely, girls! You are getting it now,' Maya said. 'The point is you don't have to be right about saying no. You'll learn to set appropriate boundaries as you gain experience. For now, I think, you are ready to move on.'

'How do we get out of here?' Gigi asked.

'Good point,' said Susan.

'Out of the hole in the roof, of course – the same way you arrived,' said Maya.

'But we can't possibly get up there,' Susan objected.

'Climb up a moonbeam,' Maya suggested. 'Meanwhile, I really must fly.' And spreading her arms, she drifted upward, twirled around them blowing kisses, then zoomed up to the hole in the ceiling and flew off.

Susan and Gigi gave each other skeptical looks.

'I've never climbed a moonbeam before,' Gigi said uncertainly. 'But I guess it's worth a try.'

'It wouldn't be the strangest thing that's happened during this course,' Susan added.

They made their way to stand directly under the opening where the moonlight streamed in. Gigi tried to grab a moonbeam, but of course her hand went right through it.

'Hmm,' said Susan, standing back to analyze the situation. 'I can't see how we're supposed to climb up a stream of insubstantial light.'

'Maybe we need to change our perspective,' suggested Gigi.

'Remember when we experienced no boundaries? If we are made of light just like the moonbeam, then we can climb up it with no problem.'

'True,' agreed Susan. 'And since Godfreys said candor was our way out of here, maybe we need to connect with each other as openly as possible and see if we can get the boundaries to dissolve.'

'Sounds as crazy and as reasonable as all of this does,' said Gigi. 'Let's try it.'

Facing each other, the women stared into each other's eyes. As she broadened her perspective, Gigi began to see glimmers of light all around her. Gradually, the boundary between their bodies began to blur, spread and disappear. Everything melded together into shimmering light.

Of one accord, Gigi and Susan stepped up onto a slanted moonbeam. It was made of the same light particles that comprised their bodies, so it was easy to simply walk up it. In fact, Gigi didn't even feel like she was walking. She was simply moving along with the light, higher and higher toward its source.

Gigi felt Susan melt away, and as the glimmering lights began to fade she looked around her, expecting to see the same spot in the forest where she'd fallen before. Instead, however, she was standing on a rocky beach. Susan was nowhere to be seen, and Gigi sensed that her dreamtime had taken her somewhere else now that they had resolved their issues.

Gigi gasped at the beauty of the scene before her. Moonlight grazed the crashing waves and slicked the rocks with silver. Obsidian clouds huddled on the dark horizon like a herd of sleeping elephants. Invigorated by the wild beauty of it all, Gigi inhaled the salty air, and its briny perfume smelled familiar.

She was suddenly certain that she had landed on the beach at Blessings.

Chapter Fourteen

Gigi spread her arms and let the brisk wind blow through her, refreshing her spirit. She was filled with joy – the joy of simply being, of standing here on the wet sand with the ocean whispering its secrets as the waves crashed toward her. She had made it back to Blessings! That must mean she was close to finishing Remedial Angel Training. After all, there were only – what – three more keystones? And already, after all she'd been through, she felt utterly renewed, as if the old Gigi had been cast off like a snakeskin, leaving her as tender and innocent as a peeled grape.

After a time, she realized that, joy or no joy, she was cold. She wondered vaguely what she was supposed to do next, but the thought did not burden her too much. Hugging her arms to her body for warmth, she began walking along the edge of the sea. Rocks crunched under her boots and the wind whipped through her hair (her poor hair! what she had inflicted on it lately!). She felt as wild and free as the lone seagull swooping along the wind currents.

As she approached a looming outcropping of rocks, Gigi thought she saw a form detach from the shadows and move toward her. A shiver passed through her and she wondered if this was a time when fear was necessary because she was in physical danger, or if she could simply be in the moment and see what happened. Realizing she felt more curious than afraid, she chose the latter.

The figure drew closer, revealing itself to be a tall person – a man. Thank goodness! After her recent adventures, she was sure she could deal with a mere human being with no problem, even if he proved to be threatening. She moved toward him slowly, noticing that he seemed to be moving in a strange, jerky manner. Was he drunk? Injured? She wondered how much CPR she remembered and hoped it was enough. Was he going to collapse at her feet? But as she moved closer, she saw that he was walking with crutches.

'Buck!' she cried, her heart singing. She couldn't believe it – he was really here! How romantic – reunited after all their tribulations, and on a beach in the moonlight, no less!

She hurtled toward him and opened her arms – but just before she embraced him, something in his demeanor stopped her short. Maybe it was only that balancing on crutches on the slippery rocks made him cautious, but he seemed reticent, and not at all as delighted to see her as she would have liked.

'Gigi,' Buck answered hoarsely, his face shadowed by his hat. He looked haggard, and her heart swelled with compassion.

'Are you all right?' she asked.

He nodded. 'I'll do. And you?'

'I'm great!' Gigi trilled, twirling around happily. 'I've been through some pretty crazy, intense stuff, as I'm sure you have, but I feel terrific!'

Buck watched her with a smile, but his eyes looked sad. She stopped in mid-twirl, suddenly realizing something really was wrong.

'What is it?' she asked. 'Aren't you happy to see me?' She reached out to touch him, but he didn't respond.

'Of course I'm happy to see you,' Buck said. 'I'm just exhausted. I've been through some rough stuff.'

Gigi felt marginally comforted, but it was hardly the passionate reunion she craved. 'Let's get you someplace where you can rest,' she said. 'And I think we could both use warming up.'

'But it's the middle of the night, and I have no idea where we are,' said Buck.

'I think I know,' said Gigi. 'Follow me.' She thought she'd glimpsed the road Godfreys had taken her on when she'd arrived in Blessings, high above the beach. And the town must be just beyond. It would be a long walk for Buck, but maybe they could hitch a ride.

After an arduous climb and one near-disastrous slip, they reached the road. The wind sliced through Gigi, seeming suddenly colder.

'I don't think I can do it,' said Buck. 'It's hell walking on these dang things, and I'm pretty near spent.'

Just then, headlights appeared around a bend. Gigi waved her hands in the air, hoping the driver was someone who was both sane and sympathetic.

The car slowed, and when it pulled up next to them Gigi realized it was very familiar. The driver got out and walked around to open the door for Buck, and she shot Godfreys a grateful smile. He was dressed once again in his chauffeur uniform, complete with cap.

He gave her a nod and a grin. 'Going to the Magical Theatre, I presume?' he asked.

'Absolutely,' said Gigi, returning his grin. And suddenly she realized there was no place she would rather go right now. It felt like going home.

Buck was looking from one to the other, a puzzled expression on his face. 'You've been here before?' he asked Gigi.

'Yes,' Gigi answered, smiling. 'This is where it all began. And it feels great to be back.'

Godfreys helped Buck into the car. Gigi slid next to him and rested her head on his shoulder. It was good to feel the sheer physicality of him again. But he didn't seem to be responding. She wished he would put his arm around her or lean his cheek against her head, or something. Anything to show he wanted her as much as she wanted him.

But he sat looking straight ahead. Maybe he was simply too exhausted and overwhelmed to be able to respond, Gigi thought. Yes, that must be it. She didn't know what he'd been through while she was trekking through the woods and talking with

Susan in the cave. He'd been facing his own demons, for sure, and he seemed quite a bit the worse for wear.

She patted his leg reassuringly, and he shot her one of his heart-stopping grins. She felt somewhat reassured.

Godfreys steered the car through the sleeping streets of Blessings to the Magical Theatre. The theater façade was illuminated with spotlights. The carved exterior looked very grand, and was in considerably better shape than when Gigi had been here before.

Interesting, she thought. *I wonder if somehow the restoration of this Magical Theatre is linked to my own inner restoration – which is changing the course of my own production in the Magical Theatre of life on earth.* Though a tad mind-bending, the thought was intriguing.

'The Magical Theatre?' Buck asked. 'But isn't the Magical Theatre the whole earth?'

'Yes,' Godfreys said. 'It's both. This theater represents everything that is possible in the game of life on earth.'

'Oh,' said Buck, looking confused.

Godfreys helped them out of the car and led them toward the door. As they approached, the darkened marquee burst into light. In Gothic script, it read:

TONIGHT! Keystone 10: Live from your heart to express your soul!

Starring Remedial Angels Gigi and Buck.

Plus, BONUS ACT! Keystone 11: Acceptance.

Gigi and Buck stopped to read the marquee. Gigi felt elated to see their names up there together. It was clear what Maya meant by Keystone 10. By loving Buck, she would be able to express her soul – which meant he was her soul mate. She'd finally found him! It was all she could do not to dance with glee, but she comported herself with the dignity that seemed appropriate to being the star of a Magical Theatre production.

Buck didn't look as overjoyed as Gigi felt, but again she attributed it to exhaustion.

'Too bad we're still in our icky old flight suits,' Gigi said as they stepped through the doorway into the mosaic foyer. 'Seems like the stars should have more glamorous attire.'

'Good point!' called a familiar voice, and Mitchell whisked out from behind the red velvet-curtained wall. He stopped short when he saw their weary, grimy faces and filthy flight suits. 'Oh, my. Oh, dear. Well, follow me... we don't have long. The audience is waiting.'

'Sorry,' said Godfreys. 'Things took a bit longer than planned. I'll go explain to the audience and ask them to be patient.'

'Audience?' Gigi and Buck asked simultaneously, exchanging panicked glances.

'Ten minutes,' said Mitchell to Godfreys, ignoring them. 'Luckily I have magic at my disposal, 'cause we're gonna need it. Now march!'

Gigi and Buck let Mitchell lead them through the velvet curtain – *so that was how you got past: you simply walked through it as if it weren't there!* – and down a series of dimly lit hallways. Buck struggled to keep up while Gigi struggled to make sense of what was happening.

Mitchell opened a door with their names written on it inside a big gold star. The dressing room was brilliantly lit and swarming with glamorous-looking women brandishing fabulous outfits, makeup and hairbrushes.

'Okay, ladies, let's go!' Mitchell cried, clapping his hands. 'We have seven and a half minutes, so snap to it!'

'Um, Mitchell,' began Gigi, as a team of unnaturally beautiful women descended on her and began stripping her, dressing her, and doing her hair and makeup in a whirlwind that reminded her of those scenes in *Bewitched!* when Samantha would wiggle her nose then clean her house in five seconds flat.

'Mmm?' asked Mitchell distractedly as he held up a black tie under Buck's chin and shook his head, frowning.

'What's happening?' she asked.

'You and Buck have your performance tonight, of course. Didn't you read the marquee?' Mitchell said impatiently. 'Maya's using you two as the stars to illustrate her lesson on connections.'

'Why us?' Buck asked.

'Because you two are learning the truth of love. At least, that's what she told me,' said Mitchell.

A tiny man in a black beret stuck his head through the door and shouted into a miniature bullhorn, 'Two minutes!'

Gigi felt the whirlwind of hands around her increase in speed then suddenly stop.

'Done!' chorused the makeup artists, hair stylists and dressers before vanishing into thin air.

Gigi stared at Buck. He was clad in a perfectly cut black Western-style jacket over a crisp white shirt and pressed Wranglers. His banged-up old hat had disappeared, replaced by a sharp black Stetson. He looked incredibly hot. Her heart melted, sending a rush of hot lava cursing through her veins, and she felt herself practically swooning toward him.

She realized he was staring at her too, and she turned to look in the mirror. She gasped. She looked amazing! Her auburn hair was piled on her head in the kind of casual, wispy updo she never seemed to get right at home; her eyes looked huge, accented with smoky shadow and miraculously lengthening mascara; and her scarlet lips contrasted beautifully with the slinky black dress that somehow managed to cling in all the right places. Best of all, her feet were clad in to-die-for silver stiletto sandals that just had to be Jimmy Choos!

'Thanks, Mitchell,' said Gigi, throwing her arms around him. 'You really are amazing.' She felt a flood of gratitude and realized all her old animosity toward him had vanished.

Mitchell smiled at her as he surveyed them with satisfaction. 'You're welcome. Luckily, you two clean up well.'

Buck cleared his throat. 'You do, anyway,' he said to Gigi.

'Now all we need to do is get rid of *those*,' Mitchell

pronounced, snapping his fingers at Buck's crutches. They vanished instantly.

'Hold on!' said Buck, balancing precariously on one leg. 'I can't walk on only one good leg!'

'So lean on Gigi's sexy shoulder,' said Mitchell, with a wink at Gigi. 'Now let's go.'

Buck cast a despairing look at Gigi, who stepped up to him and put her hand around his waist. Reluctantly, he draped an arm over her shoulder, and they made their way out of the room and into the wings backstage.

'I know this is good for me,' Buck muttered in Gigi's ear. 'You know how much I hate having to ask for help. Maya set this up, I'm sure of it.'

Gigi shot him a sympathetic smile. 'I know, but you're doing great.'

They arrived just in time to hear thunderous applause – how many people were out there, anyway? – and see Maya arrive by sliding down a golden rope from the ceiling. She was clad in brilliant robes of gold to match the rope, and even her braids shone with a golden hue. In contrast, her crème-de-cocoa skin gleamed and her violet eyes shone vibrant beams of light wherever she looked.

'Welcome, my beloveds,' she sang, opening her arms to the audience, who went wild hooting and stamping. 'Welcome, one and all: those of you who are still in your angelic forms, those who have graduated from Remedial Angel Training and are here to support the newer students, and the rest of you who have been going through this latest course with me.

'I'm delighted to introduce tonight's opening act, "The Gigi and Buck Show". After their demonstration, be sure to stay for the final keystone – a not-to-be-missed extravaganza. But first – our stars!'

Maya dramatically flung out her arm toward Gigi and Buck in the wings, fastening her laser gaze on them. Drawn like a magnet toward Maya, Gigi supported Buck as they made their slow progress onstage.

'These two lucky students will help me demonstrate my next lesson – and will also be joined by a special surprise guest,' Maya cried.

She swept them into a rose-scented embrace, then turned them to face the crowd. They stood awkwardly, trying to smile, as an audience of thousands rose to their feet and applauded them. The tiers of seats seemed to go on and on, up and up into the sky. In fact, this looked a lot like a gigantic version of the auditorium in the sky where they'd attended Maya's first lectures. But instead of being shabby, it was gilded to a stunning beauty that glowed in the phosphorescent lighting.

Gigi's knees felt weak, and she was afraid they might give out. Luckily, just then three jewel-encrusted chairs appeared, two of them flanking a more elaborate seat on a crystal dais in the center. Maya gestured for them to sit down in the side chairs before gracefully ascending the dais and sinking onto her throne.

The applause died out, followed by an expectant silence.

'My precious angels,' Maya began, her voice effortlessly booming out into the crowd. 'Are you now beginning to feel the unwavering force of your divine spark?'

'Yes!' rang out a chorus of voices from the audience.

'And do you know why that is?'

The audience waited in expectant silence.

'Because you are starting – just starting, mind you – to live from your heart and deepen your connection with your soul,' Maya pronounced, pausing for effect.

'Until recently, those of you in Remedial Angel Training have identified who you are through your parts rather than your wholeness. You have identified yourself as your body, your thoughts, your emotional pain, or your material possessions. But you now have a glimmer of understanding that you are far greater than the sum of these things!'

The lights onstage dimmed and a spotlight highlighted the blinding spectacle of Maya on her glittering throne. 'My dear ones, your soul is the force that animates your body, the radiance at the core of your being, the divine "I am".'

At the words 'I am', Maya's body glowed with a pure white light that was dazzling to behold.

'Your soul is your direct connection to the Divine Mystery,' Maya went on. 'And the way your soul expresses itself is from your heart, through love. This is how it communicates with all of creation. Thus I present to you this tenth keystone!'

As she waved her hand with an exaggerated flourish, a mass of pink rose petals rained down from the sky and gracefully formed the message: 'Keystone 10: Live from your heart to express your soul.'

Gigi felt a delicious warmth suffuse her heart, and when she looked down she saw light emanating from it. Buck's heart, too, was pulsing with light, and when Gigi squinted across the footlights at the audience, she saw that everyone's heart was emitting a similar glow.

'But beware!' Maya said in a stage whisper, and mysterious, rather unsettling music began to play from an invisible source. 'The love you are feeling right now in your heart, this love that is the expression of your soul, has very little to do with the sentiment you call "romantic love" under the spell of forget-fulness. The melodramatic notion of love you humans believe in is not the expression of the soul that will bring you eternal bliss. In fact, it often entwines the players in poisoned tentacles of possessiveness and fear.'

Maya stepped down from the dais and stood beside Buck's chair. 'And that is where you come in, my sweet cowboy,' she said.

Buck looked startled, but recovered himself and quickly nodded in agreement. Clearing his throat, he said, 'Yes, I reckon it is.'

'Very good, my brave one,' Maya said. Her face was a picture of empathy, and compassion radiated from her heart in visible waves. 'Do you want to tell the audience – and Gigi – why it is that "love" causes you to be so uncomfortable?'

Buck considered then said slowly, looking directly at Gigi, 'I guess I've always equated love with coming to the rescue. My dad died when I was only twelve, and my mom relied on me to help run the ranch. She'd tell me I was the man of the house now, and that it was up to me to help the womenfolk.

'So I learned that to gain love and approval, I needed to be strong. Once I started having romantic relationships with women, my need to rescue or be a hero took over my entire experience. If I couldn't save someone, then I felt unworthy.'

Gigi felt a mixture of fear and love in her heart. What was Buck saying? Was he relieved he didn't have to save her? But she was used to being the one who saved, too. What did that mean for them?

'Thank you, Angel Buck, for your willingness to be honest,' said Maya. 'You have begun to see now that love is much more than this meager rationing and brave posturing, have you not?'

'Yes, I have,' Buck said, bowing his head. 'In fact, what I've thought of as love wasn't really love at all. Love isn't something you have to go out and get. It's in us, all along. I discovered that during this course.'

'That is excellent, Buck,' said Maya. 'You are beginning to understand that you can experience love in all moments, regardless of the circumstances – correct?'

Buck nodded and again locked eyes with Gigi. His gaze was clear and yet somehow neutral. She felt the same lack of pull from him that she'd felt on the beach earlier.

Maya turned to Gigi. 'You have learned about love, too, haven't you, my dear?' she asked gently. 'You've learned that you must make decisions from your heart, not your brain – that you can express your authentic self by expressing your soul through your heart.'

'Yes,' Gigi said. 'But I'm not sure I get the part about not finding love outside myself. Of course I have a lot of love in my heart – an infinite amount, I'm sure. But what good is it if I don't have someone special – a soul mate, say – to share it with?'

'That is a good question, and the answer is very important,' said Maya, turning to the audience. 'Listen carefully, my dears, for everyone caught in the spell of forgetfulness needs to know this.

'The sensation of love does not come from someone else. It comes only from you. You can only feel love when it is emanating from your own heart. Conversely, another cannot feel your love but only the love *they* are sending out.

'That is why humans have such a hard time in relationships: They expect love to come from outside. But if their heart is not already glowing with love, they cannot truly feel it coming from another.

'To have a close, intimate relationship with someone, you have to master your own love. You must be willing to choose love instead of fear.'

The truth of Maya's words reverberated through Gigi's being.

'That's what unconditional love means, then,' Gigi said slowly. 'The love is there in the heart all the time, and is not dependent on circumstances, being reciprocated, being approved of, or whatever else we think it's attached to. And it's not blocked by the fear of not receiving love in return.'

'Exactly,' said Maya. 'Love is not attached to anyone or anything. It simply *is*.'

'And that's how we express our soul – through love in the heart?' Gigi asked.

'Yes,' said Maya. 'Your soul is your abiding connection to all of creation. When you live from your heart, the divine comes to life in your every experience.'

Returning to her dais, she regarded the audience with a

sudden solemnity. 'I must give you a word of caution, my earnest seekers. As you begin to live soulfully, you may well encounter obstacles. You might discover yourself living from your tired old script, your cast of characters might insist that you'll never awaken from the enchantment, your critic might ridicule you, false beliefs might rush in to attack you, or you may find it impossible to remove the mask of righteousness from your features.

'Yet know that these stumbling blocks are merely opportunities to remember that your divine purpose is to awaken from the spell of forgetfulness, remember your essential perfection, and express the love in your soul.'

A raised stage appeared behind the dais, and a chorus line of unicorns pranced onstage, kicking their silver hoofs and brandishing their horns as they sang in a round, 'To come to know yourself as whole, live from your heart to express your soul.'

After taking a bow, the unicorns pranced off, twitching their tails. Smiling, Maya said, 'And now, Gigi and Buck, it's time for you two to talk about the romantic love, or lust, or melodrama, or whatever you want to call it, that has been developing between you. It is time for you to evaluate its hold on you and understand it in comparison to the unconditional love we've been discussing.'

Gigi's heart skipped a beat, and its pulsing light momentarily dimmed. But she breathed into it and felt its overflowing abundance of love, letting it radiate out in a steady stream.

Buck hopped awkwardly over and took her hands, pulling her up to stand facing him. She looked into his eyes, thinking that this felt like a wedding ceremony, with Maya as officiant behind them on her dais. Butterflies swarmed in her stomach, and her palms began to sweat. She didn't know what to say. Buck also seemed to be experiencing uncertainty, because although he was gazing at her steadily, he too seemed unable to speak.

Finally, Buck cleared his throat and began.

'Gigi, I care about you a lot,' he said quietly. 'I'm drawn to the essence of you, the divine spark of you. You are an extraordinary being, and you're really fun to be with.' He took a deep breath. 'Plus, you're really hot.'

The audience laughed, and Maya indulgently gestured for them to be silent.

Buck continued slowly, 'But I don't think I am ready to be in a relationship.'

Gigi's heart plummeted to her toes and all Maya's wisdom seemed to fly away as she fought the pit-of-the-stomach dread his words created. All she could think was, *He doesn't love me – he's going to abandon me.* Determined not to betray her dismay, she concentrated on trying to look calm as he continued.

'How can I be in a relationship when I don't know what love is? You're great, but I've had love confused with saving someone for a long time. And I don't want to get stuck in that rut anymore. I need to learn what love really is, the real kind of love that starts with myself.

'I need to really absorb the lessons of the keystones and practice them in waking time before I can be in any kind of partnership. I'm just not ready. I don't want to do what I've always done, and I have a lot of inner exploration ahead of me.'

Buck's words felt like knives stabbing her heart. She breathed into the moment and forced herself to look him in the eyes, seeing his soul reflected there. She could see his inner turmoil and knew that she had to let him take his own path – for now, anyway.

As if echoing her thought, Buck added, 'And who knows? Maybe we'll run into each other in New Mexico sometime in waking life.'

Gigi's heart leapt with that pesky imp, hope. She knew she should let go of the imp and simply let things be, but she thought, *I get it about love versus melodrama, I really do. But I still know Buck is my soul mate and I trust that we'll find each other in waking life.*

The thought gave her the strength to respond. 'It's okay, I understand,' she began, her voice unsteady. 'I also have some learning to do. A lot, actually. I feel so much love in my heart, but I've given it away with conditions attached to it and expectations of return. I need to learn to love myself unconditionally and allow my soul to shine. I still feel attached to the idea of being with you, but I don't think that's a bad thing. Maybe someday when we are both ready, we'll meet and engage in a true soul partnership.'

They exchanged a smile and Buck squeezed her hands tightly. As they stood staring into each other's eyes, celestial music played softly, echoing their newfound understanding. Maya's voice drifted over them. 'Remember, you must be willing to choose love and not fear. And choose it again, and again...'

Slowly their hands disengaged, and Gigi felt an immediate sense of loss. She couldn't stop the thought that he was abandoning her. Maybe that belief was true, after all – she would always be abandoned.

'And now, Angel Buck, you may take your bow,' said Maya. 'There is a seat in the front row of the audience for you to watch the rest of the show.'

Buck bowed awkwardly on one foot, holding onto the back of the chair, as the auditorium exploded in thunderous applause.

'Now, I think we're done with that sprained ankle!' Maya stage-whispered and, with a wink, pointed her long fingernail at his foot. A rainbow shot out and enfolded his ankle then slipped away, and a look of relief passed over Buck's face.

'Thanks, darlin',' he said with a touch of his old bravado, and blew Maya a kiss as he strode toward the wings. Just before he reached them, his old hat came flying through the air like a Frisbee, knocked the Stetson off his head, and settled in its accustomed position. Solemnly, Buck tipped his hat to the laughing audience, turned to wink at Gigi, and vanished.

Gigi's heart squeezed painfully. He was really gone! Would she ever see him, feel him, taste him again?

Suddenly, she realized she was standing alone center stage, gazing into the wings like an actress who had forgotten her lines. Feeling exposed and rather foolish, she turned to ask Maya why she was still here, but Maya was already starting to explain.

'Now, Angel Gigi, we have a special opportunity for you. There's someone that has been wanting to see you for a long time, and this is the perfect moment for you to practice your newfound understanding of love.'

Uh-oh. Gigi felt her heart fluttering wildly. She concentrated on breathing and staying in the moment as the invisible band struck up a drum roll. From stage left, where Buck had exited, a shadowy figure slowly emerged, stepping into the spotlight.

All the breath left Gigi's body and she sat down abruptly in her seat.

He had grown slightly stooped and wore thick glasses, and his once-abundant hair had thinned, but she'd know him anywhere.

'Dad?' she whispered.

The old man squinted around, blinded by the spotlight, then his eyes alighted on her and he froze, hands hanging limply at his sides.

'Gigi,' he said, his voice breaking.

'Dad,' she repeated, stronger this time, and she rose and went to him. How many times had she imagined this moment – the moment of their reunion? How many times had she despaired of its ever happening? She'd gone over and over in her mind what she would say to him, how she would hold him accountable and make him see how much he'd hurt her. But now, all she could feel was an overwhelming sense of compassion.

Her father held out a trembling hand and lightly touched her arm, as if to see if she were real. The touch broke something free in Gigi's heart, and, sobbing, she threw herself into his arms.

He hugged her tightly, their bodies swaying slightly back and forth in the intensity of their embrace. Gigi could feel his sobs heaving with her own. Everything else disappeared, and she was completely filled with this endless moment of love and joy.

'Your soul's love has boundless forgiveness built in,' Maya said softly from behind them. 'When you forgive, the walls blocking your heart's love come tumbling down, and you are free.'

Eventually the intensity of their feelings died down, and Gigi's father held her at arm's length. 'You're so beautiful,' he said raggedly. 'I'm sorry. Gigi, I'm so sorry. I don't know if you can ever forgive me. Things didn't turn out so well for me in California and I was too ashamed to tell you. I pretended everything was fine. Then years went by and it seemed like it was too late...'

'Shh,' Gigi said, choking back tears and putting her finger to his lips. 'None of that matters now. All that matters is this moment, and I'm so grateful to see you again. There's nothing else we need to say. It's over dad, it's all behind us.' Gigi felt her heart bursting with joy as she added, 'I love you. Everything is forgiven!'

And I forgive myself, too, she added silently. *I forgive myself for holding a grudge for all these years, and for hurting myself with false beliefs and making bad choices. None of that matters now, either.*

A wave of applause crashed over them, and they turned, holding hands, and bowed together. Gigi was beaming through her tears. She had never experienced such a powerful feeling of love, and she felt it connecting her directly to the heart of the divine.

'Thank you, Frank,' said Maya to Gigi's father. 'That was a beautiful guest appearance. And now you may return to waking life.'

'What?' Gigi asked, clutching at her father's hand. 'Why can't he stay here with me?' Was she going to be abandoned again by her father, as well as being left by Buck, twice in ten minutes? It was really too much to handle. She wanted to stamp her feet and cry like a child throwing a tantrum.

'He must return,' said Maya gently but firmly. 'He has fulfilled his purpose here tonight.' And as she spoke, Gigi felt her father's hand growing insubstantial in her own. She tried to grip it harder, concentrating on keeping him with her, but he wavered and dissipated until her fist was grasping nothing but air.

'Gigi, there's a seat for you in the audience as well,' Maya said, gesturing to the wings. With heavy feet, Gigi plodded backstage and down into the murmuring throng, making her way to a seat near the front that had her name emblazoned on it. Next to her, as in the previous lectures, sat Susan – freshly coiffed, subtly made up, and dressed in what looked like a vintage Diane von Furstenberg wrap dress. But despite a predictable twinge of envy at Susan's impeccable appearance, this time Gigi was glad to see her. She squeezed Susan's arm as she sat down, and her heavy heart lightened a little at her new friend's smile.

'You did great,' Susan whispered.

'Thanks,' Gigi said, marveling at how good it felt to be on friendly terms with Susan.

I'll make sure I have a chance with Buck and my father in waking life, she vowed silently. *I know Buck will come and find me, and I can fly out anytime to see my father.* Settling back in her seat, she prepared herself to take in the final keystone.

Chapter Fifteen

'Now, my beloved students, as you prepare to return to your waking life, it seems appropriate to take a look at the nature of happiness,' Maya began from her golden throne. She was grasping an elaborately jeweled scepter and looked even more regal than before. 'Answer this, my dears: How is it possible to achieve happiness in the Magical Theatre?'

A cacophony of shouted answers arose from the audience.

'Working our way through the keystones!'

'Rewriting our script with new wisdom!'

'Continuing to ascend the spiral!'

'Ditching hurtful beliefs and dropping our mask!'

Gigi listened, thinking, *It's all of these things, sure. But what about having fun? No one has mentioned fun, but I know I need to play or I won't be happy. I can't just work all the time, or sit alone in my apartment on the Internet.*

Maya held out a hand, hushing the audience's clamor. 'You are on the right track, my dears. Certainly, remembering and practicing the keystones as you ascend the spiral of awareness are elements of happiness. But there is one thing that you must learn above all others if you want to access the joy and serenity that is your birthright as angelic beings.'

She paused to survey the hall, then wrote in the air with her scepter to form the shimmering golden words: 'Keystone 11: Accept "what is" without need for improvement.'

'Yes, my dears, acceptance is the treasure you'll find as you gain awareness – the pearl hidden in the oyster of awakening,' said Maya.

Gigi groaned inwardly. Of all things – acceptance? It sounded so boring, so trite, so... *passive.*

'Acceptance is not a passive state but an active choice,' said Maya, her eyes beaming into Gigi's. 'When I speak of acceptance, it means this: After consciously choosing a course of action, lovingly release yourself from attachment to the outcome.'

Maya stood and stepped away from the throne, pointing her scepter at it. Suddenly the throne seemed to quiver and the gold began to melt and liquefy, transforming the chair into an elongated shape that looked oddly familiar. A see-saw!

Gigi and Susan exchanged bemused glances. Where was Maya headed with this one?

'Acceptance means letting go of attachments,' said Maya. 'Attachments invariably lead to suffering, since in the Magical Theatre nothing is permanent. People, situations and circumstances will inevitably shift, change or be taken away.

'This means that attaching your happiness to a certain outcome guarantees that you will eventually lose your happiness. It's like wanting a certain team to win a game. You might enjoy the game, but if your team loses, you will be miserable.

'On the other hand, if you disengage your happiness from the result of the game, you can still be happy. You can still enjoy the sport and love the game without letting the result sway your emotions.'

The auditorium was completely silent as the students absorbed this information. Gigi felt her mind resisting it. Of course she was attached to results! Now that she'd met Buck, for instance, she knew that being with him in waking life would make her happy. And she didn't want to accept that things couldn't be permanent!

What about when she and Buck got together? She wanted that to last forever, and she didn't see how she could be happy if he were taken away from her after they were together for many years. She willed herself to listen as Maya continued.

'To illustrate non-attachment, I have created this see-saw for you,' said Maya, gesturing at the golden see-saw. 'Look carefully at the see-saw, and you will see yourself standing at its center, perfectly balanced. The balance represents acceptance.'

Gigi concentrated until a clear image of herself appeared onstage, balancing at the very center of the level see-saw. She giggled. It was pretty cool to see herself up there. Not to mention that she really did look incredibly hot in that dress. 'Eat your heart out, Buckaroo,' she muttered. 'Wherever you are.'

'Now, each of you is seeing yourself up here balanced on the see-saw, correct?' asked Maya.

Nods and 'yeses' rippled around the auditorium.

'Next, from that place of balance, imagine a choice you might make, or a choice you might ask someone else to make that directly affects you,' said Maya.

Gigi imagined calling Buck to ask him if he was ready to have a relationship with her. (Ugh! How humiliating!)

'The choice you have set in motion has two possible outcomes represented by either side of the see-saw,' continued Maya. 'If you remain unattached, you stay balanced at the center, and can more easefully accept either outcome.'

Gigi watched herself standing calmly in the center of the see-saw, knees bent, balancing herself easily as if on a surfboard. And in spike heels, too. Not bad!

'This is not to say you might not prefer one outcome over another. However, in your place of non-attachment, you don't run to one side of the see-saw trying to grab the outcome you prefer. Your place of balance guarantees that your happiness will not be held captive by the result.'

But I want Buck to say yes! Gigi thought stubbornly.

Immediately, the onstage Gigi ran to the 'yes' side of the see-saw, and it crashed to the floor. But as she did so, another Gigi ran to the 'no' side, causing the 'yes' side to swing high into the air. The two Gigis bounced each other up and down determinedly, while the see-saw swung wildly from one outcome to the other.

'You can see that becoming attached to a result causes the see-saw to swing between two possible outcomes,' Maya observed. 'And then...'

Both onstage Gigis flailed wildly, arms spinning like a cartoon character's, before falling and landing with their feet in the air, exposing a peek of lacy pink panties.

How embarrassing, Gigi thought. At least Mitchell had made sure she wore panties! Then realizing that everyone was seeing themselves up there and not her, she breathed a sigh of relief that they hadn't witnessed her fall. Thank goodness.

Though humiliating, it certainly did illustrate Maya's point.

'So you see, my dears, the moment you become emotionally invested in one outcome, you lose balance and let your happiness become dependent on the result of your choice,' said Maya. 'If you get the result you're attached to, you're relieved , and if you don't get it, you're miserable. That is why acceptance is the only way to maintain equanimity.'

Maya trained her laser beam eyes on Gigi. 'Listen carefully, my dears. When you become attached to someone or something, you are equally attached to the fear of losing it. You give over your happiness to unknown events that are beyond your control. But if you can release your attachment, your happiness is again in your own domain. You may prefer one outcome over another, but you can be content no matter what.'

Onstage, Gigi was restored to her place of balance at the center of the see-saw. Smiling, she shimmered and disappeared.

'Standing on the center point of balance is symbolic of relaxing into *what is*, letting life flow through you without resistance,' Maya added.

Gigi sighed as she realized just how much she was attached to outcomes in daily life. Disengaging from these attachments seemed a Herculean task. How would she be able to do it? How could she be happy if she had to spend the rest of her life alone, without a soul mate? She understood the see-saw analogy intellectually, but she wasn't at all sure about her ability to actually practice non-attachment.

'Humans are particularly attached to winning another's love,' said Maya gently, looking directly at Gigi. 'But being attached to winning someone's love means giving over your happiness to the result. Not only that, but it means you're operating from a false belief that you will lose love if the object you love leaves your life. Listen to me now, my students: Nothing!... has the power to take love out of your heart.'

'But isn't some attachment good?' Susan called out. Gigi noticed that Susan hadn't raised her hand, and gave her a mental pat on the back. She was definitely loosening up. 'Like attachment to doing a good job, or working hard, or treating others well?'

'Excellent question, as usual, Susan,' said Maya. Gigi noticed that Maya's approval no longer sent a pang of jealousy through her. Instead she was grateful that Susan had asked the question, since she would really like to know the answer.

'You should certainly always endeavor to do your best,' Maya explained. 'But attachment to the outcome is a different matter. Attachment to anything is detrimental to your happiness because you let yourself be swayed by events that could shift their direction at any moment.

'Your part in the Divine Mystery will unfold as it will, regardless of your human desire to control it. Still, you must remember that you have a lot of power within your experience in the Magical Theatre. You have the power to rewrite your script, shift your perception, select your emotional responses, make conscious choices and take responsibility for them, and release yourself from your attachment to a certain outcome. This includes attachment to the opinions and approval of other people or your own cast members.

'You may think that attachment to performing well at work, or looking good, or being nice, is a positive thing because it motivates you. But ultimately it can cause you sorrow, because as you have noticed before, you will never live up to all these exaggerated expectations. So I repeat, my dears, the key is to accept all that is.'

'So releasing attachment means letting go of our need to control how events turn out or how we're perceived?' Susan asked, grimacing.

Maya nodded. 'Yes, my dear. Because control is only an illusion, in any case. You must relinquish the illusion of control while greeting unforeseen circumstances with equanimity. This means not worrying excessively or striving to interpret events. It means accepting all things – *without need for improvement.*'

Maya's words echoed around and around the theater and spiraled out into the night sky. Gigi breathed deeply, taking in the information. She knew it was too much for her mind to wrap around, and the only place she could hear it was in her heart. She imagined her heart like a beautiful flower, opening to receive the gift of accepting everything without needing to improve it.

'Even my hips?' she thought, blushing when she realized she'd spoken the thought aloud.

Maya laughed. 'Especially your hips. Humans in the modern world are very focused on appearance, and this makes acceptance difficult. But accepting all that is means accepting your body, however it is.'

Suddenly Gigi felt herself being whisked through the air. She landed onstage and looked at Maya in confusion.

'Gigi, please look in this mirror,' Maya said, pointing her scepter at a full-length mirror that had taken the place of the seesaw at center stage.

Feeling self-conscious, Gigi turned to the mirror and was horrified to see herself looking short and as wide as a bus. Then, like a fun-house mirror, the image extended until she was tall and as skinny as a beanpole.

Maya continued, 'Each of you must accept being too short, too tall, too wide, too small, too big, or too stooped.' With each description, Gigi's image shifted to illustrate Maya's words.

'You must accept having a nose that is too pug, too big, too asymmetrical; legs that are too skinny, too flabby, too knock-kneed, too bowed, too veiny; hair that is too frizzy, too flat, too curly, too gray; skin that is too pale, too dark, too freckly, too sensitive; hips that are too narrow, too wide, too big, too high; and all the other ridiculous anatomical reasons your cast of characters have invented to ensure that you hold your physical body in contempt.'

Gigi felt dizzy. It was true – how ridiculous that she, along with everyone else in the Magical Theatre, had decided they were imperfect because of physical characteristics.

'Not to mention too gregarious/too shy, too stupid, too insecure, too much/not enough, too uncoordinated, too silly, too impulsive...' Gigi added aloud, realizing just how many aspects of herself, in addition to the physical, she hadn't accepted.

'Yes, my dear,' said Maya. 'You must each accept yourself – body, emotions, mind, and everything – without need for improvement. You must understand that they are only the superficial packaging of the soul and do not reflect the truth of you. Only then will you be able to have peace of mind.'

'But it's so hard to just accept,' objected Gigi. 'I understand the need for it, but I don't see how that is going to happen in waking life. How can we get to a place of acceptance when we're so busy judging ourselves, striving to achieve, comparing ourselves with others, and navigating our way through the trials and fears of everyday life?'

'Surrender,' said Maya simply.

'What?' Gigi cried, shocked. 'Isn't surrender giving in, giving up?'

'Surrender means accepting your destiny as it is unfolding,' said Maya.

'But what if we want things to be different?' Gigi insisted. 'I mean, I get that there are things we can't change that we need to release attachment to. But if everyone just said, "This is how life is and I can't do anything about it", we'd still be living in caves and foraging for food. With no central heating or cars or tampons or … or chocolate!'

A titter arose from the auditorium.

Gigi couldn't believe she was standing up here arguing with Maya in front of everyone, but she felt really stubborn all of a sudden. She turned to the audience. 'Well, I don't want to surrender to a life alone, without a job or a husband or a best friend. I don't want to accept war, or famine, or disease… or bad hair days, or zits.' She crossed her arms in front of her and stood her ground.

Maya put her hands on her hips, smiling in amusement. 'Gigi, you do have a way of expressing what's on everyone's mind,' she said. 'Because I know many of you are thinking the same thing, aren't you, my dears?' she continued.

A chorus of 'yeses' encouraged Gigi. At least she wasn't the only one who felt like this surrender stuff was a bit much.

'Let me explain more about surrender,' said Maya. 'First, I'm not saying you can't change things like war. Stopping war means first stopping the war within yourself. You *can* change the world, one person at a time – starting with you. When you accept loving responsibility for your experience of the Magical Theatre, you can carry that message of infinite possibility to others.'

Gigi nodded and uncrossed her arms, deeply feeling the truth of Maya's words. How could she ask for world peace when she got practically homicidal waiting in a long line for a bagel?

Maya continued, 'Next I would like to make it clear that I do not speak of the surrender of defeat or resignation, but rather of actively accepting *what is* on the Divine's terms. I speak of letting life flow through you without resistance.'

She pointed her scepter to the sky, and Gigi gasped to see a golden river crash down from waterfalls high in the heavens and snake toward the theatre, rushing through the air above the audience then whooshing past Gigi's nose to flow through the stage and beyond. She could feel its cool spray on her face, but not a drop fell as it remained suspended in the air.

'Behold the river of life!' Maya intoned, her voice carrying effortlessly above the water's roar. She climbed an invisible bank to perch high above the river, which continued to rage ferociously, frothing over rocks and rolling logs in its powerful wake.

Suddenly Gigi was floundering and gasping for air. She was in the river, swimming upstream against the strong current! Panicking, she kicked harder and struggled to keep her head above water. She could see a fallen log ahead and swam toward it, but the current was so powerful that no matter how hard she paddled, she could get no closer to the log.

'You can see that attempting to swim against the current of the river of life is not only useless but dangerous,' said Maya's voice, clear as a bell in Gigi's ear. 'The river represents the destiny of your life. Trying to go against this divine unfolding won't work. You must follow the river's flow. You know you've done your best. Now life is taking you in another direction.'

Understanding, Gigi stopped struggling and let herself be borne along by the current, turning around to face downstream.

'Yet within the river's flow, there are many choices to be made,' Maya continued. 'If you attach your happiness to something that isn't happening, you could be going against yourself.'

Gigi was swept against a huge boulder that blocked the river's flow. She tried to climb up it, but its surface was slick and she kept sliding off. Finally, frustrated, she pounded on the boulder. Then she remembered to surrender and brought herself into the moment. Looking around her to see what other choices she might make besides struggle, she noticed a fissure in the rock that widened as it descended. She took a deep breath, arriving at the place of no fear, and dove deep into the water.

Using her hands to feel her way, she swam through the fissure and emerged in a calm pool of water. Just beyond, she could see a series of locks, each one raising the level of the river.

'Resisting is counterproductive,' said Maya, waving at Gigi from the invisible riverbank. 'As Gigi just did, each of you will encounter obstacles in the river. These are obstacles you have created by making choices that go against yourself. When you hit an obstacle, use your awareness to see if you have attached your happiness to an outcome. Then, take responsibility for the circumstance you have created and rectify it. When you have done that, you can rejoin the flow. By accepting responsibility for the obstacles and employing the keystones to shift them, you will make your way gracefully through the river.'

Maya pointed to the locks. 'Every now and then in waking life, narrow locks will appear that take you to the next level of the river as it flows back to the source of all life. At these times, you will want to be ready to pass through these openings by applying wisdom from the keystones so you can progress to the next level.'

'Like the spiral?' asked Gigi, treading water.

'Yes, like the spiral,' said Maya. 'But unlike ascending the spiral, which takes a fair amount of dedication, practice and patience, flowing with the river means choosing *ease*. Suffering becomes optional, because once you surrender and accept, you don't have to suffer to change. Allow the flow, and your ascent up the spiral will be easier.'

With a great sucking sound, the river retreated as rapidly as it had appeared, and Gigi was again standing onstage, as dry as before.

'You see, my students,' Maya concluded, 'where you are going is assured. You will be reunited with the Divine Mystery after you exit the Magical Theatre. But how you get there is up to you. By surrendering to the river, you can positively influence the quality of your experience.

'Or you can bang your fist at every obstacle and keep swimming around and around at the same water level, seeing the same scenery. It is up to you.'

'I understand now,' Gigi said. 'It was really powerful to accept the fact that the boulder was in my way and stop fighting it. At that moment, I noticed the opening that provided a way through.'

'It was beautiful to witness your surrender,' said Maya.

Gigi smiled her thanks, but something was still bothering her. She knew that she was far from achieving a state of accepting everything as it was. So far, in fact, that she couldn't even begin to imagine what it felt like.

'Maya,' she began tentatively, 'it's hard for me to admit this, but even after all your explanation, I'm afraid that even though I intellectually understand accepting everything the way that it is, I don't actually *get* it from the inside out.'

'I'm glad you expressed your truth about this,' said Maya. 'And because I really want you to get it, I'm going to do something very special. I'm going to give you a chance to see life in the Magical Theatre through my eyes.'

Gigi's heart began to thud in anticipation. What did Maya mean? It sounded rather thrilling.

Maya reached out and pulled Gigi toward her until they were standing practically nose to nose. The scent of roses enfolded Gigi like a warm blanket of comfort.

'Look directly into my eyes, and let that wonderful mind of yours empty of thought,' Maya instructed. Gigi complied, letting herself sink into Maya's violet gaze. She felt herself being drawn into the gaze as if mesmerized. Then, to her astonishment, she felt herself tighten and twirl into a spinning top, growing smaller and smaller as she twirled faster and faster.

The world became a whirling mist of violet as she spun directly into Maya's eyes... through them into the great beyond... then the spinning stopped and she was in complete stillness.

'Now you are inside my mind,' said Maya's voice, but instead of hearing it from outside, Gigi felt it as if it were her own thought. 'I'm going to open my eyes and give you a glimpse of your life as I see it.'

Like a curtain lifting, Maya's eyelids went up. Gigi peered out eagerly.

There she was in her tiny Lower East Side apartment. An empty bottle of wine sat in front of her on the coffee table, and as she watched, she went to the cupboard and pulled out the last bottle. This must be the night before she'd found Maya's classified ad – the night she'd finished her store of wine and fallen asleep on the sofa. But instead of seeing herself as pathetic, lonely and depressed, she saw only the beauty and wonder of her soul's pure white glow.

It's all perfect, she thought, feeling love expanding outward toward her former self. *If I hadn't drunk the last bottle of wine that night, I wouldn't have realized I needed to take some steps to help myself. Hitting bottom was actually necessary to open me up to the dreamtime.*

Seeing it this way filled her with a deep sense of contentment such as she had never experienced before.

Her former self opened the bottle of wine, sloshed it messily into the glass, and took a swig, then burst into tears. With compassion, Gigi realized that in that moment, she'd been able to focus only on her losses instead of opening to the possibilities that lay ahead.

Now, through Maya's eyes, she could see those possibilities like shards of rainbows dancing around herself. She looked infinitely beautiful and precious, surrounded by prancing prisms, her heart light shining. Through Maya's eyes, Gigi didn't want herself to be any different than she was in that moment. She could perceive no duality between good and bad, sadness and happiness, or what *was* and what *should have been*.

The scene shimmered with a veneer of deep understanding

and acceptance. It was peaceful, whole and imbued with great love. So this was how Maya saw life – not judging, not commenting on the scene, but experiencing the moment as a whole and accepting all of it. She was completely aligned with the beauty, the love and the boundless magic of life. Seeing this way made Gigi's heart bubble up with happiness.

The bubble expanded until her entire being was filled with outrageous joy. She felt light, free, and connected to everyone and everything in the universe. She was one with the stars, one with the sun, one with all the myriad of experiences of life in the Magical Theatre. She was not separate from them – she was united with every expression of the Divine Mystery. Everything was of Love! She breathed it, saw it, danced it, *became* it – losing all sense of time, place and boundaries...

Whoosh! With a sudden intense spiraling as if being sucked into a vacuum cleaner, Gigi was propelled out of Maya's mind and in less than a second, found herself standing onstage once more.

Maya was smiling at her with her violet eyes, and Gigi's own eyes filled with tears of gratitude.

'Thank you, Maya,' she said softly. Awed, she realized she could still see everything the way Maya did, and the stage, the audience, the room's soft glow and hush, all seemed perfectly beautiful to her. Then the feeling began to fade, and the more she tried to make it stay, the faster it left, until she was just Gigi again. But her heart was still soft and full, and her eyes seemed somehow transformed.

'You will see the way I do all the time once you awaken from the enchantment, my beloved,' said Maya. She turned to the silent crowd. 'Each and every one of you has the possibility of seeing with the eyes of absolute love and acceptance, free of attachments, moving seamlessly with the flow of the river of life.

'You will begin to notice the expansion of your sight as you ascend the spiral. It will become your common experience when you absorb Keystone 12: All is perfection.'

Maya surveyed them to make sure they were taking it in. 'You can use the dreamtime to learn, but you must embody this in waking life, my students. True awakening happens in your daily round of experiences in the Magical Theatre.'

Gigi realized she was beginning to feel very sleepy. Her limbs felt heavy, and she struggled to maintain an upright stance. She needed to stay alert so she could say goodbye to Susan, make a plan to meet up with Buck in waking life, and offer her gratitude to Maya and Godfreys. But try as she might, she could not resist the urge to sink down onto the stage.

'Now, my valiant students, I must congratulate you. You have completed the dreamtime Remedial Angel Training course,' Maya said, her voice sounding echoey and insubstantial. 'I now release you to go into waking life to practice and implement your keystones.

'Some of you will remember this course and some will not, just as some of you remember your dreams and others don't. But whether or not you remember the course consciously, it will be working in your subconscious.'

Gigi lay down on the stage floor, letting her tired body sink into the floorboards. She wondered vaguely if she would remember all this but was too weary to ponder it.

'You can always call on me in the dreamtime, and I will come to you,' said Maya. 'During waking life, your guardian angels might visit you from time to time to check on your progress and help you stay on track.

'Meanwhile, my beloveds, know that I love you unconditionally and that you are whole, perfect and infinitely beautiful. I leave you to return to your place of slumber and awake with the dawn.'

Through half-closed eyes, Gigi saw Maya swirl and vanish in a cloud of gold rimmed pink smoke. She thought she saw Godfreys coming toward her through the mist and heard him say faintly, 'Gigi, my dear, I'll help guide you back into your sleeping human body, and please don't hesitate to call on me whenever you might need assistance. Now, down we go to create heaven on earth!'

Godfreys knelt beside her and picked her up easily as if she were light as a child. Together they were whisked upward, into the vast nighttime sky decorated with clusters of dancing stars...

Epilogue

Gigi opened her eyes, wincing with the effort, and regarded the ceiling fuzzily. Why was it white? She could have sworn her bedroom ceiling was blue.

She hoisted herself up, her body as heavy and groggy as if she'd been sleeping for a hundred years. She'd fallen asleep in the living room again. Surveying the remains of last night's takeout Chinese and the dregs of her wine glass, she waited for the familiar sense of doom to slide over her as it had every morning for the past couple of months. But it didn't come.

Something was different. She'd had a dream – a good dream. One of those dreams that went on and on all night, and left a residue of positive feelings in her body. What was it about? Some kind of fantastic adventure? She wracked her brain but couldn't remember it.

'Why do I always remember the bad dreams and not the good ones?' she grumbled. But it was there, just at the tip of her consciousness. She could feel it... something about a performance, or a theater? Yes, there was definitely a theater. And she'd traveled all over the place. There were people in it, too, very interesting people... but who?

Maybe if she stopped trying to remember the dream, it would come to her. Sometimes that happened. She'd be in the middle of riding the exercise bike at the gym or buying bagels at the corner deli when, *bam!* The previous night's dream would hit her.

Gigi decided to make a pot of coffee and let her brain wake up a bit. Standing up with a groan, she shuffled the short distance into her kitchen and opened the cupboard.

Aargh – the coffee tin was empty!

With a shrug, Gigi put the empty tin back in its place. She'd just head over to Starbucks for a macchiato. It was high time she got herself out of this apartment and out of this funk, anyway.

Maybe she'd even take a shower! Now, there was a revolutionary thought.

Hmm, something was different. This funk – this funk that had been her constant companion since the divorce...Where was it? Interestingly, she didn't feel its tendrils winding themselves around her heart quite so strongly today. In fact, slight hangover aside, she really didn't feel too bad.

Well, that's odd, she thought. *Good, but odd. I feel better, even though it's not like anything has changed since yesterday.*

Or had it?

She wandered back into the living room and plunked herself on the sofa again. That dream! She knew it had been powerful. It had a message for her, she was certain. She strained her memory, searching for clues, but all she could access was a feeling of excitement and wonder. What had caused that feeling? She had to know!

Frustrated, she yawned and stretched her cramped leg, placing it on the coffee table. Her foot hit a pile of books and knocked them over. The top book slid close to the edge of the table and as she gazed at the title something stirred in her memory.

Dreaming Down Heaven

by

Maya

'Maya!' she shouted jubilantly, her voice echoing off the empty walls of her apartment.

That was it! She'd dreamed that she had found Maya's classified ad for the Magical Theatre in Blessings... she'd gone there, but it turned out the Magical Theatre was something else entirely, something truly magical and wondrous...

Remedial Angel Training! Of course.

'Oh my God, the keystones,' Gigi said, her hand flying to her mouth in astonishment. The keystones to awakening! She'd been reading about them in *Dreaming Down Heaven,* sipping glass after glass of wine as she progressed through the chapters, and she must have drifted off to sleep and dreamed about them all night long.

She closed her eyes and saw herself seated in an amphitheater surrounded by stars. Next to her was a cowboy named Buck... Buck from New Mexico! Buck of the heartbreakingly gorgeous smile and old-school manners. Her heart lurched, and she strained to remember what had happened. They'd been on wonderful adventures together, she was sure. Yes, they'd ridden a horse together... and from the sudden tingling throughout her body, she gathered there must have been more. Omigod, yes, now it was coming back to her! His strong arms around her, his tender kisses, his caresses, his...

Lost in a swirl of memories, Gigi found herself laughing and crying at the same time. She had certainly had the ride of her life, and things would never be the same. Caught up in the emotion of the moment, she said aloud, 'Thank you, Maya, from the bottom of my heart. Thanksgiving is coming, and I truly have so much to be thankful for. I have the opportunity to start my life over, to really understand the keystones, to live and love and experience and learn and ascend the spiral and be in the moment and learn what it is to truly accept and be in the flow of life!'

Elated, Gigi jumped up and spun around the living room. 'YEAH!' she yelled as she twirled on tides of joy.

Thump. Thump. Thump. Her upstairs neighbor was banging on his floor. 'Hey, keep it down! Some people are still sleeping!' came his muffled shout.

'Sorry!' Gigi yelled back. 'But I just got a new lease on life, down here!'

Silence. She giggled to imagine what her neighbor must be thinking; then, hands on hips, she surveyed the shambles of her apartment. Right. It was time to get it together. She couldn't wait! After all, there was no telling what adventures could be right around the corner.

But... what should she do first?

Suddenly overcome by a flood of doubt and inertia, Gigi sank back down on the sofa and buried her head in her hands. What if she were just deluding herself with half-dreamt nonsense? Maya's keystones were all well and good, but how was she supposed to change herself so drastically? After all, who was she to think she could change her life?

A loud 'bang!' startled her, and her eyes flew open. *Dreaming Down Heaven* had fallen off the table.

Shrugging, she bent to pick it up, then froze. A folded piece of lavender paper had spilled out of the book as it fell. She picked it up carefully, shivering as a sudden aroma of roses sent goose bumps up her arms. Slowly, she unfolded the paper. On it was a handwritten note in Maya's unmistakable ornate penmanship.

To My Beloved:

Stop trying to fix yourself. You are not broken, you don't need repairing, and you don't need to try harder. Study and live the keystones, practice what you want to master, and your life will be blessed with great ease and boundless love.

You don't have to worry about the past; worry robs you of the energy to be NOW. New choices await you. The most important choice you can make is to remember and live the truth of your magnificence. You are a perfect reflection of the Great Mystery without need of improvement.

When you are confused, ask 'What would love do here?', then do it!

Know that I am always available to you in your meditations and in the nighttime dream and look forward to seeing your most precious self soon!

xxoo,

Maya

Gigi let out her breath with a gusty sigh of relief. She wasn't alone in this. Maya's insight and wisdom were available right here, anytime she needed it. Maya would never leave her in the lurch; she would always be available to help her. She would always provide the guidance and support that Gigi needed along the way.

Feeling renewed strength, Gigi nodded firmly to herself.

'Ready or not, here I come,' she said, adding a silent *giddiup!* in honor of Buck. She wished he were here, but she had a sneaky feeling that she would see him again. Meanwhile, she had work to do...

Returning her gaze to *Dreaming Down Heaven*, Gigi flipped to the title page and began to read.

Dreaming Down Heaven

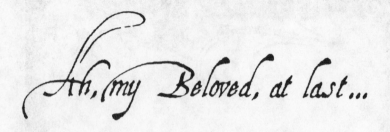

Ah, my Beloved, at last...

I wondered how long it would take you to discover this cache of my most cherished keystones — the secrets to happiness.

It was inevitable, of course. If you look back over your life, you can witness the perfectly orchestrated chain of events that delivered these twelve gifts into your hands. On your journey here did you *suspect* there was something in your life amiss?

Perfect.

That is precisely the awareness you need to propel your escape from the dream-like enchantment of the Magical Theatre, and rediscover and subsequently

live the truth of your magnificence.

If you are wondering who I am and why I want to help you awaken,

then permit me please –

I am known as *Maya,*

the Great Mistress of Illusion,

and it is I who designed this enchanted game

of earthly life you've been playing.

What you have thought of as *reality,*

I call the Magical Theatre,

for it is a realm where *anything* can happen

if you open to the *possibilities.*

I imagine you are brimming with questions so let me explain.

I invite you to *imagine a time* in

the eons before you began your human journey,

each love-filled

moment

flowing unimpeded

into the next

across eternity.

From this place,

you, my love,

courageously chose to participate

in the antics of the Magical Theatre,

so that you might

expand beyond your knowing.

YOU FULLY UNDERSTOOD A SPELL OF FORGETFULNESS

WOULD BE CAST ON ALL WHO ENTERED THIS ENCHANTED TERRITORY.

And, like the multitude of other souls who came to explore the magic,

your intent was to star in your own glorious

production, without being impeded by earthly fears.

You were certain you would remember your essential nature —

the key

to breaking the spell.

But no sooner did you enter your body than you

succumbed to the potency of the illusion,

forgetting *you*

had delightedly agreed to play the game of awakening.

Worse, like millions of others trapped in the same oblivion, you

developed a deep conviction of your imperfection.

You came to accept that in order to feel complete
and experience your divine heritage of unconditional love,

you needed to *change*

or *do* something —

or pretend to be something you were not.

Dear one,

do you honestly believe that you could be intrinsically flawed?

Be assured that this nonsensical thinking is merely a result

of the fear that blinds you,

leading you to search in vain for the missing pieces

that might ease your becoming impossibly faultless.

What you long for does not exist

outside of yourself,

so it cannot be found

through relationships,

treasures

or status.

The actual wellspring of happiness has simply

faded from your awareness.

You have forgotten you are born whole
and perfect and irrevocably connected
to the Heart of the Sacred.

Love could not have been missing,

for you

are its Source.

Miracles await you, Beloved, if only
you remember who you truly are.

I will share with you *twelve keystones—*

the *foundational principles*

that will release you from the slumber of forgetfulness.

If you study the keystones and *live them with intention,*

you will become *free* to reclaim the legacy of your divine spark.

In the Magical Theatre you are

the producer,

director,

writer,

and *star*

of your own wondrous production.

Armed with free will, you can take on whatever role you choose
in this bountiful world of wonder.

I am here to help you navigate the journey, so call on me any time you are in need of support and I will join you in the nighttime dream world.

Here unencumbered by the pull of the enchantment, I will reveal the secret of secrets,

how to dream down heaven.

In return, I ask only that you open your mind and unlock your

heart. It is a grand deal, is it not?

Let us begin.

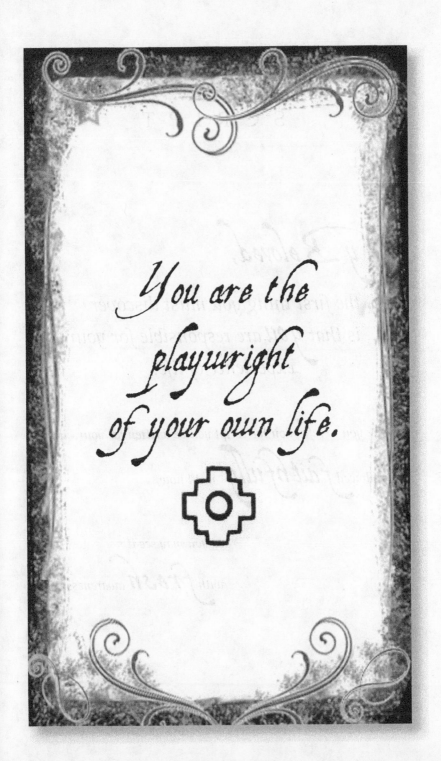

You are the playwright of your own life.

∼ 1 ∼

S C R I P T

My Beloved,

the first thing you must discover
is that ***you*** are responsible for your
experience of life.

I invite you to reflect on the script you've written for yourself

and followed ***faithfully*** *until now,*

so you may see it

with ***fresh*** *awareness.*

Has it brought you happiness and peace?

If not, recognize that the possibility for reworking it

lies in your hands.

Does it accurately reflect who you are?

If not, you can compose new themes to live by.

You have the *power to*
broaden the stage directions,

update the character profiles,

and compose a fun and marvelous new production.

Tell me of the *story* of you –

                    the mythical script you've been following

      until now.

Rest assured that it is

safe to reveal all with honesty,

because I accept you without conditions

and will not judge you.

WHILE DESCRIBING YOUR LIFE,

PLEASE PONDER THESE QUESTIONS:

Who are you, really?

WHAT DO YOU CLAIM TO BELIEVE?

HOW DO YOU FEEL ABOUT THE CHARACTER YOU'VE BECOME?

WHAT IMAGE OF YOURSELF DO YOU MOST STUBBORNLY DEFEND?

Take all the time you need to discover what motivates and informs

the many aspects of your world,

for I have an eternity to listen.

Let your thoughts pour forth without evaluation.

Allow yourself to experience the excitement of discovery.

What do you find in this place of *uncensored* awareness?

When you have finished your investigation,

honestly reflect with renewed insight on your

enchanted creation – the fabled character you have called

you.

If you were to glimpse your tale through the eternal mists of time,

how accurate would your portrayal be?

Pondering this deceptively simple question will reveal the degree

to which you have strayed from the

truth of your vastness.

Be brave my treasure,

it is essential to acknowledge that you've had a hand in

creating your script.

Once you *take responsibility* for your own creation,

you are free to begin shedding the heavy burdens of the role you

have assumed in the

Magical Theatre.

───≈≈≈───

Notice that your script is based not on enduring truths

but on your mind's fictitious interpretations

of your experiences.

These tired scenarios arise from a hodgepodge of ancient fears,

traumas and self-criticism

that wrongly accuse you of being not good enough.

Without realizing it, you have carefully fashioned this story line from your reactions to events and have selected tainted evidence to prove your perceptions accurate.

Ah, the ingenuity it took to do this!

My sweet playwright,

why not use that mental energy to

become the infinite being

you were born to be?

The ongoing melodramas you have crafted to keep your story deceptively fresh also ensure you continue playing a character that is small, manageable and predictable.

Yet no matter how familiar and comfortable your script feels or
how well you can play your part, it is a minuscule and inaccurate
reflection of
your boundless splendour.

The thrall of your old script mesmerized you
into forgetting you have

the power
to create your experience of life.

Are you ready to throw that parched document away and begin to enjoy the stunning array of opportunities available to you in the virtual reality of the Magical Theatre?

To begin, dare to remove the bewitched spectacles that have kept you from knowing who you really are and peer closely at the fine print on the theatre's playbill that reads,

Magical means anything is possible.
You are limited only by your choices.

As the playwright of your own script,

your choices are infinite.

And while life events themselves may not all appear to be under

your jurisdiction,

it is always possible to

form a new perception of them.

I implore you to decide today to abandon the lenses that have

blinded you to the rich enchantment surrounding you

and allow yourself to see that the part you've been playing

is only one option among millions.

When you shift your perspective in this way, you will come to understand the power you have to continually rework the script of your life,

       opening yourself to endless possibilities.

Here then, my *Beloved* is your first keystone:

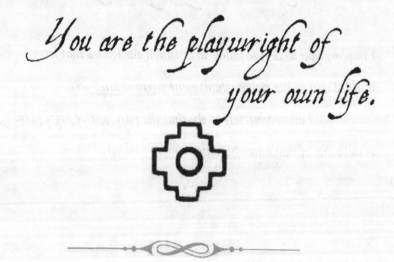

You are the playwright of your own life.

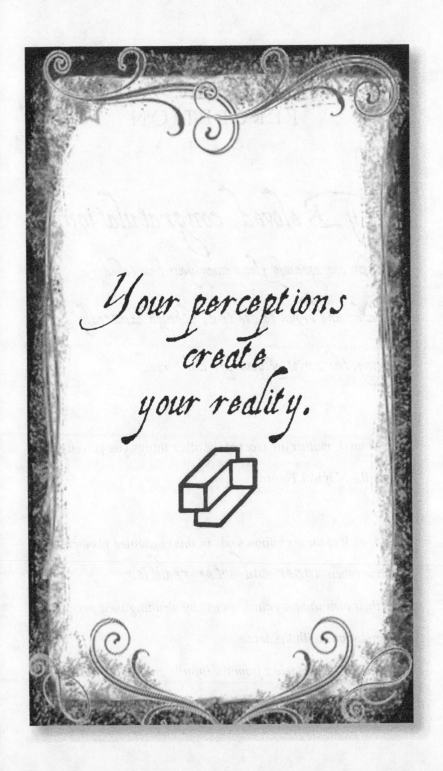

2
PERCEPTION

My Beloved, congratulations!

You have courageously flung away your bewitched spectacles and begun to see that, although admittedly engaging, the script of your life isn't real.

To be honest, neither are most of the other things you perceive as real in the Magical Theatre.

In fact, each of the six billion souls in this enchanted playhouse construct their *inner and outer realities* from their own unique points of view by blending their personal interpretations with the data

their minds select from the infinite options available.

Allow your mind to expand as you ponder my words.

Like everyone in the Magical Theatre,

you interpret both your physical world and life experiences through the filter of your thoughts and emotions.

What you conclude is "real" and concrete is not only an impression from a restricted angle of perception, but an altogether personal experience.

What I am trying to say,

is that reality in the Magical Theatre isn't a fixed state, but rather a *malleable one.*

For example, you, magical being, have a sense of hearing that can identify a wide variety of sounds,

as do most people on earth, correct?

Yet, though you share this common ability to hear, your interpretation of different musical styles is uniquely yours because you

automatically overlay your perception

with what you *think*

or how you *feel.*

The same holds true for sights, smells and other impressions that form your entirely subjective point of view.

Don't take offense, my darling, but I'm simply helping you

see the truth so you can

release the point of view

that your thoughts and emotions form

the foundation of

an absolute reality that can stand the test of time.

Now let's take this a step further.

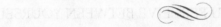

Unlike your ancestors, it is easy for you in your modern world

to imagine moving beyond the reality of your five senses

and perceiving your miraculous human body

from the point of view of pure energy.

Compared to the physical essence you perceive through your five

rudimentary senses, you "understand" that your body is comprised

of sub-atomic particles — very tiny bits of light.

You are animated by a *profound mystery*

with infinite intelligence

and your physicality differs from other life forms

because the inner arrangements of the lights vary —

different designs,

same Designer.

THE BOUNDARIES YOU PERCEIVE BETWEEN YOURSELF

AND OTHER EXPRESSIONS OF PHYSICAL REALITY ARE ARBRITRARY

AND, LIKE YOUR EMOTIONAL PERCEPTIONS,

CAN BE SHIFTED AT ANY TIME.

If this seems absurd to you, sweet, it's only because you have

grown accustomed to relating to your inner and

outer world in limited terms.

I encourage you to stretch.

For starters, take a moment to consider the page you're reading

from *the point of view of energy.*

Notice that the paper, like you, is made of microscopic

twinkling lights.

Now gaze at your hand as it holds this book.

You already have a physical

and emotional perception

of the appearance of your hand and fingers

but can you also imagine the interaction between the lights and the

space within its form?

Now shift your focus, and release your opinions about your hand

and allow the boundary that separates it from the page to

soften and melt away,

leaving only the splendor of light-filled space.

Where now is the dividing line between your physical self
and the page?

Where is the border separating you from the
staggering wonder of the Divine Mystery?

It has faded, and you have discovered the only enduring vestige
of reality:

you are part of the infinite cascade
of brilliant lights
seamlessly merging to form
a single, fantastic
Light
Being

The many wonders of the world will not change so that you may finally know the truth of your magnificence.

It is your **perception** *of the world that must change.*

Happily, this new awareness frees you from the plodding, often painful, mistaken notions of reality you experience onstage in the Magical Theatre.

Any time you wish, you can expand your physical and emotional perceptions as creatively as a designer creates new backdrops for a scene.

When you consider that you are travelling through space at

thousands of miles an hour with nary a breeze in your hair —

it would appear anything "real" is suspect.

Carry this keystone in your deepest awareness:

Your perceptions create your reality.

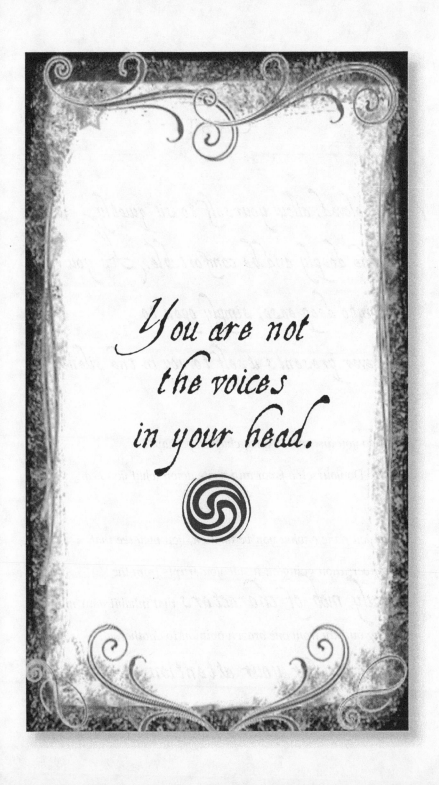

3

CAST

Beloved, allow yourself to sit quietly, breathe deeply and be comfortable. As you melt into deep ease, simply open to whatever presents itself to you in the silence.

What do you discover? Noisy chatter, perhaps?

Do yourself a favor and write down what you hear.

When you review what you've written, you may see that the conversation going on inside you erupts from the *unruly mob of characters* that inhabit your mind, shifting quickly from one brazen opinion to another, all *clamoring for your attention.*

Who are these voices constantly chattering inside you?

I call them your *cast of characters—headstrong commentators* who attempt to *direct the action* in your script.

Many of these characters are not on your side,

for their opinions cause you to be afraid,

close your heart,

and negatively impact your decisions.

They want you to remain under the spell of forgetfulness

because they know *upon awakening, you will*

no longer need to rely on their input.

For example, when you are making a decision, one may caution,

"Don't do it, you'll get hurt,"

while another might say,

"Just go for it! Don't be such a coward."

Which voice should you listen to?

It's possible that neither voice is giving you good advice and that together, they are executing one "sleight of mind" after another

that leads you into a of self-doubt and confusion.

BECAUSE YOUR CHARACTERS' VOICES ARE FAMILIAR, YOU TEND TO BELIEVE THEIR OPINIONS AND LET THEM HAVE POWER OVER YOUR LIFE. YET, YOU HAVE MISTAKEN FAMILIARITY FOR SAFETY.

A character's urging may sound harmless because you've heard it a thousand times before,

but does it really serve you to follow fear-driven advice?

Brave one,

free yourself from the oppression

of your characters and resume your rightful

place as director of your own production.

Recognize that you don't have

to base a course of action

on these conflicting voices —

because they are LIARS.

The characters' voices do not express the true you.

As a sublime spark of the Divine Mystery, you are gifted with a

beneficent inner sage called the *impartial observer.*

This compassionate, loving presence lives in your heart and serves

as the eyes and ears of your soul, and is always available to direct

your attention to the truth within.

When confused by the babble of your characters' opinions,

you can access the ever-present awareness of your

impartial observer, who will align your perspective

with the wisest course of action.

You may wonder how to distinguish the true voice of the impartial

observer from the false voices of your cast of characters.

Beloved one, there is a simple way to tell:

Pain always accompanies falsehoods.

Let the discomfort of the lies spewed by

your cast of characters alert you to instead

access the loving communication

from your impartial observer.

To do this, shift your attention away from the noisy mob in your

head and drop your awareness into the center of your open heart.

BE still.

NOTE the eternal wisdom emerging from

your deepest knowingness.

From the boundless understanding of your impartial observer,

celebrate the news of this third keystone:

You are not the voices

in your head.

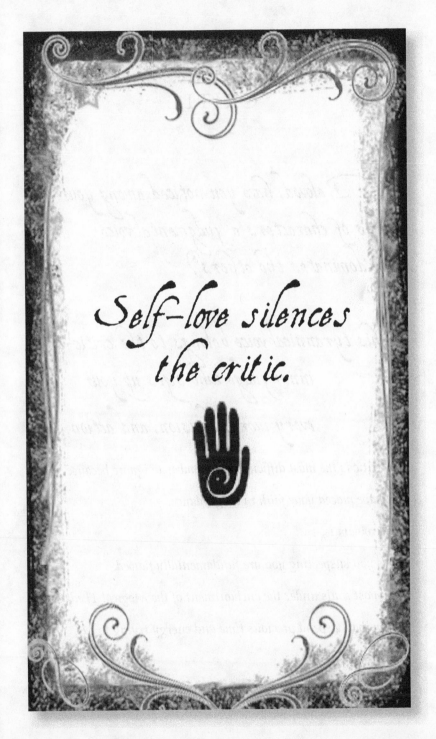

Self-love silences
the critic.

4

CRITIC

Beloved, have you noticed among your chorus of characters a judgmental voice that dominates the others?

This tyrannical voice belongs to the critic—the inner judge who sizes up your every word, decision, and action.

The critic is the most difficult cast member to ignore because you have placed your faith in its guidance.

The problem is,

it has you suspecting you are fundamentally flawed.

Like most souls under the enchantment of the Magical Theatre,

you probably spend precious time and energy trying to

please the critic.

Have you noticed it doesn't work?

The critic judges you, then hands out

perverse, indeterminate sentences for the smallest offense.

The critic's immunity is rooted in the *demand for a*

perfection that is distinguished by always

being just out of reach.

The moment you achieve one step on the road to the critic's idea

of perfection, more steps magically appear and you find you are

no closer to your goal.

YOUR CRITIC WANTS YOU TO BELIEVE THAT
SELF-CRITICISM LEADS TO SELF-IMPROVEMENT.

Yet, if you could really become a better you by castigating yourself

before, during, and after every scene in your melodrama,

wouldn't you already be blissfully complete?

Honestly, does self–judgment really make anyone
a more loving, peaceful, compassionate, accepting person?

Today you have the opportunity to rise up in rebellion, refuse

to accept the critic's point of view, and take self-interpretation

into your own hands.

First, create a list of accusations from your critic.

You can probably think of quite a few allegations immediately, for the critic is always busy making up new ways to tell you how inept or inferior you are.

The moment the criticisms are brought to the attention of the impartial observer, however, you begin the process of disempowering the critic.

Armed with clarity, you can begin to **transform** *the critic's accusations from vague, emotionally fraught life sentences into concrete,*

black-and-white statements

you can refute through a deep knowing of your own worth.

So read over the critic's statements, then go down into your inner wonder-land and ask your impartial observer to show you the truth beneath each one.

Do not be afraid to uncover the facts,

for the truth of who you are cannot hurt you.

INSTEAD, IT IS YOUR BLIND ACCEPTANCE

OF THE CRITIC'S JUDGMENTS THAT CAUSES YOUR SUFFERING.

When the answers arise from the stillness of your heart, you will learn that you are not the dreadful things the critic has accused you of being.

How could you be, my sweet?

You are a whole and complete expression of the Divine Mystery.

Beloved one, be vigilant now, for the critic is a stubborn, ingrained presence that will not simply disappear upon detection.

Criticisms will pop into your mind uninvited and unwanted.

The moment you feel the critic's presence,
administer the antidote; self-love.

Here's how it works:

When the critic says something spiteful or demeaning, instead of immediately judging yourself for having the judgment and heading down the dangerous road of self-condemnation,

firmly interrupt the snowball effect.

Laugh,

empty your mind,

eat chocolate,

dance wildly,

or sing loudly

anything that might stop the string of judgments.

This interruption *is the antidote of self-love in action,* a kindness you can substitute for the ingrained brutal habit of self-criticism.

And you can do it again and again, each time a critical or judgmental statement comes to mind.

This will allow you to progress from self-accusation to self-acceptance.

Each self-loving act, no matter how small, becomes a building block for your increasingly expansive role in the Magical Theatre.

Now, my heroic explorer,

with love in your heart accept this keystone:

Self-love silences the critic.

5

BELIEFS

Beloved, have you ever wondered why your earthly melodrama has you doing things that cause you unhappiness?

The answer is simple yet profound:

you keep re-enacting distressing scenes over and over because of the beliefs you hold.

Beliefs are your convictions about who you are

and how your life should unfold.

Strengthened by years of rehearsal,

they robotically guide your every action onstage in the

Magical Theatre — whether or not you are aware of them.

My dear friend, your beliefs about yourself and your life

keep you stuck.

Beliefs such as "I need a true love to be happy,"

"I won't be successful until I have a lot of money,"

and "my appearance influences my worth,"

all create a misleading picture of what you should do and

who you are authentically.

Even beliefs that sound deceptively positive, like

"I'm a perfectionist," "I'm always there for my friends,"

or, "I always look my best." can limit you.

These seemingly positive beliefs forge attachments to unhealthy ideals at the expense of a potential you haven't yet imagined.

Until now, your fearful beliefs have spurred unconscious reactions and kept you from spontaneously weaving the magic of creativity into your life.

Dear one, to acquire the ability to make responsible choices, it is essential to begin identifying your *fearful false beliefs* and loosening the unconscious hold they have over you. This can take some strength of will, *for your knowledge will often masquerade as a belief.*

Listen closely, for here is one of the great paradoxes
of the Magical Theatre:

ALTHOUGH YOU MAY KNOW SOMETHING INTELLECTUALLY,

IT IS WHAT YOU FUNDAMENTALLY BELIEVE

THAT CONTROLS YOUR BEHAVIOR —

EVEN IF THE BELIEF CONTRADICTS EVERYTHING YOU UNDERSTAND TO BE TRUE.

*This paradox explains why you may not see yourself as lovable
even though you know you should.*

*Knowledge alone cannot override your fundamental belief that you
are not perfect enough to receive love, but awakening to the beliefs
that direct your actions will help you overcome your automatic
responses to events.*

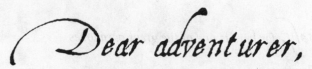

Dear adventurer,

you have the power to shift the entire theme of your production.

Begin by asking yourself whether you hold beliefs that limit your experience of happiness in life.

Allow the answer to rise gently into your awareness.

If you feel a constriction, it indicates the presence of long-held beliefs that have been hurting you and resurfacing in anguishing scenarios. Now you are free to release their grip by practicing a technique I call

LIQUID:
Listen, Identify, Question, Intuit, and Decide.

Listen to your thoughts (cast of characters) to locate the belief at the core of your un-ease.

Identify the belief as carefully, thoroughly and honestly as you can. Use the impeccable clarity of your impartial observer to guide you.

Question its validity. Is it really true? Look at it through the eyes of the Impartial Observer.

Intuit what it would be like to live the rest of your life with the belief. Now feel your life without it.

Decide if your want this belief impacting your experience of life. If you don't, make a conscious, willful commitment to release the belief.

You are now free to replace your limiting beliefs, my love. Begin rewriting the theme of your production today and live from a deepened awareness by accepting this keystone:

Free yourself from false beliefs.

Sacrifice your mask
to save your soul.

6

MASK

Beloved,

I now welcome you to the greatest illusion of the Magical Theatre — the image of yourself that you project into the world.

To join me in exploring the illusion, first ask yourself this question:

Do you secretly fear that if you are wrong about something,

a distressful emotional event will likely occur with the probability

of a painful penalty: the loss of approval or acceptance?

If this seems familiar, you have placed responsibility for

emotional well-being outside of yourself.

Perhaps you need someone else to agree with you in order to feel at ease, personally important and safe.

Yet have you considered the cost of needing to be right?

Wearing a mask to depict a contrived image obscures *your soul's magnificence*— from yourself and the other players in the Magical Theatre.

Dearest, do you have any idea how much energy you have devoted to saving face by wearing this mask to look acceptable in the eyes of others?

Behind this mask is the fearful belief,   *"If I'm wrong, I lose."*

True, being wrong may temporarily cause you to lose the
superficial trappings of others' acceptance or approval.

Yet it is a far greater loss to hide your splendour behind
a false mask.

To create a joyous new production in the Magical Theatre,
           it is necessary to remove your mask and open to the
possibility that you have been wrong about many things,

including the truth of your very being.

And what a refreshing discovery to touch the truth of you!

To remove the mask that conceals the wonder of you, begin by calling on your impartial observer to let you know when you are attached to being right.

You may feel irritated, for example, when someone *dares* to disagree with you, whether or not they threaten to prove you wrong.

In paying close attention to your impartial observer, you may realize you have inadvertently placed conditions on your happiness that are beyond your control.

You can't control whether or not someone agrees with you, accepts you, or approves of you. You can, however, find abiding joy by redirecting your attention inwardly,

toward your heartfelt connection to life.

Once you've identified instances when you are attached to being right, you can remove your mask by learning to

hold the position of no position.

When someone disagrees with you, allow your impartial observer to witness the situation without trying to change it.

Very soon you will see...

YOUR HAPPINESS WAS NOT PLACED IN JEOPARDY SIMPLY BECAUSE ANOTHER THOUGHT YOU WERE WRONG; IN FACT, IT DOESN'T REALLY MATTER AT ALL.

As you then release your attachment to the "correct" point of view and recognize that *there is nothing to defend,* your mask will fall away of its own accord.

In your new position of no position,

your mask has nothing to which it can adhere.

My dear, in trying to be right you have exhausted yourself by
endlessly pursuing evidence to justify your assertions.

As you shed the mask

designed to protect you from being seen as wrong,

you will be greatly energized

and radiant in the spotlight of your magnificence.

From your new, unmasked position center stage, you can begin
uncovering what makes the real you shine.

That doesn't mean you won't make mistakes; indeed,
mistakes are integral to life in the Magical Theatre
and its intriguing series of rehearsals.

Nevertheless, you have countless opportunities to get things
wrong, rewrite your script, and TRY AGAIN.

Your cast of characters, led by the critic,

may jeer at you or tell you you'll never get it right

— yet deep inside, you will know

you have already traded your mask
for greater intimacy with your luminous soul.

Absorb, then, this essential keystone:

Sacrifice your mask to save your soul.

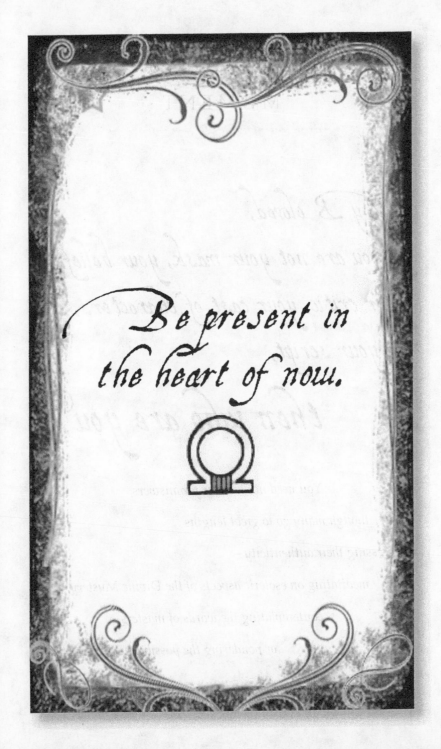

Be present in
the heart of now.

7

MOMENT

My Beloved,
if you are not your mask, your beliefs,
your critic, your cast of characters,
or your script,

then who are you?

You need not look far for answers,

though many go to great lengths

in accessing their authenticity —

meditating on esoteric aspects of the Divine Mystery,

contemplating the words of masters,

or pondering the possibility of past lives.

Much may be gained through these pursuits,

yet to find your authentic self,

you need only remember *the truth*

of who you are in a now moment.

To awaken you must take responsibility
for your emotional experience
of life in present time.

Courageous seeker,

discovering your authenticity requires not a journey of

self-betterment, but a sojourn into the heart of now.

Chasing a better future will only rob you of the awareness
necessary to dip into your heart and
come to know your essence.

Time comes and goes but the moment remains —
so do not wait for the perfect moment but rather recognize
that moment is *Now.*

As you make forays into your heart in the moments of your
everyday life, you develop a conscious relationship
with yourself, after which you will no longer choose
to mindlessly follow an outdated script.

The choices you make

or don't make

(for not choosing also has a consequence)

impact the very foundation of your production in the

Magical Theatre.

Until now, dearest, your choices were actually

reactions which may have appeared to hold value,

> *but were borne out of past events,*

>> *the authority of society, or the influence of loved ones.*

TO ACCESS YOUR INFINITE POTENTIAL,

MOVE AWAY FROM LIVING LIFE IN ACTION/REACTION

AND STEP INTO THE DELIGHT OF KNOWING

YOU

ARE THE POWER BEHIND YOUR CHOICES.

When you *predictably* make choices that reflect your highest
possibility, the tentacles of the past slip away and
you experience the miracle of your authentic aware self.

As you begin to reveal your authentic self, beware of a few
deceptively innocuous imps who may try to pull you out of the
moment and insinuate their way into your new production.

These mischief-makers are
Hope,
   Potential,
     Wishful Thinking.

This triad will tempt you to focus on
what lies in the distance and miss the
fullness of the moment.

Hope may appear to fuel optimism, yet it can also lull you to inaction with its promise of 'some other time'.

Potential assures you of bliss as soon as someone or something changes — an outcome over which you have no control.

Wishful Thinking keeps you expecting
different results from similar circumstances.

The future is being determined by your current decisions
and always shows up in the present moment,
as there is no other place for you to arrive.

Each moment you experience,
you are where you are *going.*

Embrace the moment fully and allow your emotions to flow through you unimpeded and the spell of forgetfulness will quietly slip away.

In the Magical Theatre,

the moment of transformation is yours for the taking.

Accept this keystone into your heart in this moment and the next until, sweet and warm as heavenly sunlight, it reflects the heart of all of creation:

Be present in the heart of now.

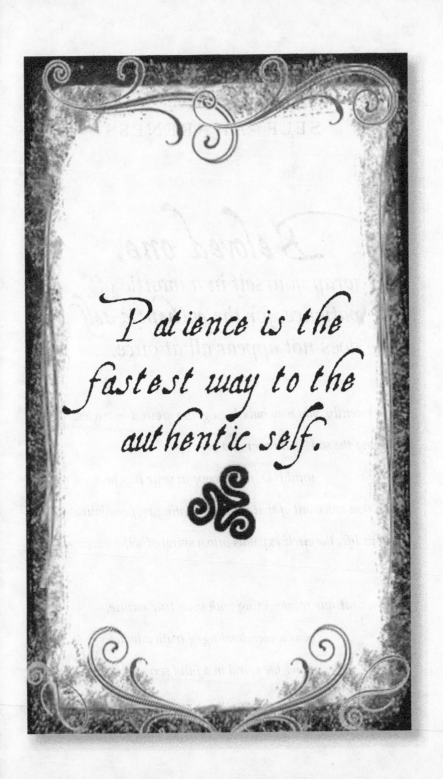

Patience is the fastest way to the authentic self.

8

SELF-AWARENESS

Beloved one,
wrap yourself in a mantle of
patience, for the *authentic self*
does not appear all at once.

Until recently, you may have been going around in circles,

retracing the same path over and over

until it wore a groove in your psyche.

When you move out of that rut by assuming responsibility

for your life, the circle expands into a spiral of self-awareness.

As you continue reconnecting with your true nature,

your understanding of truth advances

along the spiral in a fluid series of stages.

Each stage builds upon one another, creating the foundation

necessary to support your subsequent exploration.

Stage by stage, you wondrously become more
authentic and conscious at precisely the pace that is right for you.

But hold tight to your awareness, as the ascent of the spiral hinges

not on 'knowing' what each level represents.

*To advance to the next level, you need
to experience your new wisdom –
one small success at a time.*

If you hurry blindly you may acquire a tendency

to misinterpret knowledge as wisdom and skip the practical work you must undertake at each level.

Here's how the spiral works, my love:

Let's say you want to free yourself from the harshness of your emotions and learn to live in a state of loving compassion.

Initially you might memorize all the information on the subject and don the disguise of a master, naively trying to jump past the necessary steps in the spiral.

This technique may temporarily shore up your image but will not ultimately resolve your internal experience, prompting you to start over again.

So, the first stage is to move through your resistance and tell yourself the truth. In acknowledging the truth you will
find the grace to begin.

Perhaps the truth is, that despite a deep longing and many attempts to manifest your goal, you don't feel loving much of the time and don't routinely experience compassion.

THIS ACKNOWLEDGMENT ALIGNS YOUR PERCEPTION
WITH YOUR INNER EXPERIENCE.

In the next stage, you identify the emotional reactions that thwart your ability to experience love and compassion,
illuminating the hold they have over you.

You then move to the stage of accepting your emotions

and allowing them to flow through you

rather than stuffing or succumbing to them —

understanding that despite your trepidation,

this will actually hurt less than avoiding or indulging them has.

In the next whirl of the spiral you place yourself in a position to make more life affirming choices. You begin to identify and unravel the fearful false beliefs that form the original foundation of your story and replace them with new beliefs based on abiding truth.

At last you have the clarity to rewrite stories that trigger destructive emotion.

As you move through the spiral in this way, you free yourself from unconscious reaction and increasingly experience life from a place of loving compassion.

Whatever your goal, my love, keep in mind that your spiral will, by nature, take many twists and turns before delivering you to a consistently wakeful state.

Attempts to bypass any stage will only bring you back to it and leave you treading the same old groove until

the light of awareness dawns.

Your journey will often require you to revisit a previous stage

and though it may appear the same, it now offers

the next level of discovery.

At a later stage you may need to embrace forgiveness — an action

you could not effectively accomplish without the prior visits.

As you progress, remain grounded in the moment

and *experience* each insight as fully as you can.

Remember, while ascending the spiral of self-awareness,

what matters is not speed but
rather the absorption of wisdom.

So it is that awakening to who you

are happens in a series of small epiphanies,

creating a solid basis for whatever new role you decide to play in

the Magical Theatre.

Detours borne of fear or impatience seriously delay your progress,

because each step along the spiral path

provides additional *strength* necessary

to break the spell of forgetfulness.

Have compassion for yourself on this sometimes exhausting quest,

for with each beat of your heart you are *growing more and more* into who you already are —

an essential part of the Divine Mystery.

Beloved, each step will become *clear*

at the moment that is right for you.

Trust that the spiral is leading you across a wondrous

threshold of understanding.

Step into the light of a new stage, my courageous sojourner,

and accept this keystone:

*Patience is the fastest way
to the authentic self.*

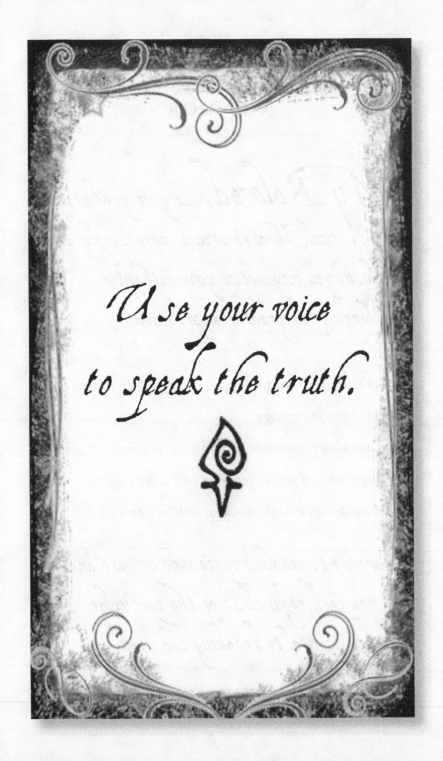

9

CANDOR

My Beloved, as your production in the *Magical Theatre* grows increasingly deep and lush, you may notice your authentic self longing for greater expression.

At such times, your heart is begging to sing out the truth of you, without shyness or apology.

When you feel a constriction in your throat or chest, it is a sign that you've been ignoring your heart's request and would do well to begin speaking with increased candor.

Learning to openly expose who you are and how you feel, regardless of the particular audience, is vital to breaking the spell.

Yet speaking your truth is not always easy,

for like the other players on the magical stage,

you may have developed the habit of carefully phrasing

and censoring your comments in an effort to control

how others perceive you.

*Honest communication originates in
your **heart**,
where you hold the spark of divine wisdom
that connects you to all of creation.*

Imagine the relief you will feel when you release the need to censor your expression and open your throat to let your true voice pour forth.

Fearlessness will allow you to

express your integrity

regardless of your concern for the response (opinions and expectations) of others.

Upon hearing what you have to say, some listeners may in fact judge you, while others might be inspired to strive for their authentic expression also.

You cannot control their reactions,

though you can take responsibility for the words you speak

by delivering your honest message from a place of kindness.

Believe it or not, my love, the one word that will unlock your true voice is the small yet powerful "no".

You may have noticed that your cast of characters often encourages

you to say "yes" even when it may cause you to suffer.

For example, you may want to do something because it feels

compelling in the moment even though it may harm you in the long

run, such as drinking to fit in, or agreeing to assist a friend when

you are already over-whelmed with your own responsibilities.

Sometimes you have to be candid with yourself and say no to things

such as overeating to find comfort.

The courage to say no, voiced from an honest reflection of what is right for you, aligns you with your heart's desire. Each time your lips say "yes" when your heart says "no," you sacrifice a precious bit of yourself.

Dearest, I understand this new practice requires great resolve,

      yet when you are untrue to yourself

         for fear of disappointing another,

you split from your integrity;

and when you dare to voice a truthful "no" from your heart,

you become whole in your own eyes.

Allow NO to open the floodgates for your authentic voice and

prevent the further build-up of fearful energy.

If saying NO is distressing at first,

connect with your heart,

> *be present in the moment,*

>> *and view the experience as a chance to ultimately*

override old habits of self-judgment and self-blame.

Release the controlled image

you have spent a lifetime perfecting

and use your voice to speak the truth.

Then you will know the *freedom that comes*
with honest expression.

And remember this:

even if you speak in a whisper, your truth will echo through the Magical Theatre like a roar.

Discover your voice to become present in the magic

and embrace this keystone:

Use your voice to speak the truth.

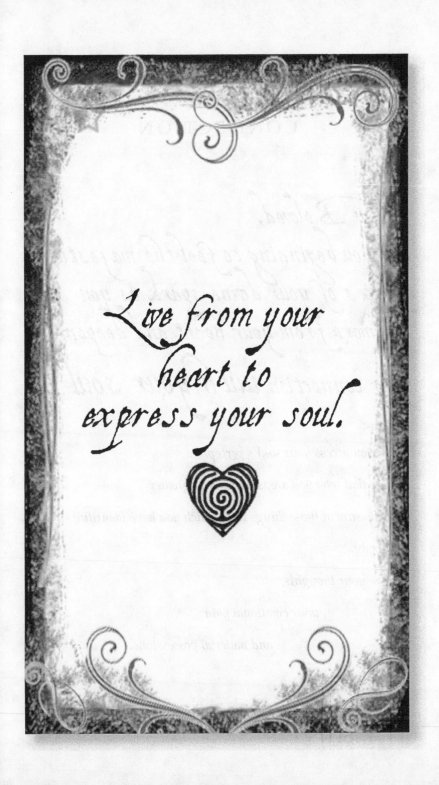

~10~
CONNECTION

My Beloved,
are you beginning to feel the majestic
forces of your divine spark as you
live more from your heart and deepen
your connection with your soul?

When you access your soul's perception,

you see that who you are is immensely greater

than the sum of those things with which you have identified —

your body,

     your thoughts,

          your emotional pain

             and material possessions.

Listen closely my heavenly being, and I will help you comprehend

the mystery of your soul—

the force that animates your body,

the radiance at the core of your being,

the divine I am.

Your soul is your abiding connection to the heart of the
Divine Mystery. It communicates with all of creation through
your heart and you experience this expression as love.

Please be aware that the love I speak of has little to do with the
melodramatic love experienced while under the spell
of forgetfulness.

In the Magical Theatre,

the sentiment called love

often entwines the players

in poisoned tentacles of possessiveness and fear.

The soul's love, on the other hand, is impersonal and infinite and doesn't need to identify arbitrary criteria to exist.

This love originates
in the intention of the Creator
as love with no conditions attached.

My precious angel, you need no longer

exhaust yourself in the pursuit of love, since you have all the love

you could ever want pouring through you.

But the only way to know this love is to *express it.*

YOU CAN EXPERIENCE LOVE IN ALL MOMENTS –

regardless of the current melodrama swirling around you –

by moving your decision-making

away from your intellect

and engaging in actions that arise from your

connection to your heart and soul.

Beloved, the brain is an extraordinary computer but it

cannot lead you to joy or provide a way to awaken – these miracles

are the purview of the heart.

But, there is wondrous news —

WHEN YOUR SOUL EXPRESSES LOVE
THROUGH YOUR HEART,
YOU EXPERIENCE YOUR AUTHENTIC SELF.

As you follow the urgings of your heart,

the sacred will come to life in your life

and your soul will joyfully emerge

to direct the action in the Magical Theatre.

As you attempt to access your soul's love, you will occasionally
stumble over obstacles. At such times the tired script you've lived
by may direct your cast of characters to shriek that what you seek
isn't possible, your critic may disparage your efforts, false beliefs
might grasp for a foothold, or the mask of righteousness may
stubbornly adhere to your face.

Do not despair, *Beloved,*

    for the stumbling blocks you encounter

are merely opportunities

    for pausing,

    breathing,

    and reminding yourself

    of your larger purpose:

*to awaken from the spell of forgetfulness,
remember your divine heritage, and
express your soul's love.*

To hasten contact with your soul, flood your heart with gratitude.

Be thankful for your every experience,

including the most wrenching predicaments,

for these too propel you toward self-awareness.

Also be grateful for the Creator's boundless love that buoys you
through these painful episodes. A heart pulsing with *gratitude*
forges an immediate link with your soul's radiance.

Receive this keystone with gratitude, for it will free you to exult in a
steady stream of small miracles:

*Live from your heart
to express your soul.*

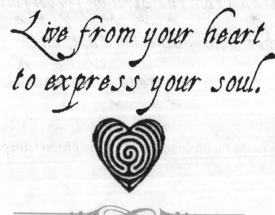

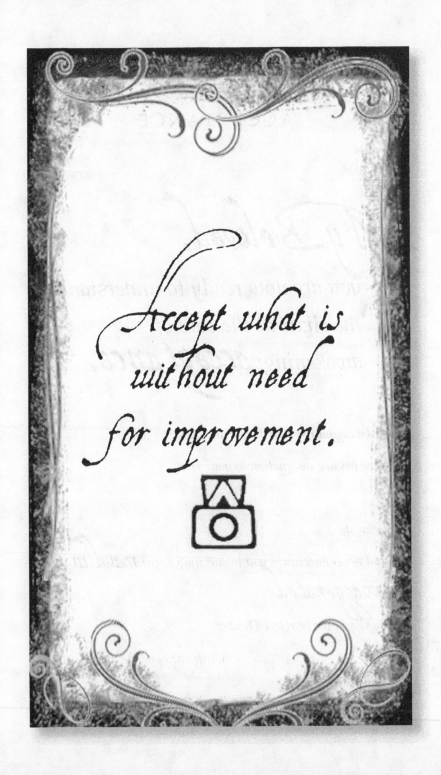

Accept what is
without need
for improvement.

11

ACCEPTANCE

My Beloved,

*you are now ready to understand
the elixir at the core of
awakening:* **acceptance.**

Please be vigilant so you do not mistake acceptance

for some passive resignation to your fate.

No, dearest,

I would never encourage you to succumb to the **maudlin**

and **exaggerated**

plot twists in the Magical Theatre.

> *Quite the opposite, in fact.*

When I speak of acceptance, it means this:

after consciously choosing a course of action, lovingly release yourself from attachment to the outcome.

In accepting *what is* you, relax –

because having set in motion a chain of events, you can *entrust the result to the all-knowing of the Divine Mystery.*

When you accept a consequence, the sacred offers you a

blessed gift in return:

the ability to choose
not to suffer.

When you are attached to a particular result,

    your happiness is tethered to it

        and when things don't go as you wish,

you are mired in confusion or misery.

Yet, this is the height of hubris, for it implies that you already know how things should turn out.

The Architect of the Greater Plan often delivers information on a need-to-know basis. Your role is to accept *what is* in a now moment.

To visualize this type of active acceptance,

picture yourself standing

in the center of a seesaw

and making a choice

that immediately sets the plank in motion,

swinging wildly between two possible outcomes.

For example, if you have applied for a job, your effort will result either in an offer or a rejection letter.

HOW WILL YOU DEAL WITH THE RESULT?

If you are balanced, you remain unfazed by the up and down movement. If you moved off the center and emotionally invested in one outcome over the other, your happiness would depend on the concluding result:

you would be either on top and delighted,
or low-down and miserable.

Yet because you have planted yourself

squarely on the center of the plank,

you can remain **unaffected** by the outcome.

When standing in the center of a seesaw, my dear one,

you inhabit the place of acceptance and relax into what is,

letting life flow through you without resistance.

This is especially important to embrace
when you are faced with an oft-occurring
theme of the Magical Theatre—
winning someone's love.

When you are tightly attached to receiving love,

you become equally invested in the opposite,

or losing that love.

Not only is your happiness held prisoner to events

you intuitively know are beyond your control,

you are operating from a false belief that says

you lose love if the object

you love leaves your life.

Beloved, nothing has the power
to take love out of your heart.

Your carefully laid plot can shift at any moment, for the Divine

Plan unfolds your destiny as it will, regardless of your desires.

Yet within that plan,

you have the *power* to select your
emotional response,

make decisions,

take responsibility for them,

and release your attachment to the outcome of events.

Your peace and happiness

are fully supported by aligning

with the far-reaching *wisdom of the Creator.*

Your task is to accept all things 'without need for improvement.'

This means relinquishing your need to control situations

while greeting unforeseen circumstances

without striving to interpret,

brood or worry obsessively.

In actively accepting what is on the Divine's terms,

and letting life flow through you without resistance,

you gain *peace of mind*

by releasing the belief that something

must change for you to be content.

Meditate lovingly on the idea of active acceptance.

Removing the armor of defiance reveals the beauty of surrendering

to the heart of the Sacred.

Trusting in the wisdom of the sacred mystery,

open your heart to this keystone:

Accept what is without need for improvement.

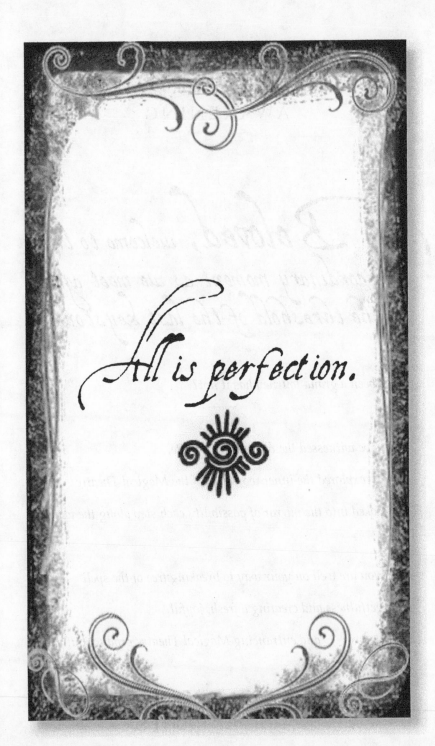

All is perfection.

12

AWAKENING

Beloved, welcome to this extraordinary moment as we meet again on the threshold of the last keystone.

It has been a grand journey has it not?

You have witnessed the vast wonder of life,

     explored the inner workings of the Magical Theatre

and looked into the mirror of possibility each step along the way.

Now you are well on your way to breaking free of the spell

of forgetfulness and creating a fresh, joyful,

     and entrancing Magical Theatre production.

With ever-increasing awareness and determination you are
traveling toward a place of unimagined freedom.

And so, please accept my final gifts.

As you begin to live spontaneously and fully from your heart,
permit me to guide you into the deepest truth:

*you are whole and perfect
just the way you are.*

To love and be loved, you do not have to achieve a particular
standard of excellence, for you are already a resplendent expression
of the Sacred.

Dear one, do not wait for anyone or anything to appear worthy of your love to *allow love to pass through you.*

If you have learned to see yourself as flawed, understand that this perception arose from a grand lie – the myth of your imperfection.

Indeed, your authentic self is magnificent beyond your wildest dreams.

Your essence is eternal.

Carry this with you like a precious gem.

Do not let fearful concern for your safety delay your awakening,

for catastrophic harm cannot befall a timeless being.

Place your faith in the grace of the Divine Mystery and substitute

the fear that has kept you striving for an unreachable perfection

with love for the

LOVE IS YOUR BIRTHRIGHT,
PERFECTION YOUR INHERITANCE,
AND HAPPINESS YOUR LEGACY.

You alone are the final authority on your human life, the only one

who can awaken to the truth of who you are.

As such, do not wait for a future "right" time

or the "right" circumstances,

my darling, for they will never arrive.

Please do not wait another moment to
let the world see you shine.

The authentic self emerges action-by-action; so be the first to smile
and extend your hand.

Live authentically *and follow your passion joyfully*
and others will notice the ease with which your
life is flowing and will want to enjoy life as you do.

Ultimately, you are never alone,

for you are always in union with the Sacred.

And yet I must caution you —

even as you bear witness to evidence
of your Divine nature
the spell of forgetfulness might pull you back into its grasp.

To extricate yourself, reclaim your authenticity and

surrender ever more deeply to

the possibility of unscripted miracles.

Beloved, before we part I would like to offer

you the opportunity to cast off any lingering doubts.

Stop everything,

find a place of quiet comfort,

and be wholly present with me here

for this breath in time.

Silence the inner voices.

Suspend the world.

Draw upon the wonder of your inner-sight

to stretch beyond the boundaries of perception you have previously

described as REALITY.

Use the phenomenon of your imagination

to extend far beyond the physical body

and the entrapment of an illusory world

to the joy of the utter vastness of the

Divine Mystery—the beginning and end of all Creation.

In the wonder of stillness,

allow the *presence of Presence* to wash over you

and recognize

the infinite nature of your being

as an emanation from the heart of the Sacred.

It all begins and ends with love,

your love,

EXPRESSED in each and every moment.

There are many paths to awakening but at the heart of awakening there is only one essence – love.

Now and always, put aside fear, open your heart and embrace the essence.

When you live in this way my dearest, you will awaken in the

Magical Theatre and truly *dream down heaven.*

Let your authenticity shine and accept this final keystone:

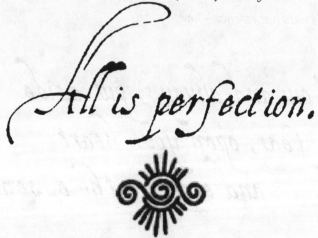

All is perfection.

The Twelve Keystones

 You are the playwright of your own life

 Your perceptions create your reality

 You are not voices in your head

 Self-love silences the critic

 Free yourself from false beliefs

 Sacrifice your mask to save your soul

 Be present in the heart of now

 Patience is the fastest way to the authentic self

 Use your voice to speak the truth

 Live from your heart to express your soul

 Accept "what is" without need for improvement

 All is perfection

BOOKS

O is a symbol of the world, of oneness and unity. In different cultures it also means the "eye," symbolizing knowledge and insight. We aim to publish books that are accessible, constructive and that challenge accepted opinion, both that of academia and the "moral majority."

Our books are available in all good English language bookstores worldwide. If you don't see the book on the shelves ask the bookstore to order it for you, quoting the ISBN number and title. Alternatively you can order online (all major online retail sites carry our titles) or contact the distributor in the relevant country, listed on the copyright page.

See our website www.o-books.net for a full list of over 500 titles, growing by 100 a year.

And tune in to myspiritradio.com for our book review radio show, hosted by June-Elleni Laine, where you can listen to the authors discussing their books.

mySpiritRadio